a concrete sky

a concrete sky

BY

KRISTEN JEX

ISBN-13: 978-0615715117 (Kristen Jex)
ISBN-10: 0615715117

Visit
www.aconcretesky.com
for original music from the book.

Journal / Prose

Flashback

Song

Letter / Poem

Email

Flashback Email

Narrator's Aside

1988	San Antonio, TX
1988-92	Harrisville, MI
1992-94	Plattsburgh, NY
1994-97	San Antonio, TX *1st - 3rd grades*
1997-98	San Antonio, TX *4th grade, new school*
1998-00	Yokota Air Base, Japan *5th - 6th grades*
2000-01	Prattville, AL *7th grade*
2001-04	Sumter, SC *8th - 10th grades*
2004-06	Fort Walton Beach, FL *11th - 12th grades*

introduction

One in five people who are in a mental institution have Borderline Personality Disorder. I am not one of them. Institutionalized, that is.

I have Borderline Personality Disorder. I know, it sounds scary. I hesitate to tell people because I worry it will make them uncomfortable, and I want them to like me. Still, I want them to know.

I want them to know because the truth is there's something wrong with all of us. Borderline Personality Disorder just happens to be what's wrong with me, and that's nothing to be ashamed of.

You hold in your hands my truth, pieces of my high school past, a mess I couldn't untangle until I was diagnosed.

BPD is officially identified in adulthood, though signs can show up in childhood and adolescence. A patient must experience five of nine specific symptoms to be considered Borderline:

1. Fear of Abandonment. *It's not a fear of being left alone; it's the fear of being thrown away.*

2. Exhausting Relationships. *It's mostly a consequence of something called "Idealization and Devaluation." It means you only view people (including yourself) in absolute extremes. They are either good or bad. The slightest provocation can switch your vision immediately, so everything is a dramatic, unstable and passionate affair. This sort of black-and-white thinking is applied to other things as well, not just people.*

3. Inconclusive Sense of Identity. *Your self-image is inextricably tied to other people around you, similar to a chameleon changing with its surroundings. It is difficult to establish yourself as a separate, single soul.*

4. Impulsivity. *The self-destructive kind. Taking unnecessary risks. Like gambling, promiscuity, reckless driving. Binging and purging. Uninhibited shopping, drug addiction. Pretty much anything that feels great at the time, but that you regret and feel guilty about later.*

5. Suicidal Behavior. *Thoughts about self harm or suicide. Suicidal gestures, like running a pen across your skin like a knife. Attempted suicide. Cutting yourself.*

6. Erratic Emotions. *Intense mood swings. Your emotions are hyper-sensitive. Reactions to small and constant changes that occur in a typical day are disproportionate. You feel everything so deeply. Because the emotions are so intense, they are hard to control or suppress. This criterion is independent from mood disorders like Bipolar. Not the same thing. BPD mood swings change circumstantially, even hourly.*

7. Emptiness. *Chronically feeling empty. Like a mixture of loss, boredom, and isolation sitting on your empty lungs.*

8. Rage. *Frustration so overwhelming that you explode in anger you feel powerless to stop. Afterward, you often feel like a horrible person, and because of #2, conclude that you are, at which point you will manipulate other people into comforting you by being ridiculously self-deprecating and apologetic.*

9. Paranoia. *Kind of. Being hypercritically aware of yourself, believing no one likes you.*

These are the criteria, but the cause is *invalidation*. Growing up in an environment where your thoughts and feelings are continuously unacknowledged.

Often abuse, whether it's physical, sexual, or disguised as neglect, is at the root of BPD. Because underlying the abuse or neglect is the idea that you don't matter.

I am not a professional psychologist. This is a memoir. All I can offer is my experience and point out the clues to a developing disorder.

But rather than allowing my present self to describe my entire story, I think it is only fair to allow my past self to tell you in her own words what she felt, who she loved, and the reasons she feared growing up.

chapter one

the scarlet crayon

"We'll fly by wheat fields and water towers. We'll go."
- OK GO

July 15, 2003

Everything is changing. It makes me uncomfortable. I feel like I've been running so fast I didn't realize what I was leaving behind. Now that I've slowed down, I don't know where I am.

I'm in the air, actually.

I love riding airplanes because the way I see it, it's the closest I can get to heaven. I forget where I live, where I came from, where I'm going, or WHAT I'm doing, and for once, I just live in the moment. One second at a time. Looking back makes me realize how one thing can lead to another and change everything. Nothing is the way I planned it to be.

It makes me sad to know I'll be 15 soon. Maybe the reason I'm so uncomfortable with this change is because I haven't changed. I guess I was running, but in the wrong direction. Maybe I was running backwards.

For the first time, I feel insecure.

I don't know where I am.

You ever get the feeling you're being forced into this little box? Encased in this little cube, where everyone is hidden beneath something that everyone else understands, or sees through, but you can't? Or don't want to? Nothing makes sense to me.

Maybe I've lost something.

Wednesday, July 30, 2003 10:55 AM
From: alex

Hey kristen. I'm tired. I just got home from New Mexico last night. My dad called too. I'm leaving. I'm going in September. Good old Saudi Arabia. I don't know what to think. I'm not sure I want to go. I had a scene for you and me to take to Drama Competition. I guess we can't do it anymore. Well. I guess I should go. Peace out girl scout.

-the one, the only Alex

July 30, 2003

Alex is moving.

I can't think. I don't know what to say.

School starts next Thursday, and I'm NOT ready for it to start.

I'm turning 15 soon. Can you believe it? 15. I keep shutting my eyes real tight and hoping this all could disappear. That things were back to the way they're supposed to be. . .

September 1, 2003

So I'm 15. (sigh) Yesterday was Sami's birthday. She's 16. Tomorrow is school again. Darn it.

Wednesday, September 17, 2003 5:08 PM
To: alex

As soon as I got home, I put your toilet race car right next to my guitar.
~kristen

Thursday, September 25, 2003 9:28 AM
From: alex
Subject: It's not easy

Hey Kristen. I know I told you already, but I read your letter in homeroom after I was about 10 minutes late. . . I really liked it, and I'm glad I was able to just be part of your life. I mean, what were the chances two air force kids like us would meet up in a crazy place like Sumter, South Carolina?

It was really hard to say bye yesterday. It was harder than I thought it was going to be. I mean, you and I both have had to say "bye" so many times in our lives, but this time it was so much harder, and you meant so much more than most everyone that I had to say bye to. I love you, Kristen. I know we don't say it enough, and it's not the drugs talking either. . . I'm really going to miss you; I'm gonna miss everything about you. I'm gonna miss everything we ever had planned for the year—or I had planned. I was already looking for stuff to take for competitions. Well, that just would have been too easy. I'm really gonna miss you

Kristen. I need to go, I'm leaving soon for Columbia to fly out of this good ol' country. I'm gonna miss you kid.

-the one, the only Alex

To my Alex –

I'm guessing you're reading this in some hot sandy room in Saudi, tired and exhausted and feeling like Wednesday morning in Melton's room is a billion miles away (or you could've cheated, and you're reading this on the airplane). I would've sent this by mail so this would be waiting for you when you got there, but I figured I could save some postage and just let you send it to yourself.

I'm sitting here, looking out the window and thinking of you. A thousand memories rush through my head. I laugh as I think of each one of them. You know, you've never failed to make me feel twice as good as I was before. It's strange, how much I find you in me, myself. I feel like I have a little Alex inside of me smiling and clapping and shakin' his li'l fro. It makes me wanna tell random, loud stories and drink chocolate milk, or listen to the Foo Fighters and tell people, "In England, it's Teenage Mutant HERO Turtles."

I feel like time stops when I'm with you. No one else makes me feel that way. I love being with you. I want us to always be friends, because I need that.

People don't like you because you're funny, Alex. They like you because you're honest and sincere, they just don't know it. They like you because you're open and cheerful, considerate and cool. Anyone can not be those things and be funny, but people like you because you are all those things, and you're Alex. I just want you to know you've made a profound impact on me—you've set my life on a different course, and I hope you'll do that with whomever you meet. I'll miss you.

— Kristen

Foil Letters

*I'm sitting here just looking out the window
and thinking of you
A thousand memories rush through my mind as I
think it through
And I am guessing that you're feeling like a
A billion miles away
I would've wrote you sooner but I didn't know
what to say*

*I am standing
Falling into what I feel
Understanding nothing to believe this is real*

*You said
I won't lie I admit that I read your letter
Don't you worry I always knew
you were something better*

Dreams of tomorrow now can't be so
'Cause that would be too easy
We could've been anything, anything
We wanted to be

Now we find ourselves falling into what
that is now taken from us
Now we can fly away back to the past
where memories are waiting

You never knew how much of you was
the missing part of me
Never again will I ever find myself.
Myself

And I am standing
Falling into what I feel
Understanding nothing to believe this is real
I miss you I miss you

Friday, October 3, 2003 4:28 AM
From: alex

Hey Kristen! I can't go much longer without telling you about all that's happened here so far! I mean, you told me all your Japan stories, and now it is time for the WHITE BOY IN SAUDI ARABIA CHRONICLES!

So my first experience in Saudi Arabia consisted of a urinal, my dad, and a man with a gun. I know what you're thinking. . . Well, not really. It's hard to tell with that. In the airport my dad and I go into the bathroom, and there's a nice little man with an AK-47 as I gently pee into the Saudi urinal.

Well after getting through customs and getting through security onto the compound I finally GET SOME SLEEP. . . until about 4:30 in the morning, when I awake to "UMNILLAAA! SHULAMMAAAACHIKAAAA!" and I think the world's on fire and I'm like, "WHATS GOING ON?!" and then I realize it's just call to prayer.

So I started school, and we go in our bullet proof van with the military escort and we take a different bus and a different route every day.

Of course I learned this when, on my second day, we start driving through this junk yard and I was like, "Uh, are we going to school?" And another thing—the roads here are. . . SCARY! It's like a 2 lane road, or I'm guessing it's a 2 lane road 'cause there are no lines! And we're squeezing about 8 cars in the turn lane and you know as soon as it goes from red to green INSTANTLY cars way behind start HONKING LIKE CRAZY! And it's like mahaam. Is that how u spell mahaam? Probably not, but it doesn't really matter. Peace out girl scout.

-the one, the only Alex

October 7, 2003

Today, on October the 7th 2003, I, myself, Kristen Kiyomi Jex, received my first kiss. (eeep!) STAGE kiss that is. I shared it with Tim. Tim Threet. Yeah. It actually felt kinda awkward. Nothing I really expected. Well, you know.

Anyhoo—I miss Alex a lot. I never realized how much I took him for granted—how much I counted on him to be there for me. Anyway, I have to get my beauty sleep.

October 14, 2003

Another gloomy day. It didn't end as bad as it started, but it was pretty sucky. Tomorrow will be better. I've just got to live one day at a time. That's all you can do.

I do miss Alex. And Robert. And Sami. I miss my life. I miss Zach. I miss Flipside.

October 17, 2003

Dad came home today, but he's leaving again for Iraq. Anyway, I've got drama rehearsal at 9:00 a.m. tomorrow so goodnight. ♥ Kristen

November 7, 2003

Today was my first day working at Cici's! Did I even tell you I got a job there? Yeah. It was crazy. I don't know if I really want to go back.

I've been feeling lonely lately. Just, really lonely. Alone. It's weird. I'm usually not like this. But I guess everyone has their down.

November 8, 2003

I really do hate this. I haven't had a real crush in like, FOREVER. Well, since Alex left. This is driving me crazy!

I just feel. . . Bad. Everyone has been driving me crazy and I just haven't been myself.

Okay, about the crush thing—that was stupid. My point was, Welp—I can't help but see everyone in pairs lately, and, and, I just miss my friends! I miss Zach, Robert, and Ted and Alex.

AHHR! I need friends. I need someone who will help me for a change. Yes. Someone who will help me. I need someone who will help me. Like Robert. I miss him.

Sarah, was Robert's younger sister. She had been my best friend since I moved to South Carolina and continued to be throughout high school and college. But girl friends really weren't enough to make me feel valued. I needed boys.

Robert was sort of the first male I could rely on. He was three years older than me. He took me under his wing. He instilled so much confidence and passion in me.

The very first time I laid eyes on a real-life guitar was in Robert's room. The memory is clear. He sacredly lifted his sunburst Fender Strat over his head, and as soon as he brushed those strings with his hand, it was love at first sight. I was fascinated, enamored, and demanded he show me how to play.

And he did. He encouraged me to sing as well, something I was never proud to do, but he insisted. We formed our band Flipside together. He traded in an heirloom acoustic to buy me my first electric guitar. He has the twin; they're bright orange.

So when both members of the band moved, and Alex moved, and I lamented my best friend Ted moving the year before, I realized I had no best boy friends.

I didn't care about girls. I didn't need their approval. I wanted boys to approve of me. So I was into the things they were into. Even the girl friends I had were tomboys, because they were into what boys were into too. I needed boys to think I was pretty and really cool. I needed their hugs and their attention.

November 23, 2003

Man, I've been so slack these past days. All I can think about is GUITAR, GUITAR, GUITAR, GUITAR. I've just been working, going to detention, and practicing.

Did I tell you? I got a gig at the coffee shop on the 19th of December. I'm real excited.

Well, tomorrow is School,

♥ Kristen

November 29, 2003

Thanksgiving was all right. I spent the night at Kristel's house Wednesday. Kristel is pretty cool. I went to the mall today hoping to see friends, but no one was there.

November 30, 2003

Last day of November. Last day of Thanksgiving break. So sad. Two weeks until Christmas break. Gosh. Already? Man. It seems like forever ago Alex was here.

December 2, 2003

How are you? I'm kind of hyper. And it's 10:41 p.m. Scary huh? I made cookies for my youth group just to be nice. I talked to Joanne today. I can't wait until we perform!

Tuesday, December 16, 2003 11:22 AM
From: alex
Subject: Alive and in pieces

Hey Kristen! How are you? Hearing you talk about the show really made me miss being backstage for a Sumter High show, such as. . . Night of Originals where I couldn't find my legs from yours, or me trying to get pumped for Drama competitions and shaking like a baby, and of course, cowering in the corner with you during our Drama one "First block holla!" yes, good times.

I miss you Kristen, ok I'm over. . . well, not really, I really miss our insane conversations like "ah! Ah! AHHHH!" with the hand movements of course. Or like the time you put my shoes on over yours. Haha! One day you and I are gonna take on the world, okay? With our powers combined, we are the ultimate partners in crime. As we steal candy from on top of the vending machines and try to stomp the evil roach dogs of the world. Well, Kristen life here is somewhat becoming normal if there is such a thing as "normal" and if there is such a thing as "life" here. Peace out girl scout!

-the one, the only Alex

December 21, 2003

So, the coffeehouse thing was great. Joanne and I did really well. I'm so glad everything turned out awesome. I'm so so SO relieved school is OUT! Whew! I made it. For Christmas, I got a bottle of perfume from Kayla, a book from Tim Threet, 2 stuffed dogs from Marshall, and a burned CD from James Bond (yes, that's his real name). Aren't they sweet?

I wasn't really prepared to go to New Hampshire (I'm in the car right now) 'cause I had the coffeehouse thing on my mind, you know, so this was just all last minute for me. My room is a mess!

Sami was supposed to come with me on this trip. I'm so disappointed she couldn't come. I really hope I meet someone, a friend or something up there! I really do. I guess it's nice to run away from it all. Go on a trip and leave it all behind.

Robert will be home for Christmas break when I come back. What a relief. I can't wait to see him again.

December 22, 2003

Today was great! I forgot how awesome Snowboarding was. I've been reading the book Tim got me. It's kind of bizarre. They're the works of D.H. Lawrence. I love the feeling of riding on snow.

Wednesday, December 31, 2003 4:07 PM
To: alex

Yeah I've been out of town for a week. I went snowboarding in New Hampshire. I played a show at this coffee shop last week and I played your song "Starbucks," and I was like, "Um. Well this whole song is basically one big inside joke, so you won't get it, and I don't think you want to try to, so I hope you can just enjoy the melody." I got some interesting looks after I spilled the first line.

My friend Joanne really likes it though. She said, "I mean, do you know of any other song that starts with 'If only I could buy the world's best egg roll'?"

Merry Christmas! ~kristen

Thursday, January 1, 2004 2:05 AM
From: alex

Hey Kristen! How are you? The other day I reread the lyrics to the song you wrote me. I really like it, and it still makes me laugh out loud. That's cool you played it at the coffee place, haha, I can just picture the looks on people's faces.

You know what I just thought about? The day when Marshall and I came over and you guys locked me in your closet and I put on all your clothes and then we started filming it! HAHA, it was so bizarre! And I was like yelling at Marshall the whole time for no reason. And I kept falling over because the clothes were so small! Do you still have that video? 'Cause when I come back we're getting a huge glass of chocolate milk and cups with coffee beans in them all over the room and we're gonna watch it! haha, Sounds like some horrible romantic mood I would try and create. . .

Yesterday we went downtown after our compound was attacked. But that's another story. Anyway we have to radio into the base every time we leave, you know "Base 2 Alpha 46 departing 128 for 7" type of thing. And there's this lady on sometimes and last night I started talking on the radio and I was talking all slow in that "hey sexy baby" voice and I said "Alpha 46. . . plus 2 arrive 128. . . over." and there was a long pause. . . and she just quickly says "base 2 roger out" and we all started laughing in the car. I love messing with her.

Well, I need to get going, but Happy New Year! May this new year bring lots of chocolate milk to the middle east, and spread Twinkie joy all over the world. Well peace out girl scout.

– Love, the one the only Alex

Saturday, January 10, 2004 7:14 PM
To: alex

ALEX! guess what I found on my doorstep this morning! Your package! I LUUUUUUHHHHHHHHVVVE IT! You are the coolest, Alex. I brought it downstairs, and showed my mom, and she started dancing to the music.

And I put that li'l Post-it note under my amp switch so it says "push here!"

~kristen

Hey Kristen!

How are you? So, I'm sitting in Arab marketplace one evening and I hear this music, this Arab music. And I turn around and there is this big camel singing and flashing red satanic eyes at me. And it was bigger than any singing camel I had ever seen and it made me think of you. So, I bargained and got it for about 20 riyals.

I don't know if they have camels in Turkey, but either way consider this your "wish you were here" from Turkey. Maybe you'll get stationed here after all, who knows. You know there aren't any Kristens here. No one really has those absolutely strange and bizarre conversations that we used to have.

I hope everything in Sumter is going alright. Everything here is slowly becoming normal. As scary as it all seems. Good cocktail conversation for later in life: "Yes. Well, when I lived in Saudi Arabia. . ." people will either think it's interesting or yell "Bomb! Ahhh!" And they'll throw me in jail where you'll have to come bail me out with all the money made from The Kristen and Alex Show. *And then we'll be broke and homeless living on the steps of Patriot Hall hoping that someone will pick us up. Or wait for the cops to deport us to Iraq where we planned to be all along. It's amazing how things work out so nicely like that isn't it?*

Well, I hope you enjoy the happy happy camel that is translated to sing "We can do it! We can do it!" Well

Kristen, I miss you, but I'll see you this summer. I love you girl scout. Peace out.

Love, Alex

Saturday, January 24, 2004 12:01 PM
To: alex

Are you really coming back? I hope you are. Sad thing is, I'm moving. Yeah. . . I just found out I'm moving to Ft. Walton Beach, Florida. But it's an actual CITY with a BEACH, so I'm half excited. I'm moving mid-June. So you better hurry up and get your butt down here!

Have you heard about Ted? My gosh. . . He called me the other day. And his life is seriously effed up. It's so bad. Like all he does is weed. That's all he talked about on the phone. It was rap, girls, and weed. He is nothing like he was in 8th grade. But you know. . . he's still TED. He still makes funny impressions and does stupid stuff. . . but yeah.

Did you hear about Dallen? Dallen Alexander from Mrs. Sherer's class? Yeah well, a few months ago I guess, we found out Dallen had hanged himself in the bathroom. Tess was crying and Grayson was bawling like a baby when he found out. Isn't that sad? Just to remember Dallen laughing and having fun in class. . . and then to hear that?. . . How could, how did he end up that way? It just makes you think.

I can't believe how much everyone's changed. It's crazy. I dunno, sometimes I feel so lucky, like a SURVIVOR almost, because I haven't ended up like that. Makes me wonder what everyone will be like in 2 years, or 4, or 9 years from now. Do you ever worry about that, what you'll do after high school or college?

Somehow I feel like there's this certain passion that children have. They always have some kind of DREAM that motivates them, that keeps them alive. And yet, when you reach the point of becoming an adult, reality has a tendency of crushing all those dreams out. I don't ever want that to happen. See, maybe that's why I love being around you. Because you remind me. You bring something out of me that keeps that dream alive? Yeah. That's it. I want to keep that forever. I don't want to lose that. Am I making any sense? Anyway, just a random thought out of the mind of Kristen Jex.

~kristen

Tuesday, January 27, 2004 10:11 AM
From: alex

Hey Kristen! How are you? That's neat about moving to Florida; I don't know if I'll get to see you this summer or not now, but we'll have to see. And I had heard from somebody that Ted was messed up now or something. It's really sad. I mean I guess people change, but I don't want that to happen to me. I worry about a lot of my friends changing like that. Like my friend bugs me because he needs to stop smoking. But we don't need to get into that. I had heard about Dallen from a lot of people. That's really sad, but I mean. . . coward. I hate to sound harsh or something but people who do that are just cowards.

I'm glad I'm forever a child to you. I want to stay a child forever. I worry sometimes that I'm not like that and then I go play with little kids and it just gets in me even more. I love kids and I love being one. . . I think I've found a balance of yea, being a kid and having responsibilities without ever really growing up. I don't want to grow up. I just hope people will unite with me to never grow up. Yea, college. . . job, maybe a job if I can ever get one. I mean being an actor already means not a lot of security, but I LOVE THAT. I love that. . . Maybe I'll grow up one day and won't be so stupid. . . but I like this all. Peace out girl scout!

-the one, the only Alex

20

February 2, 2004

Man. I dunno what's wrong with me. I can't sleep—I can't concentrate, I'm eating toast with nothing on it. How depressing is that? But seriously, WHAT'S WRONG WITH ME?! I'm not happy. And I don't know what will make me happy.

February 15, 2004

Yesterday for Valentine's Day I went out to San Jose's with Kelly Renko and a bunch of Drama people. Tim and I talked about the LDS* church almost the entire time. ♥ Kristen

* Latter-day Saint, as in The Church of Jesus Christ of Latter-day Saints. (I'm a member)

Tuesday, March 2, 2004 10:19 AM
From: alex

Hey Kristen! How about talking to you on the phone Friday was the highlight of my week! It's been an awesome week altogether, but I mean that was just a great way to start it. I went to school Saturday all pumped, but at the same time there was a point of realization where I was sitting in Drama class throwing scripts everywhere trying to cast the show with everyone standing in front of me. . . I miss you. Anyway, I realize I got distracted from whatever it was I going to talk about, but. . . oh well. Next time. Hopefully we'll get a chance to talk again soon. Peace out girl scout, I really miss you!

-alex

Thursday, March 4, 2004 10:25 PM
To: alex

I just got finished doing the Complete History of America Abridged. I'm exhausted. I climbed your tree behind the Drama room today before the show. It reminded me of how we used to sit on the hood of your brother's car and just sit there. Do you remember that one time you bought that Fanta soda during REACH, and I said it was pronounced FAHNta, because it was so FAHN-TAHstic? You know that hill you used to run up and down? The one in front of the school? It's completely gone now because of construction. It's really sad. . . and ugly. But anyway. Man, I cannot tell you how much I want to be over there right now, or for you to be here right now.

But really, I miss you. And that's all.

~kristen

March 6, 2004

I've been doing a lot of thinking. I feel so alone. No. Not alone. Not anymore. I used to feel alone. Completely alone. But now I'm alone, but I know why. I'm not making sense. But I am making sense. Life is so short.

I need.

You know what? I miss Alex.

I miss Alex.

I bleed just like this pen. I think people hold on to childhood because they're afraid of the real world. It creates a world—a world of safety. Like that world we lived in when we were younger. Something to hang on to so we don't have to deal with the harsh realities of life. That's why I miss Alex. He saw that. He lived it. He made me feel like a kid again. He created that world so I didn't have to live in this one.

I fool myself sometimes. I forget myself in a world I try to create, but only to really fool others. Yet in doing so, I ultimately forget and fool myself. But it's just so fake that way.

I can never. . . grr! I'm just not as happy as I used to be and I feel like it's because I'm growing up too fast and no one understands, no one can relate. Everyone else is going through their STUPID high school drama! No one sees the Big Picture. I feel like I'm too far ahead, and too far behind. I know I've said this like a billion times.

Would you think I was sick if I told you sometimes I think about taking a cold knife and just. . . Sometimes I feel like I can't take it. I can't hold it in. I want to let it out but there is no one to listen.

There's just too much pressure.

It's all stupid. It doesn't matter. Who cares? Look at this. These whole 2 pages. Nothing. High school drama. I contradicted myself. I can take it. Everyone goes through it. Everyone is above it. It doesn't matter. You just live life. That's all there is to it. Eventually the sun shines right? Right.

God, I miss Alex.

I feel dark. And alone. No one understands. I just don't see how.

NOBODY KNOWS. I'm shaking. I'm so alone. Where is God? I'm cold. I feel my very soul being eaten up inside me. I can't even express myself through music anymore. It's so dark here. I shake.

Where is God? Everybody else lives in their own little world. Away from me. How did I end up like this? How did it get this far? Nobody listens. There's too much pressure. I'M SCREAMING.

Leave me alone. It's all my fault. It's all my fault I feel the nothing eating me inside. Like everything is being sucked into this bottomless pit of nothing. I live in a world where everything is so close. So close. I am so close but nobody knows.

No one can hear me. I'm tired of hearing people's problems. Who will hear mine?

I hate this world. I hate it. So many people want attention. WEAK people.

So where do I stand now? I am weak. It's all my fault. I'm just like every other stereotypical teenager. Depressed. Right? I hate them! Where did I reach rock bottom?

I miss Alex. I miss him so much. One day. One day I'll escape. We'll be together. It will be Fall. The air will smell like Spring. Everything will be beautiful. I'll be happy.

Why am I not happy? I don't understand. I'm just not happy. I wish I could just melt away. What should I do, I'm screaming. I miss Alex. Happiness. I can barely remember.

I can barely remember.

For me at least, there was this idea that all the alternative, punk, and goth kids were depressed, cut themselves, and did drugs, and that all that was part of the image. So I didn't feel like my being depressed or wanting to cut myself was out of the ordinary.

To be clear, wanting to cut or cutting yourself is serious. It is a major indication to seek counseling, no matter what kind of group you associate with.

Sunday, March 7, 2004 3:55 PM
To: alex

Actually Alex, I DO have to wake up at 5:30 every morning. I go to early morning Seminary at my church every weekday. (It's like Bible study).

But I did get some sleep finally. School is just really hard, and we are trying to sell the house now so I don't really have a home anymore, or a room. There are weird creepy stranger people in it all the time! The weather here is like, PERFECT right now. You know how there's a certain smell when spring comes around? Those few weeks in the whole year where it's not hot or cold, it's just warm and breezy, and there are no bugs. And the sky is unbelievably blue. So blue it has no depth. It's awesome.

~kristen

March 12, 2004

I hope I'll meet new people in Florida. People that can temporarily substitute for the people I miss now. You know?

March 13, 2004

Today I packed. Then I went to Firefly Summer's "opening CD party" thingy. I had a good conversation about religion with Mike Strickland. He's Charlie Brown in the other cast. There's two, so everyone can have a lead part. Anyway, it was amazing talking to him.

March 22, 2004

I'm sitting here in the airport waiting for Dad. Snowboarding with him was fun I guess—a little lonely, but fun. It always seems that way.

I'm listening to Incubus. I can't believe it's been one week! It seems like forever. I can't wait to go back to school.

Oh. There's Dad. –later

April 4, 2004

DUDE! You will not believe what happened Saturday at Battle of the Bands!

First of all, Mom and I got in a CAR WRECK on the way to Lakewood High School. We were about one minute away and I would've had to WALK 15 min. if it weren't for the guy we hit's mom. She came and drove me to Lakewood.

I was supposed to OPEN and be the first to play, and I just barely made the meeting they had for all the bands and band members. If I wasn't nervous about playing first, I was nervous then because of the car wreck. Oh and before I went to Battle of the Bands, I went to *Charlie Brown* rehearsal.

So I played first and everything was fine. I messed up in a couple of places, but kept going and did fine. My voice and mouth also got really, really, REALLY dry around the second half of my set which is really frustrating. But so finally they were announcing the winners and they announced category winners first, like best guitarist, drummer, etc. . . Joanne got best vocalist yay! She so deserved it.

And guess what? I won something! I got best SONGWRITER! And I won $20!

Dude I was—what am I talking about—I AM so excited! Like 2 adults who heard me last year said I improved, 3 guys offered to record me, and another 3 wanted to play with me. I actually got some respect! I am so, so, so EXCITED! I cannot wait! I can't believe how far I've come with all of this.

Honestly—I owe it all to Robert. He taught me guitar, and he opened the door and shoved me into making that first step. It's all so unreal! I really am kind of speechless at this point. I'm so EXCITED. I AM A SONG WRITER!

January 20, 2003
If there's one thing that gets my mind off of everything, it's

band practice. It makes me forget about everything else. I'm completely unaware of anything or anyone around me. I guess that's why I love performing, too. But as soon as the song ends, it all melts away, this trance, and I go back to the world again.

Being on a stage was addicting for many reasons. I loved it. It was an opportunity to command attention. An opportunity to make the audience fall in love with me. The applause and approval was validating. I could be whoever I wanted on stage. A character in a play, a comedian, a musician, a dancer, a rock star. Funny how it feels you're free to be yourself while pretending to be someone else. In a period where everyone was still shaping who they were as young adults, I think being someone else for a while was a relief.

This was especially true in Drama. Alex Kyger convinced me to join Drama Club. I would've chosen the JROTC step team otherwise.

I know. Me, in JROTC. It's quite unbelievable to me now. But I suppose that was a character too.

I chose Drama Club because Alex would be there, and it changed my life. It was a guaranteed place to laugh so hard I'd cry. I would be surrounded by people who worked hard to play. We all respected each other.

That Sumter High Drama room was my refuge, our own little island of misfit toys. Mr. Melton was the best teacher. He was ridiculous and goofy, smart and ethical; he was our leader and hero, and most of all he respected us. He was a very weird adult, and we thought he was the greatest person ever.

> I embraced Drama. Acting is about cataloguing human emotion, using imagination, and creating a duplicate reality. It's about overcoming fear, going with whatever stupid random thing we thought of because we learned self doubt can hinder the greatest discoveries from being made.
>
> It was so much fun.

April 8, 2004

I am so tired
Of waiting to feel
Like I am inspired
To spin this wheel

April 12, 2004

I've been thinking about a lot. Which is usually not a good thing.

Frau Wright said I was whiney today. She gave me a Post-it note and pen and said I had to color every single part of the note with pen before I could leave school. Isn't that retarded? And she called me whiney! That really hurt my feelings.

I hate stupid teachers! They make me cry.

Sometimes I really hate people.

Friday, April 16, 2004 3:04 AM
From: alex

Hey Kristen! How are you?

Sorry I haven't emailed in an eternity, but things have been pretty interesting lately. Uh, we've been on lockdown for a while because of threats on the embassy and on us, so we didn't go to school that day, and that night they found 3 trucks loaded with explosives heading into Riyadh, this after 3 straight nights of shootouts downtown with grenades and rockets.

Yesterday was a pretty shaky day because of meetings and briefings all day, and for some reasons I can't say over the internet and reasons they won't tell us. . . we're coming back soon. I'm not allowed to tell you when, but I can tell you I'll be in Sumter. So, I'll get to see you before you leave!

We're evacuating! Haha, crazy stuff, right? Yeah, I know. . . They're obviously not giving up all the details, but I'm guessing these hostage situations aren't helping, and I wouldn't be surprised if the explosives and weapons they found in those trucks were what they've been looking for in Iraq. Things are really out there right now. BUT I'LL GET TO SEE YOU! I won't see Charlie Brown, but we'll get to hang out and try on each other's clothes and. . . Kristen. . . if there's one good thing from all of this, I'm happy to see you before you go. If I don't email you right away it's because. . . things are going to be getting crazy soon. Talk to you later kiddo. Peace out girl scout, see you soon!

-Alex

April 22, 2004

Our first performance tonight was good! I was great, Snoopy was awesome. The performance was absolutely fabulous. Yes, I'd say it was fabulous. Everybody liked me!

Kelly gave me a ride home today. I just lay down in the back seat and closed my eyes and listened to Something Corporate and then looked up and watched the clouds.

It was one of those "I'm 15 and feel free" type of moments.

I really can't wait for Alex to come home. I feel like I've opened a Christmas present and know what I'll be getting— but I'll have to wait until Christmas to open it—and maybe my reaction then won't be as grand as it really does make me feel. Anyway, it's late. Love, Kristen

Monday, April 26, 2004 1:26 PM
From: alex
Subject: Pre-flight email

Hey Kristen! How are you? I'm pretty worn out, today was my last day at school and I've been packing and I'm just. . . exhausted. Not to mention I have, like, 15 hours of flying ahead of me and then an hour in the car. I guess that you've heard I'm finishing up school over the internet, so I'll have a lot of time to spend with you guys, and apparently Melton has placed me in shows coming up and I should be able to do REACH, or "help" with REACH considering my school district is in Riyadh. All flights here are in the middle of the night. None of that daytime stuff.

Crazy Arabs. I'm guessing you heard about the bombing on Wednesday . . . interesting stuff. Crazy crap constantly here. I don't know. I need to, uh, finish packing and stuff. Peace out girl scout, I guess I'll see you soon!

-Alex

April 27, 2004

Today was one of the coolest days in my entire life. I feel like I'm on top of the world. I could not be any happier. Okay, first of all, Tim, Ray, and I hung out at the mall all afternoon. Well, we went in, walked all the way around, bought candy at the $1 store, then just hung out in Ray's van for 3 hours. It was awesome! I can't explain it! We did absolutely NOTHING and it was the most fun I've had in forever.

I got home around 8:00, and around 9:00 the doorbell rings and I see Tim again at my door. AND THEN ALEX. Yes finally, Alex Kyger runs out from the side of the house. I couldn't believe it. I still can't.

We sat on the porch and talked for like an hour and a half and came up with this really AWESOME plan. Okay. This is really, really bad. Tomorrow after Seminary, Tim is going to pick me up from church. I'm going to his house and then Alex, Tim, and I are going to spend the whole day together. I'm skipping school! Shh! I can't wait! ♥ Kristen Jex

April 28, 2004

So how about today was the single COOLEST DAY of my entire existence. Okay. I wake up at like, 5:00 because I'm so excited. I go to Seminary and everything and Tim is waiting in the LDS church parking lot for me at 7:30 a.m. I jump into his car and we drive over to his place. I have a bowl of Cinnamon Toast Crunch and teach him some guitar. At 9:00 a.m. we pick up Alex from the hotel and we go to this gas station. Then we get this brilliant idea to DRIVE TO FLORENCE, a whole other city like an hour away. So we spent 4 hours in Florence, it was insane!

First we went to this book store and there was this little boy about 5 or 6 and we watched previews for *Toy Story 2*. Tim was sitting directly behind this boy and the boy goes "Quit breathing on me!" His mom prolly thought we were college kids. We kinda looked like it. I felt like one anyway. Then we went to Chik-fil-A and got lunch and Tim started throwing waffle fries at the birds, and they were all fighting for them. Then I chucked this HUGE waffle fry at the flock, and this tiny little bird was trying to lift this HUGE potato and Alex and I DIED. It was hilarious!

Then we went to Best Buy and you know how they have the aisle with all the big boom box stereo systems? Well we all changed the station to what sounded like the Mormon Tabernacle Choir, and there was some Baptist devotional going on and so it was so funny walking down that aisle of just Gospel hymns blasting through the tricked out subwoofers and stuff.

Then we walked around the mall and made a wish in the big wishing well. Then we went to Toys R Us. We got these big bouncy balls and found this secluded aisle in the back and bowled with random stuff. It was really fun! And this is when Alex called Tim a "squirrel head" because Tim has a mohawk and he didn't spike it today, so he really did look like a squirrel head! Then Alex and Tim sat in those toddler car seats on the shelves. They were all scrunched up. And then we found racing cars and we played with those. Tim also taught me how to smash peanut butter M&Ms in the bag so when people buy them they are all smashed.

Then we sat and chilled and had to drive home. I brought my guitar so I played on the way to and back. Man I missed Alex so much. This is a dream come true. I've never ever been so happy in my entire life. I feel so liberated. FREE! I can't believe I skipped school. It feels AWESOME! I can't believe we did all of that in just 6 hours.

May 1, 2004

Today Alex and Tim and I went to have breakfast at Shoney's and we saw Fred and then we were going to go to

Columbia but we drove out and sat in fields all day instead. You know, those. . . fields.

You see them all the time but this time we did what I've always wished to do when I see those fields. We got out and walked around in them. It was amazing being nowhere with people you could spend forever with. Today was the happiest day of my life, and yet I got home and I cried.

Today was perfect. So perfect it shouldn't be real. It's too good to be true. Why can't we sink in, out of the world that's so cold. It's sad to think we're so scared. We're so desperate to hang on to that innocence of life. Something so beautiful that can't exist in the real world. Why can't it? Maybe bits and pieces—but why can't it be like that? Why can't I spend forever like that? Maybe that's what heaven is. The feeling you get where you just feel like you could spend forever feeling this way—It's so sad. It'll all be gone from me. I really wish Tim and I could've been friends earlier.

I feel like I've created this perfect secret world I go to, to escape this awful one. But that's cheating. You can't do that. It's too good. Maybe the downside will come when I'm gone.

Krist-o-rino: Ugh, what to say. Thanks for liking my mohawk, teaching me bar or power or whatever chords, lying in a wheat field with me and Alex, and being such a rock-hard awesome person. I hate when people say, "Don't ever change," because that's so stupid, how can you help that? Just promise me you'll never lose your passion for life and your guitar-wailing, face-melting, song-writing greatness. Just keep being you and I'm sure you'll be set. I wish this wasn't goodbye, but since it is, thanks so much for everything. Keep rocking!

Timothy Threet*

Hey Kristen!

How are you? Well, it's been a really interesting year, but I'm just glad I got to come back and see you. I was scared I'd never see you again. You're probably the only person I could see myself lying in a field with. I'm glad you kept emailing me. Your emails always made me feel better. I'm really going to miss you, but I can't forget all the times we spent together in Drama, or the day we skipped school and went to Florence. I'm so glad that I was evacuated, in that I could surprise you and just see you again. It never was the same without you, and it won't be. But just stay in touch and maybe I'll see you again sometime. Peace out girl scout and I'll see you around. If you can't be good, just be.

Love, Alex Kyger*

*From my yearbook

Thursday, May 6, 2004 10:19 PM
From: tim

Okay, let me ask you a question because I value your opinion. If I get started now with my exchange student program for my senior year, I'd basically have my choice of country and junk. Well tonight I was thinking about maybe going to Japan. It would be a totally different experience and I just wanted to hear your opinion on it. I'll be getting a yearbook, so yeah, I'll save you a couple of pages, haha. Tm thtttt

~100 Percent Cotton~ - "the touch, the feel of me. I'm the fabric of your life."

May 10, 2004

Two more weeks of school left. Two more. Agh. Makes me sick.

I called Sami's mom today and she "okayed" me to stay over there in July. I can't wait. This summer is going to be crazy. First Girls Camp, then Youth Conference, then Sami's place. Crazy! I can barely focus on what I'm supposed to be focused on right now. I'm writing in my journal instead. I can't help it.

I don't want to move away from it all, but at the same time I want to. Ugh. Help me. I keep wondering what Florida will be like. I'm sick of thinking about all the people I'm leaving here though. It makes me sad.

May 12, 2004

Man! I am so slack! I didn't do anything today. I got home and wasted 2 hours.

Doing nothing. Just thinking.

I'm so hopeless.

May 13, 2004

This morning was the last day of Seminary. Kind of sad.

Night of Originals was tonight! It was awesome! It was really good. Afterwards, we all went to Dairy Queen, and then Tim drove me home with Alex in the car and Matt Wilt drove behind us. So then we have to change Tim's tire, because it's flat. I changed the car tire, 'cause they didn't know how to.

I like the color orange. I don't think that there is enough orange in this world.

Goodnight, Kristen

May 17, 2004

Dude! Tim and Matthew Eldridge made me feel so good today! Tim was like "OMG! Marry me! You are so kick-a!"

They listened to my CD. Matt and Tim both said their favorite song was "Hate to Waste." Isn't that awesome? I have the best friends in the WHOLE ENTIRE WORLD.

May 18, 2004

I love it here. I love Melton. I love Tim and Alex. I love everyone at church. Joanne.

Everything. Will it really be gone? What about Sarah? Meagan?. . . Why?

Life. That's why.

April 24, 2000

The movers are coming May 5 and 6. I wonder if I'll like Alabama.

I'll miss Japan. I'll miss Chris, Robin, Carissa, Erika and most of all my Japanese friends.

May 19, 2004

I realized I'm going to miss Molly a lot.

I'm going to miss a lot of people a whole lot.

Is this really happening? It's all going to be gone. But how could it?

Change. Maybe it's not a bad thing. Maybe it just is. Things just are.

I hate change. It's the only way we ever progress in life. The only way we get anywhere. Ignorance is bliss. Yes it is.

Why can't we be happy and stay there? Why do things have to change? Then when change does happen you have to adapt and try to achieve happiness again. And it's always happier the 2nd time and you feel glad you changed but you wouldn't have known that difference if you just stayed where you were.

I wish I could just pick a moment, call time-out on life and stay 15 for three years in that one moment with the people I love. But time. Time is what it is. Time is what brings about change. Time FORCES you, AGE forces you to change.

Let me melt away. I don't care anymore. I just don't care.

May 22, 2004

First day of summer. Read July 15, 2003. That's exactly how I feel.

I can't believe I'm almost going to be 16.

I organized my room today. I'm trying to get everything together before the movers get here. Friday night before "The Big Cheese Awards" Alex, Tim, and I watched *Orange County* together.

I hate moving. Here we go again. Just rip my soul out and make me start all over again.

Bleed. Bleed into this empty room. Empty. Memories echo back to haunt me. I cried today.

I cried today.

June ?, 2001

I haven't written you in a week. The movers are here now. I'm not sure what date it is 'cause they took my calender down.

I'm full of thoughts. My mind is racing. It's always like this when I move. It's like, in this stage or time frame of gloominess. It hurts so much to lose something you once loved. I mean, you think it wouldn't hurt as much since you knew all along you were going to move, but still. . . you almost wish and hope SO BAD that you could bring back the past.

Gosh. My room looks so dead. It's like. . . colorless. lifeless. empty. with only the echoing memories and spirits of all the happy and sad times I spent in my room with friends or by myself.

(sigh) I think the #1 reason people cry is not because they miss the place or the people but the past and memories they spent with the place and people. People and places change. Whether you go back or not won't make a difference. It just won't be the same.

May 23, 2004

It's raining. Just as if the sky were crying with me.

After church, we stopped by Bro. Whittaker's house and he cut Mom and I the roses from his garden. What a beautiful thing to do. He was telling us that his friend died last week, and it made him remember when he was a little boy he'd always see those June bugs and their shells. His friend was just getting a new shell.

I feel like I'm just getting a new shell too.

Movers come tomorrow. Great. I'm leaving. They all are gone.

Life is sad.

May 24, 2004

The movers are here. I've forgotten just how hard it is to move. God help me.

I'm almost 16. 16 years old. It scares the crap out of me. It really does. I hung out with Joanne. I'm so proud of her. She framed this quote, "Everything comes with great risk, so risk it all, risk it all."

It's kinda our song lyrics combined. I love it.

Wednesday, May 26, 2004 1:36 PM
To: alex

I wish I could've gone to REACH today. Leaving yesterday was so sad. I'm going to miss every part of that Drama room. It's just not fair. I'm really going to miss Melton. After we graduate, dude, we're going to come back to Sumter, pick Tim up, and go on a road trip. Got it? So start saving now!

I hate this right now. The feeling you get when you're not totally sad yet, but you're just depressed, because YOU KNOW you're going to be EVEN MORE depressed in just a little while. And I always have the tendency to think that life is a whole lot more optimistic than it really is. . . so I'll block it all out; think it's not really there. . . but it is. I think you and me and Tim, I think we all hate accepting reality and so we try to bend the possibilities of life. I hated crying in Jay's car yesterday. It always makes me feel like a sissy when I cry in front of guys. It's very 2nd grade, I know.

I'm glad I have someone who understands what I'm going through. That's really important because this is when I feel alone the most. I told you I read all my journals from the past 3 years spent here. And I started counting the pages that had your name on it. More than half of the pages mention you, Alex. For the first year it was more of a stalker kind of way like, "Omg Alex is so funny! I like him so much! Alex is blah, blah, blah," but most of the time it's how you were my best friend. How much I could talk to you and the funny jokes you would tell me and how I couldn't wait to get your next email.

You are loved, Alex. Remember that always.

~kristen

Thursday, May 27, 2004 3:17 PM
From: alex

Hey Kristen! How are you? You know I'm sure we'll end up here again for some strange reason and we'll all hang out again, it just seems hard to think it would all work out like this again. I really do think this is an endless cycle.

You know it seems like not long ago I was down in that business center staring at the screen knowing I had like 2 minutes before I had to leave for the flight to Saudi Arabia. Just sitting there staring at the screen. Thinking that I was gone forever and that I'd never see anyone ever again.

I don't think I ever told you about the flight to Paris. That flight sucked really bad. I mean it was really late and dark and everything and EVERYONE else is sleeping but me. So I'm just sitting there bored and tired and worn out and just wishing I could either sleep or see my friends again. And I pulled out my notebook and I read your note again, and again, and again, just trying to find an answer and I started crying and no one was there. They were all sleeping in their little dreamy worlds and I was sitting there miserable and crying.

That flight really sucked. I just hoped that no one would wake up and see me and be all like, "What's wrong with him?" or maybe I wanted someone to wake up so they could realize I am a HUMAN BEING! Yes, that's right folks. I am human. I'm human, other guys are human. Yes, I know it's hard to imagine we can handle the whole being human, but yes.

It's so hard to be human. That's really funny to hear about your diary. I never really kept a journal or anything, so I could never tell you how many pages you were on. I mean, I just go by memory. Let's see, I remember laughing til I cried just about every day with you. I remember learning more about myself through you than I ever have.

I'm sorry, I just feel dead. I'm tired and I'm trying to pound it into my head that tomorrow you're leaving. I can't do it.

I know it's sad leaving the Drama room and leaving this life behind, but, but in many ways that's a good thing. It's not all bad and I hate to sound like you leaving is all good. I mean, you should know of all people, there is good stuff in what you're about to experience.

Peace out girl scout. . . never lose touch, I know you won't.

-Alex

May 28, 2004

I said goodbye.

The Goo Goo Dolls were playing in Sis. Dennis's car when I said goodbye to Robert and Sarah. I think that was a perfect moment. Saying goodbye to Alex and Tim was. . . like. . . growing up. Like. . . I was 5 years old and then turned around and realized I was 40? It's hard to explain. Said goodbye to Alex AGAIN. You know, I might just marry Alex Kyger. Who knows. Why did I write that?

Why do we grow up? Why? Let us live in our dream. We're dreamers.

Gosh, I'll miss them. I'll miss my friends. I guess I'll make new ones, but geez. It won't be the same. Sam keeps hope alive that I'll see Alex and Tim and Sarah again though, because I'm gunna see her this summer. I can't wait for that. I'll miss Drama with Melton so much though. SO MUCH! I'll miss Tim. I love him. I do.

It's all been one long dream and I'm waking up. I'm waking up alone. I'm all alone.

But I can always fall asleep and dream again.

Love, Kristenacious J

October 20, 2002

I played Robert my song "Pancakes" when he dropped off Sarah's stuff. They were both the 2nd people to hear my song. Kayla was the first. I don't think Mom and Dad know I have a song.

Pancakes

What's your name?
I'm a nerd, dork, freak, whatever
It's all the same
I like your pants
Hey talk to me you're cool
Are you thinking the same by chance?

Are you?

I knew you would.

I'm stupid weird and odd
You always see the good
I hope that we
Can laugh a lot together
Have fun just you and me.

'Cause time goes by like rain,
Seconds turn to days
I don't want to drown
It's sunny with you
Clouds will turn away

Hey hey
Everything just sucks
But you just made my day
You make me smile
I didn't think you'd notice
It makes it all worth while

Live each day
Like you haven't got a future before
This slips away
Don't make me cry
Never make yourself believe
This is goodbye.

One day we will run
And nothing will have changed
I'll still make you smile
Make sense of all that's strange

One day we will run
We will run away.

What's your name?

in boxes

"*The distance is quite simply much too far for me to row. It seems farther than ever before. I need you so much closer.*"
- *Death Cab For Cutie*

Kristen,

I don't know where to start. I still don't think it has sunk in that you are really leaving. I guess by the time you read this you'll actually be gone. That's sad.

Think back. Me, you, and Alex hanging out in Florence. That was the most fun and the happiest I'd been in a long time. It was. . . or maybe just is, like a dream. It was so awesome, you can't hold onto it. I remember it being great, but it hurts to think about, a little. It was a lot of fun.

I wish I had gotten to know you and hung out with you before the month before you moved. Kristen, you are hands down the coolest person I've ever met. And I mean that with all of my heart. I admire your musical and songwriting talent; I respect your honesty. Your friendliness blows me away. You have this deep passion for life and a curious nature that I hope you never lose. You are so funny and so great to be around, I'm happy just to have known you. I don't know if I should tell you or not and it may freak you out, but for a bit I thought I was in love with you. I realized though that it was just this want to be around such a cool person.

I don't know why I'm telling you all of this. I'm only writing it because I think I sound better in print.

Kristen, please don't lose your love of life. Keep playing those guitars, keep searching for answers. Don't get tied up in some gross desk job, unless you want to. In which case you still have to be kick-A.

Thank you for making May 2004 one of the best months of my life. And if I don't ever see you again, ROCK ON!

Your friend,

Timothy Threet

June 2, 2004

Could it really be? It's June already? It's like, 4:00 in the morning. I'm not tired. At all. I spent the entire night unpacking. It's so unreal to me. Moving. I don't feel like I'm HERE, I still feel like I'm in Sumter.

I've been so nostalgic lately. I can't help but wonder what everyone else is doing in Sumter. I bet they're having fun.

I feel so indifferent to everything. Like I don't know if I feel like. . . well I don't know if I feel more like a 6-year-old or a 20-year-old, I just feel like I have no age.

March 24, 1999

I am so confused about my future and my past. I have a lot ahead of me, but I miss Brittany and San Antonio soooo much. I miss my friends. I have so much stuff going on, I'm the "c" word.* (confused).

* Thanks for the clarification, 11-year-old Kristen

This place is too perfect. I feel like I'm trapped in Pleasantville.

I feel like I've lost a sense of reality. Maybe that's why I haven't felt much emotion. I wish I could go back. That's all. Go back in time. Live some moments over and over again.

What am I doing? I feel so LOST! Why am I NOBODY? I've lost all friction. I don't think I'm myself. I'm not who I used to be because so much of me was parts of Sarah, Meagan, Tim, and Alex, and Joanne! And they're gone! So where am I?

Who am I?

I'm nobody.

I am a blank sheet of paper.

Thursday, June 3, 2004 3:11 PM
From: alex

Hey Kristen!

REACH is going well. . . It's exciting. . . but it feels odd without you. I guess I feel like, "Oh, she'll be here tomorrow." It just hasn't hit me yet I guess. It never does. This life has made me that way. Don't feel anything, just hyper CONSTANTLY, or at least most of the time. You know that. You understand. I'm afraid no one else ever will. That made me want to be close to you, I felt that I could trust you and that you could be a friend and not be like everyone else. You made it all better, all the time, whether you knew it or not. It's crazy the guy with the most friends in the world: one person understands him. Thanks for that.

I just want to be there for you like you always were for me. You're special, Kristen. I wish things were the way they once were, but of course that'd be too easy. I'll talk to you later. Peace out girl scout!

-Alex

Dearest Sarah,

Oh Sarah, lol. I LOVED your letter. And Meggo's letter. Both make me laugh really, really, really hard. They depict your personalities so well.

The other night I was crying because I felt like I was such a NOBODY here. Like I wasn't even sure of my personality anymore. I was so LOST! But I realized that I would find my personality in you guys and that I can just carry you with me always.

I miss your house. It's really weird I guess. . . but I miss the shed and the jam sessions, and I miss Katherine's bedroom where we used to play truth or dare all the time. I miss your fridge.

Keep writing me. . . I love ya, Sarah. You understand me so well.

Love, Kristen

When you solely depend on the ones you love for your sense of identity—self esteem, sense of humor, interests—you completely lose who you are when they're gone. What's left? You are a shell of a human being, barely hanging on to the scattered shreds of your soul. You have no self worth. There's nothing you feel like doing. You are reduced to laugh at only memories of things that used to happen in your former life with the people you are torn from.

When you are abandoned, you feel empty. Alone and empty. Like you're aware of your body; you know you are breathing, but you're not sure if you're alive.

June 6, 2001

I miss school so much. I miss all of my friends. I. miss. it. so. much.

I'm all alone. I wish we could visit the past. I mean, not to change things but just to see them over again.

June 7, 2004

Fender is on my bed. What a great dog. She's so cool.

Looking at pictures of Robert, Sarah and Meagan is just so weird. They seem so far away. That's sad.

Tuesday, June 8, 2004 8:01 PM
From: tim
Subject: Aaand roachie. . . and roachie. . .

Your birthday is like, August 11th, right? Or something. Because I want to send you a present. Not to give it away or anything, but you would wear a small tee-shirt right? And then you get it in the mail and it's a football phone or something. Haha. No, I want to get you that shirt that says "Kristenacious J: Set the Artist Free" on it. And copies for me and Alex. The gift that keeps on giving.

Talk to you on the flipflop,

t-bone

June 9, 2004

It's weird. I keep thinking, not even 3 weeks ago I was sitting at the Baskin Robbins table in Sumter with Meagan, Robert, and Sarah. The same Baskin Robbins Joanne used to work at. The same table we ate free ice cream at the day we played the coffee shop, December 19.

It's crazy. I can't stop thinking about it all. I'm screaming and crying inside. I know it. But I haven't really cried about it yet. It scares me. I'm moving way too fast.

I wish Sarah was here.

Hey Tim— Guess what I found this girl had today? FUDGE Hershey kisses. I totally freaked out and took like. . . 12. They made me think of you. And sure enough I had little foil balls in my pocket. I miss hanging out at your place.

June 10, 2004

It's a beautiful thing. When you are a kid you have no schedule, no real comprehension of time. You just live. Each moment at a time. That's what I imagine heaven to be like.

I love looking out the window of a car when the sun's going down. It gives you that feeling. . .

The whole time I had flashbacks of my life. All the greatest moments of my life. It makes me cry. They're moments so great—moments you can't touch. Something that feels so far away. Like the stars. I get the same feeling at night when I'm all alone and I look up at the stars. Makes me want to reach up and touch them. To fly up and escape everything. From it all. I yearn to. And that feeling is so overwhelming I get choked up.

And so we live.

I think how many millions of billions of people throughout the world, through the world's entire existence, have looked up at those same stars and felt the same thing.

Monday, June 14, 2004 1:19 AM
From: tim
Subject: Great galloping hula hoops!

Hey, so, what if you could have any power or ability that you wanted, what would it be?

At first, I'd say invisibility, but it's SO hard because you can still be heard and felt, so people will freak out if you aren't extremely careful. And I don't like heights so I don't want to fly. I think I'd want the ability to create destruction with my mind. In church or the library or something, just think really, really hard and I can make all the windows explode and then be like, "What in the world was that?!" or to be able to speak any language at all. Including sign language, the language of love, music notation, computer 'ones and zeros', Morse code, and that African one where they just click their tongues and blink a lot. That's a language right?

Gotta go. The roaches are reading over my shoulder, and I think they're out to get me fired! See you when my eyes fall out and I ship them to Florida in a little box that's not big enough for anything else so you just have to display it.

-teerht mit

Monday, June 14, 2004 11:55 PM
To: tim
Subject: Good question

I think I'd want the power to stop time. . . wait no change that. No I don't want that. No, no, no, no, no. Okay, okay, okay, okay. I want the ability to visit any memory in my mind, whenever, and however many times. Ha. So you don't have to go back in time in order to relive moments. . . because that's really, really dangerous, and it prolly won't be the same. It won't be as you REMEMBERED it. . . sooooo yeah. The ability to visit any memory in my mind, to relive the memory, even the ones I've forgotten. Yes. That's a good one you have to admit.

Flight. . . I don't know why, but I have this incredible, like a tugging within my heart to just fly up there and touch the stars (or at least get closer) every time I look at them. And that's the only time I'd want that.

Ooh! Oh! But another power is to be any place, any time with just a thought, in an instant. Like, as a "there's no place like home" type of thing. Think of how much time we'd save without travel. Then I could visit anyone, anytime. No problem!

I sometimes wish the Earth (the planet itself, the environment) would act according to my emotion. Like when I'm crying I want it to rain, when

I'm really angry I just want a window to explode and shatter in a million pieces, when I'm discouraged I want things to melt away, you know? Wouldn't that be cool? Expressing yourself with destruction? It would be a little selfish. . . eh. But still, that's a cool power.

Okay so top three powers are:(in no particular order of preference)

1) Mind travel—being anywhere whenever you want to, in a second

2) Memory travel—being able to visit any memory

3) Expression through destruction

You know one thing I could change, instead of expression through destruction it should be expression through nature, so it doesn't have to be only when you're in a negative mood. A flower should blossom if you're in love. A breeze should come when you're satisfied. The leaves should fall when you're having fun. It should snow when it's Christmas! Yeah I like that a lot. Okay so,

3) Expression through nature. (or the environment around you)

There. That's my top 3.

*netsirk ylsuoicanetsirk

Thursday, June 17, 2004 12:07 AM
From: tim
Subject: Ultimate powers

Good question? Good FREAKING answer. That was the best effing email I've ever read. Good, good answer.

So I'm hanging out in Georgia right now with my dad. I drove down by myself, which was awesome because my mom lent me her car—air conditioning and a CD player/radio! Luxuries to me. It was very adulty. Loads of fun, blasting Tenacious D and Rush and The Doors and singing and driving 85 mph down the interstate and back roads by myself.

I also saw a van that had this huge thing painted on the back of it: "I know why divorce costs so much—It's worth it!" in humungo letters. I was embarrassed for him.

I'm still working on guitar. Spending a lot of time on my dad's acoustic. I really want to get one, but the 350 dollars I have I'm saving for a trip to England. And my mom would buy a 40 dollar one for me, but I would break it and kill myself with the jagged, plastic bits.

Breathlessly awaiting your reply,

Your secret admirer (but it's Tim)

Thursday, June 17, 2004 4:52 PM
From: tim
Subject: Am, F, C, G—

Kristenacious J!

You rock my world. No, I haven't gotten your letter yet, but I can't wait. I'm getting together a box of stuff to send to you; pockets and stuff. I ripped off one pocket for you and it destroyed my shirt. It was hilarious. I was in the living room with my mother and I thought, "I should give this pocket to Kristen," so I reached down and ripped really hard at it and it just, chunked this huge pocket-width stripe out of the side of my shirt. My mom was like, "What the freak?" and I was crippled with laughter. It was great.

You need to read Catcher in the Rye and The Perks of Being a Wallflower. Seriously, dude, do it now while you're young. You would really, really appreciate them. They are #s 1 and 2 on my ever-changing favorites list.

Hey, I'm writing a song for you and Alex. You inspired me. I was messing around and all of the sudden it started coming out, so I wrote it down.

-gringo threet

Thursday, June 17, 2004 9:25 PM
From: alex

Hey Kristen! How are you, darling?

I'm in New Mexico now. I've been spending a lot of time just thinking lately. It feels like everywhere I go people are pressuring me to know what I want to do in my life. I'm still searching. It's all I've ever done so far. You know things felt so clear with you around. But I guess I just need to do some more growing up.

Sorry to make it seem like when I email you that I'm just some lost puppy dog wandering around. . . but maybe that's what I am. Who knows kiddo. It's just good to talk to someone I guess. Hard to find someone who might understand as all I hear is, "Your brother's really going places!" or, "Yea, they have real talent" or, "They've got it all and will take the world by storm" and maybe that's just not me. Although it would be fine to make some noise every once in a while. I think I've made a lot of noise, maybe just the wrong noise? AHHH WHO CARES!? It doesn't matter and the only time I really think about it is when I talk to you because I figure you should understand. . . maybe just a little? Peace out girl scout

-Alex

Thursday, June 17, 9:49 PM
To: tim

Remember that Tuesday we hung out in Ray's van? It's crazy to think about. That was the first time we ever hung out! Makes me think, what other people have I not met that could be my best friend, ya know? Remember I asked you guys in the field, "I wonder if there are other people like us in the world. . . I wish we could meet them."

*jristen kex

Friday, June 18, 2004 3:14 AM
From: tim

I don't know if it's all the coffee I've had, or the fact that it's 3:00 a.m., or because I'm holed up in my dad's house with little to do but play guitar and read teen-angsty novels, but I'm totally in love with you.

I hate that all we can do is email all the time, but they'll make due, I guess.

I'd rather hang out. I feel high, but you are the best person ever. I don't know. I just want to talk to you over coffee and cigarettes in New York or something.

I made cookies tonight called "sand tarts" and I have no idea why they aren't just called "sugar cookies" because that's what they are. My dad got called in to brief his squadron on some drill thing, so he was gone from 6 to midnight, after working a full day. So I was hanging around, working on my song and reading Perks of Being a Wallflower and I wanted cookies, so I found a recipe. They're pretty boring.

I should be reading my summer reading (Lord of the Flies and Mayor of Casterbridge) but I didn't bring "flies" and I don't even have "mayor" yet. We have to buy our own copies this year because kids always steal and damage the provided ones. I really don't mind, I always steal my copies anyway.

I need to get back to Sumter and hang out with some people. I feel really lonesome. It might just be tonight, but I'm sad. Is it bad that I don't really want to hang out with anyone other than you? Alex and I haven't done anything together since you left.

Sorry to be weird tonight. It's 3 a.m. and I just felt like talking.

Love always,

underdog billy

Friday, June 18, 2004 3:24 AM
From: tim
Subject: november 7, 1991

I forgot. In my last email I wanted to copy down a little of Perks of Being a Wallflower for you because I like it so much. But I got sidetracked. As soon as I'm done with it, I'll send my copy to you, if you like. It's really good.

Love always,

henry the 8th.

Friday, June 18, 2004 4:26 PM
From: tim

So this morning I went to a diner for breakfast—called "Waffle King," if you believe it. If I was going to be king of something, it'd be a lot nicer than waffles—with my dad because we like those sort of things together, but I wasn't very hungry. I ordered a coffee and a water and a piece of apple pie, warmed with a piece of cheese on top. I've always been so effing curious about that. What is that? Does that taste good? Who knows. I still don't, because she discovered they didn't have any. But she offered me carrot cake which I promptly accepted saying, "My friend Kristen would really want me to have the carrot cake." She half nodded and gave it to me, completely lost, but I enjoyed the carrot cake anyway. You were right—it was delicious cake. And it didn't taste like carrots, which is the taste I was expecting.

I'm hitting the road myself again tomorrow. Driving back to Sumter. Wish you and Alex were going with me.

Ton ami,

benoit

Friday, June 18, 2004 7:35 PM
From: alex

Hey Kristen! How are you? We just saw Eternal Sunshine of the Spotless Mind with Jim Carrey. It was amazing. It's about this guy who lives the life we constantly never want and he meets this girl. An amazing girl who gets him away from this life, but they eventually separate and she goes to this doctor to have him erased from her memory. He finds out so he tries to do the same and erase her. As it goes on, the two of them realize they have to run away from being erased, that they like their life together. And it comes down to the last memory. . . the one where he meets her. . . and she says to him "So, this is it. Soon it'll all be gone. . . What do we do?" and he says, "Enjoy it."

YES! I LOVE IT! It was. . . It was amazing and it was crazy. I mean, I just sat up in my seat and just stared at the screen thinking those lines over and over again in my head. "Soon it'll all be gone. What do we do?" "Enjoy it." They don't run anymore.

You HAVE to see this movie. I loved it. It meant so much. I mean, I sat there and just. . . I left that theatre with it running in my head still. "Enjoy it." It was perfect. You know in moments where you feel like you can never make decisions, I certainly felt it all made sense when Jim Carrey said that line. It all became clear to me.

I'll talk to you later and peace out girl scout.

-Alex

Saturday, June 19, 2004 1:14 AM
From: tim

Hey. I'm sorry I keep writing you so much. I was lying in bed just now trying to get to sleep, and I couldn't keep my mind from racing and I got more and more awake, and sometimes I get a little panicky about stuff. I thought if I just went ahead and asked you some questions, I might get to sleep.

As soon as this weekend is over, I'm going to call Ray. Because I haven't hung out with him since that one Tuesday, and we were going to be the hang-out team. I need to just sit with someone who understands life and music. I haven't had that since you left and it was amazing before.

I was thinking about all kinds of stuff and for some reason I got really, really sad about all the people who jumped off the World Trade Center when it was hit by a plane because they'd rather hit the ground than burn alive. And I got extremely sad for them. And I felt what it was like to be them and to jump and then close my eyes and wait for—what? They wouldn't have felt anything, but I think because of air pressure and stuff they would have known when the ground was coming close.

Also, I want to know what you think about drugs. I mean, I know you're Mormon and have a pretty clean plan for life, but honestly I wouldn't be against trying them. Perks of Being a Wallflower doesn't glamorize them, but it makes me want to try something. It might just be an experimental youth thing, and I know you're going to say, "DUDE. . . Don't do drugs! They will totally mess you up, Tim. You don't need drugs to experience life." But I'm all about trying everything at least once (well, to a certain extent. I don't ever want to murder someone). You only have one life to live, this is it—why would you not want to experience everything? And go everywhere?

And also, what should I do with my hair?

Yeah, sorry for all that again. I just get sometimes where I feel like I need to cry but I can't, and I feel very alone all of the sudden like I'm the only one who understands anything, and I thought if I said it all to you that I could sleep. But I still feel a little weird. But I don't know, I value what you have to say. Haha, sorry about all this. You don't have to reply if you don't want to.

Love always,

t

September 19, 2001

It was when I came home that day that I really started thinking about what happened. I started thinking about all the people who died and all the people who tried to save them. I think about it in my head, trying to imagine how many people have died. It's all there is on the news. It's really depressing. The only I thing I can bear to watch is cartoons.

Sam has called me almost every single day to make sure I'm alive and well. I miss her so much. I've never grown so close to a person before. She's in Nebraska. We talk, like, all the time, but it just isn't the same. I miss my friends. I always do when I move; I miss everything. Then I think it's okay, then we move again, and I miss it.

Today was a pretty good day because Dad's coming home. He was in Saudi Arabia when the planes crashed in New York, and he couldn't tell us anything after that, but today he called and said he was coming home.

Saturday, June 19, 2004 2:30 PM
To: tim

Last night I pretended I was on E! or something and I was talking to Jack Black and it was really funny.

I laughed at some of the things we talked about and then I thought about what the perfect first kiss would be and then I thought about my life and the past places I lived and friends I've left behind. . . then I cried when I thought about Ted. I mean I cried for like a whole hour.

February 25, 2002

Ted's moving this summer. I cried Friday all afternoon. I cried myself to sleep. I'm gunna miss Ted a lot. I don't like thinking about it, but I know he's gunna have to leave. He said he found out today he's going to move to Albuquerque, New Mexico.

I haven't talked to Ted in, like, a year. But it just sorta hit me. Ted used to be this amazing person with all these great ideas and viewpoints. The Ted I knew is gone. He's dead.

You know. . . I've thought that same thing. This is life. Why not try everything? And I really do think if it wasn't for the family I have and the gospel I believe in, I would've totally done it a long time ago. Sometimes it's hard to suppress the curiosity.

Don't ever be afraid to tell me anything. I'm your best friend! The other day I made someone's wallet talk by doing your "ELLO! My namez Ritchardzen!" voice. I was disappointed; I think they would've laughed 10 times harder if you did it.

bis spater ~gabi

Saturday, June 19, 2004 10:04 PM
From: tim

Okay, you've convinced me on the drugs. Ted was really cool and now he is pretty sad, and I made the direct connection between that and the "bullets of meth" he shoots.

p.s. I got your letter in the mail. It was great to see your handwriting again. You're still alive!

Snow angels in July,

Richardson

Monday, June 21, 2004 9:42 PM
To: tim

I love airplanes. I mean, you're nowhere. For once, you're nowhere. It's like an escape. And all there is is the clouds. They're so beautiful it's a shame you can't touch them. I mean that there's nothing to touch. This is the first time I'll be flying by myself. So I'm kinda going on one of your road trips to Georgia. . . 'cept it's on a plane. I feel kinda adultish too.

Later ~kristen

Tuesday, June 22, 2004 2:58 PM
From: tim

Yeah, I'm not a big fan of airplanes. They scare me because I have this huge overactive imagination, so I can't not picture it plummeting to the ground and how it would feel to get ripped out the window and how would it feel to see some random couple get picked up and slammed into the ceiling. . . It's not cool. I get a little panicky.

Wishing you all the happiness and cheese-puffs the world has to offer,

timbo jonesy

Tuesday, June 22, 2004 11:35 AM
To: alex

Alex, You're a tough kid. It broke my heart every time you talked about Saudi when we went on those "skipping school" trips. It really did. 'Cause I knew you missed it. I mean, even I didn't realize until the day you came back that you were going to miss all your friends and stuff there. Everybody thought that this was just going to be great for them 'cause Alex was back. "Alex wants to see me, Alex wants to hang out with me, Alex didn't have friends over there so he'll be happy to see me." That sorta thing. I sat up in bed one night and actually thought about it and it HIT me. The whole terror behind the whole thing. I almost cried. My word Alex, it's just sad. And having your dad over there and stuff. . . and knowing all your friends are still there.

How did we ever know life was going to take this turn? I would've never imagined. . . makes me think. What kind of future will I have? Really you can't plan life, if you do, it doesn't matter 'cause it'll STILL end up being something you never imagined. Sometimes I feel like it makes us grow up too fast, you know? And I hate that, but it's good at the same time I guess. ~kristen

Tuesday, June 22, 2004 3:34 PM
From: alex

Hey Kristen! How are you?

I blew my nose in the most wonderful tissue this morning. It was magical.

It's funny you tell me I'm a tough kid. The director I worked with in Riyadh would always ask me, "Alex, is there anything that would rattle you? I mean does anything affect you?" I get that from my dad. The whole, "Oh, ok" attitude about most things. Of course being an emotional teen-ager at times I do tend to go "NOOO! BUT I DON'T WANNA! I DON'T WANNA EVACUATE! I LIKE IT HERE!" Living there was like living in a nice little bubble. Sure, a bubble full of terrorism and threats, but a nice bubble none-the-less. Back to reality. No more terrorist days off of school. Those were the best.

I think moving does make us grow up faster, in a good way. Then again, it's taught me to never get attached to anything. Kind of sad. Sad when you don't feel anything for anything half the time. I mean this house could go up in flames, I wouldn't care. You know, I'd care if I lost you for good. It's never for good, I've learned that. Just hope it continues.

You know Kristen, the Thursday I found out I was being evacuated (on a day I wouldn't know til the day of, and for reasons I was never allowed to know), I was at school walking around with withdraw forms and transfer records and kids were looking at me with big eyes, and my close friend Nikki was crying as I walked to the office. I just walked past them all. I can't get that image of her out of my head. Just bawling. And I just kind of gave a little smile. Just something that may have comforted them. I'm still not sure who was more confused. Them or me. They had no clue what was going on. I felt like I was leaving them behind. Something big was about to go down and I was leaving, and they were left in fear. Lost . . . just searching for anything that could comfort us.

You know what I found comfort in? Coming home. I thought about you, I thought about my friends back home. It still hurt to say bye that day, unsure of what was ahead of me or them. All of it was so. . . so fast. . . standing on that picnic table by the 10th grade lockers telling them that I'd be back. . .

Not so sure of that anymore. Driving to the airport at 2:00 in the morning in the armored van with the escort. Walking through security and looking back at my dad. And sitting on that plane, reading the letters from my friends same as when I left Sumter. . . Only this time I didn't cry. I smiled. I smiled at the experience. No regrets.

You have no idea how exciting it was pulling up to your house that night. I just couldn't hold it in. . . and I ended up hitting Tim with a bottle or something. I realize now that a lot of people don't like me anymore because they get angry at me for wanting to go back. I told Katie M. that I was going to see friends from Riyadh in Denver and she was all, "NO! No you're not!" and I got so mad.

They wouldn't understand. . . you understand. They never will. Thank you for that.

Last night you sang me to sleep. I couldn't sleep. I just. . . I have this feeling in me and I don't know what it is. And I feel horrible. I feel sick almost. I feel bad and yet there's no one I can tell. I mean, who would I tell? So I keep staring. And I want to talk to someone. I always just want to talk to someone. Just. . . one problem. No one to talk to. The only person I can talk to is you.

My dad comes in today. I'm really excited about that! Yeah, things are looking not so nice over there, but there is hope that maybe one day I can go back and be with my dad. I'd like to go back, but then again I want it too bad, so I'll never get it. You never get what you want, which leaves me hesitant for almost everything I think I want.

Kristen, I'm not a tough kid. My dad. . . now there's a tough kid. I don't want to end this email. Man, I miss Riyadh. . . putting soap bubbles in the general's fountain, running away from the MPs in a ballerina outfit, asking the MPs if they want to play manhunt. . . just being free in my little bubble. Dangerous bubble. Of course it wasn't all great. Not being able to sleep at 3:00 in the morning, walking to the bathroom and seeing on the door "Alex, no school today, go back to bed," seeing smoke in the sky, helicopters flying around the school.

You know nothing's perfect. It's just how you take it. I'll talk to you later kiddo. Peace out girl scout.

-Alex

On the morning of September 11th, 2001, I was in Mrs. Sherer's 8th grade English class. Alex was in that class too, though we didn't really know each other then. We were desks away, and had no idea how those planes would change our lives, or bring us together.

It sent Alex to Saudi Arabia. It sent my dad to the Middle East for months at a time, leaving my mom practically a single parent for two years.

The summer before Alex moved, my dad thought we were moving to Turkey. It was a sliver of hope for me, because it could've been a way to see Alex in Saudi Arabia, but we didn't. In the Air Force you never know for sure where you are going to live from one year to the next or how long you'll stay.

People always want to know where you're "from." It's customary, I know, but I don't really know where I'm from. I moved nine times before I graduated high school. So I don't know how to sum up my origin, between 6 different states and a different country.

Alex was right. It did make us grow up too fast. We had to uproot our lives before we had even finished growing, and lay them down again, over and over.

June 28, 2004

I feel like I'm nowhere. Somehow I keep telling myself home is in Sumter where Alex is. But it's not. And he's not.

I miss Sarah.

There was a girl here I saw with a guitar and I tried to say hey but she seemed really busy so I left her alone.

Tuesday, July 6, 2004 5:35 PM
From: tim
Subject: KRISTEN!

I love/adore you and haven't talked to you in weeks! I feel like I slipped into a wrinkle in time to an alternate dimension where you don't exist (horror!). What's happening? How was flying, how was your trip? I want to hear all about it.

Your box is on the way, and check it out, check it out! I finished my song for you and Alex. It rocks so hard and it all came together and I'm so very excited. I'm so proud of myself. I finished it; I've written a song with a GUITAR that really expresses true emotion/period of my existence. I need to, like, tape myself doing it or something and send it to you, but it'll sound all crappy on tape. I need to do it in person. So that settles it, you're moving back. Lol.

Lots of little meow meow goods,

timborufus from bananna-ramma republic

July 18, 2004

Sam's house. I'm so glad nothing's changed between me and Sam. It's a good feeling. It really is. She's special. She's like a key. A key that can fit every door, every personality. She's so optimistic. That doesn't mean she's never sad. . . but she's. . . I dunno. I've never had a fight with her. NEVER. She's just funny and sweet and loving. Her smile is just so honest.

Seeing Sam again was like coming home. Almost like going back.

I've changed so much, yet I haven't at all. Personality is a funny thing. I think personality stays constant. . . It's just the way your personality is perceived changes with your behavior.

And how smart you are.

Anyway, I've had a lot to think about this summer. About who I want to be. Who I am. What I'm grateful for. I'm so lucky. My life is SO much easier than anyone I know.

Thursday, July 22, 2004 4:28 AM
From: tim
Subject: Hey Kristers-

How was your time with Sam? A wild and crazy girl party? Any rock and rolling? I hope so—girl bands are cool. I was sad the other day because I was ready for school to start back so I could see my friends, but I realized that most of them, including you, won't be at SHS next year. A depressing state of affairs.

Missing our email discussions wildly,

timfrutig the barig gut.

Thursday, July 22, 2004 5:16 PM
To: tim

TIM! I got your package! Thank you for the pockets. I now have 9. I finished Perks of Being a Wallflower. I liked it.

I'm extremely sick. I mean the kind of sick where you're sore and achy all over and you wrap yourself up in a blanket and sleep all day and wake up at 2:45 in the morning only to peel yourself off the covers and your head is buzzing constantly.

But anyway. Here's all what I did at Sam's house:

We went to Linoma beach (Which is really a lake. . . I thought it was hilarious they called it a beach.) It was really cool; they have these big inflatable glacier things that you can climb up on. Sam would always do some fancy double flip dive off the 25 foot one. She's a showoff. She's really athletic though. Like. . . she's really pretty and flirty, and really funny. . . and she's a total tomboy. I mean like, she can really kick a guy's ass. No kidding. So she's like every guy's perfect girl basically. And she's SO much fun to be around.

I also saw *Spider Man 2* and Sam grabbed me at this really scary part and I screamed. And she laughed. It was great!

I think the highlight of my stay at Sami's was going to the 311 concert. People came all the way from Chicago to see them play in their home town. It was the first rock show I'd ever been to and it ROCKED! There was this blue tarp thingy that people were popping people on, like. . . you know how 2 or 3 kids hold one towel and fling water balloons over a net? It was like that, 'cept they were popping a kid up in the air. So anyway, Sam wanted to do it really bad so she did and I did too. I went like 10 feet up in the air! Then I went crowd surfing and that was like a dream come true. I've always wanted to try it, and it was everything I imagined it to be. It was great. Except when I got up front close to the stage some punk grabbed my boob and WOULD NOT LET GO. I was like, "What the eff!" but eventually and luckily one of the bouncer/guards—whatever— pulled me down. So it was awesome! A little scary. . . but awesome! I even bought this really cool 311 t-shirt. I told Sam all about you and she thinks you're a very cool kid.

I can't wait to see you in your next email. . .

~kristenaciously kristen.

Tuesday, July 27, 2004 3:22 PM
From: tim

I'm sorry you're sick. If you still are. I hate being sick, especially when it makes you weak and you just sigh and roll over in bed and blow your nose.

I totally want to meet Sam. She sounds almost as cool as you, which is not easy, let me tell you. Guys like kick-ass girls—girly psycho girls who need all this pampering and attention are total b.s. If you're a girl who I can make out with, but also hang out with the guys and not be all, "You guys are slobs," that's cool. But you don't want a girl who is more manly than you. It's a fine line, Kristen.

Hugs and kisses to Fender.

-totally turnip

Wednesday, August 4, 2004 3:05 PM
To: tim

Hey guess who's birthday is this month on the 26th? I don't know why people have to call it my "Sweet Sixteen" though. It makes me feel really weird. Like I'm turning into Emily Chance or something.

So school starts tomorrow. Yikes. Yes, I'm afraid I'll have to go back unwilling and ill-prepared. Write back soon,

~meep zorp.

Wednesday, August 4, 2004 3:52 PM
From: tim
Subject: Watashi-wa ofuro-ni hairi-mashita. Ebi-ga keki-o tabe-masen!

Boy, it seems like yesterday we were skipping school to hang out with Alex or sitting in Ray's van after school. This summer flew past. (It really scares me how everything I write to you anymore is about how old we are or how fast time flies. I don't like that.) I hope you have a great time, anyway.

I know having to switch schools when you don't want to kind of sucks, but you'll have 100s of friends in no time. And probably better teachers;

Florida's education is better than S.C.'s (Seeing as we're what? 49th in the nation? 50th now?). I wish I was there with you.

I love and adore you,

Spankers Fluff McTriggerson.

chapter three

pages of me

"So many faces, I don't know the names.
So many friends now and none of them mine."
- The Bravery

Thursday, August 5, 2004 4:04 PM
To: tim

So today, the first day of school, went perfectly actually. . . That was nice.
I got this overwhelming feeling at lunch, though, when I looked over the
entire cafeteria and couldn't recognize one face. And then I imagined
how many faces I would've recognized at Sumter High. I about cried
right then and there. I guess it goes to show that no matter who you are,
high school is tough. I just felt stupid for some reason. I felt really stupid.
It sucked. Bad. So lunch was really, really, really depressing. BUT! I DID
meet friends. I met this girl named Hailey. She's in my Improv class.

That's all I know about her 'cause attendance called me up in the middle of Improv class so I could take an ESL test because they thought English was my second language. I've never felt so insulted. But the lady there was really nice and she figured I knew English so she let me skip to the end to write a short essay. And through the whole process I met a Filipino guy named Ricky who was in the same situation. He was someone to share my frustration with.

So let's see, Hailey, Ricky, Oh! And this guy named Nathan? I think. Some blonde surfer dude who sat next to me in Physics. He was really nice. And he is also in my English class. And that's about it. I also had to ride the bus home, which is always a pain because the kids who normally ride the bus are just outright raunchy, lousy people. So I hate tolerating that. But I survived. It's good.

I miss it being the way it was though. And here we are on the "time" subject again. Gosh I dunno. I feel like I'm lying to myself when I try to be positive, because I'm trying to be positive in a sucky situation. And no one is truly positive in sucky situations. I'm sorry I'm being negative.

I miss you horribly. Yes, lots and lots of hugs. ~kristen

P.S. I loved your Japanese subject line. If I'm correct, you were trying to say "I have entered the bath" and. . . "Shrimp can't eat cake." Nice. Perfect!

Henji o haiyaku kaite ne!

~kuri

August 7, 2001
I'm not sure I'm making friends too well, but I'm trying.
Love,
Kiyomi

Monday, August 9, 2004 1:07 AM
From: tim

KRISTEN! I love (emphasis)you(end emphasis)! You make me feel ecstatic!

I wish I could have been the face in the strange new cafeteria that you saw across the way, and I caught your eye and you were all, "TIIIIIM!" That would have been nice for you. Sucks that you moved. But it sounds like you're already the most popular girl in school. Or among Hailey, Ricky, and Nathan. They sound like fake people because I don't know them, you know? I'm a face person not a name person, so until I meet someone they are, like, nothing in my head.

I've been thinking about some great birthday ideas for you, but they're all going to take time, so you have to wait and get a (maybe extremely) late birthday present. I'd say I was sorry, but I don't think it's too big of a deal, is it? You know I slack (said in urban voice).

Hugs and mint candies and dreams and clouds and the best song in the world,

Couch Tomato.

Monday, August 9, 2004 4:56 PM
To: tim

TIM! OH MY GOSH, what took so long? I've missed you so, so, SO, SO MUCH! Already most popular kid in school? You gotta be kidding me. Okay the people I listed were people I TALKED TO at school, who were gracious enough to let me have a little human contact. But geez Tim, popular? I'm a long, long way from it. You would be disappointed if you saw the way I act at Fort Walton High. It's totally not me. I don't say anything, I don't approach people because they just won't "get me," ya know? I dunno. I guess I shouldn't be so cynical. But you should see these kids! I'm like cherry Jell-O in chocolate pudding. I'm totally see-through and people don't even know I'm there. I just take up space. And I won't try to get their attention because they're too thick to understand. (OMG! What did I just do there?! How awesomely deep was that?!) Yeah, so I'm the cherry Jell-O.

You know you said you wish you had been the face I'd recognize from across the cafeteria? Well this is really weird. . . but I imagine you and Alex, and Kelly and Matthew and Matt Wilt and everybody else; I imagine that you guys are all there at school with me, I just can't see you, and it makes me feel better.

When I did this today I thought to myself, "Self, you are insane. What's wrong with you?" And I'm here to tell you loneliness can drive a person insane. . . which I am right now. I miss you insanely.

Tell me more about you, Tim. Did you get my package yet?—With all the fudge Hershey kisses in the world to give,

~kristen

June 9, 2001

I met Garret yesterday.

There was this passageway between the right and left side of the gym. I went in and heard echoes of the past in my mind. Past plays and stuff. There was this old piano with the keys chipped and I imagined it new and someone playing it. I noticed an old hymn book open on the piano. Then, right when I walked out of the hallway, the sounds and echoes stopped. All of the sudden, this guy starts talking in my mind.

I mean, it was hard to know whether it was just me making Garret up or if he was real. He told me his name and he said he had died in a car accident 50 years ago.

Garret had to make a choice whether to come and move with me to S.C. or not. He stayed.

The amount of content I wrote between the ages of 12 and 17 is impressive, to say the least. Seven volumes of journals, two binders' worth of songs and lyrics, two composition notebooks of thoughts on literature, and an entire cabinet of files filled with everything else: letter drafts, stories, poems, original scripts, drawings, notes I took on religious talks, and letters I never sent. It's a tremendous indicator of how lonely I was. I liked to pretend I was with people, and I liked to pretend I was writing to someone.

And sometimes I fantasized I had friends.

It felt like moving completely destroyed who I was. Sadly, when you don't know who you are, and hate the emptiness inside you, it's hard to befriend people. How are you supposed to find new people to define you, if you don't love them yet? How can you allow someone you don't love to define you? How can you be sure who you are if there's no one to love? How will anyone love you if you are a nobody?

Tuesday, August 10, 2004 2:00 PM
From: tim

I'm writing sooner this time. I've started working at WRJA again, (I know, I said I hated it and it's like Jack Black talking about doing one little thing you hate over and over and you ruin your life, but I don't plan on doing it forever, and now Matthew Eldridge works there so it's lots better) and the last two weekends I've been out of the state with the church band, so it took me a while to respond.

YES, I got your package, and it almost made me cry it was so great. After I opened it I couldn't quit smiling. I liked all of it. I haven't put the bumper stickers on yet because I can't decide where. There isn't much room on the back of my car with the 20 I already have, but I'll figure it out. And the veg stickers were great.

School will get so much better, don't worry. You've only been going for a week or so. These friend things take time (apparently; look at us, it took years, haha). But I gotta tell you, they probably aren't going to come to you. You have to break through that newcomer mentality and actively try to meet people with your interests. That's what's so great about Drama—you're forced to meet people and then get closer through play rehearsals and stuff.

Timony Cricket

Wednesday, August 11, 2004 5:07 PM
To: tim

You are so, so, so right. Be friendly. That's what I need to do. Go to them.

There's this kid Ryan in my Algebra class, who sits behind me and is extremely gay. (There's a lot of gays here, and I don't think I've ever met a dude that's gay.) But anyway, Ryan is really funny to me 'cause every two seconds he says to himself, "Greeeeaaaat. THANK yooouu!" and the other day he goes, "Hey! Hey you! Yeah you!" (speaking to me) "Is this getting annoying yet? 'Great, thank you?'" and I said no, but it was getting there. So he said, "Great. . . Thank youu!" and he didn't even mean it as a joke. It's like the only thing he can say! He is the prettiest boy I've ever seen. He's just this skinny, dark haired, blue eyed guy, with perfect skin. Gosh, it's just weird. I can't imagine him as a straight guy, and I can't imagine him as a girl. He's just supposed to be gay I guess. But see the funny thing is that he's so prissy. Like he talks to you like he's too cool to be talking to you, like he's at the top of the popularity chain. And I guess you could say he is. . . just 'cause he hangs out with all of the preppish girls. It's funny. It's really funny. What a fun personality to sit in front of in Algebra.

We have to do this reading journal for English (everybody did theirs this summer) that I have to do now. Mr. Urquhart said I could write about Catcher in the Rye if I wanted, even though it wasn't on the list. Isn't that awesome?! Man, I love that teacher.

You know what's really annoying? Umbrellas. For one, they're hard to open and close, and two, you get just as wet trying to get in and out of your car with an umbrella, as you would just standing out there in the rain without.

Hey, random question—Did you ever stick to that "no shaving" policy this summer? Do you have a beard now? Because if you do, I'd like to imagine you with a beard now. You know, to keep my mental pictures up to date. Speaking of which. . . I got a haircut yesterday (so, SO UGLY!). Glad you can't see me in person for once. Thank goodness hair is something that grows out.

Hershey hugs of fudge ~kristen

Thursday, August 12, 2004 12:26 AM
From: tim

Ryan sounds like a trip. I guess if you're comfortable enough with yourself to be that out there, more power to you. He sounds like a good character to be put in the sitcom of your life.

It's so awesome that your teacher (Erquerharter or something?) let you write your reading journal on Catcher in the Rye. I'm sure you've got a lot of intelligent stuff to say about it that will really wow him.

I totally feel you about the umbrellas. I've often wanted a better system.

No, as it stands right now, I'm beardless and have an ugly bowl-head haircut. The beard is just too uneven right now to be cool. It starts looking redneck long before it looks hippie, so I just have to wait on that look.

I feel really sad all of the sudden. I can tell that this is not the direction that I wanted to take this email, and you don't have to respond to this portion, because I don't know what you'd say. I just am apprehensive of the change of friends next year and I'm listening to really sad/ heavy music ("Knife Party" by Deftones, for the curious). I feel infinite, like Charlie talks about in Wallflower. I feel like this night is going to last forever. I feel really small in relation to the world right now. You ever get that feeling? I can picture millions of people sitting at their computers right now writing email just like I am, with the same blank stare, but to me this is really important. It's scary. Feeling infinite is not always great. Sometimes you feel huge, like you could fly, but right now it's really scary, thinking about mortality and stuff.

I had a dream once where I was being held captive on this island by this couple and they kept talking about killing me and shooting me in the head and stuff. And they were getting ready to when a whole bunch of cars with adults pulled up to the hideout, and they ran in and handcuffed the couple. Nobody came over to me or anything, so I was still sitting on the floor and I remember feeling extremely disappointed that they hadn't killed me. It felt real, you know, so I got excited that I was going to heaven or afterlife or whatever, and when they didn't kill me, I woke up feeling really, really disappointed. I get weird like that in real life sometimes.

Well hey, enough of all that. I love and miss you and hope we'll meet up soon. Even if it's only in our dreams.

Tim

Thursday, August 12, 2004 12:37 AM
From: tim
Subject: "Lost in You" by Ash

Listen to this, if you can find it. It's really pretty and it made me think of you. For you dude, I've decided to grow some random beardage. Just whatever I can that doesn't look nasty. I think that'd be funny if slowly over the first few weeks of school everybody is like, "What the. . . ew." I'd laugh at them, 'cause it's like nothing, but people fixate on little things. Haha, in their face.

August 12, 2004

Joan Didion: *On Keeping a Notebook*

"We forget all too soon the things we thought we could never forget. We forget the loves and the betrayals alike, forget what we whispered and what we screamed, forget who we were."

It's bad enough that life passes you by without having to forget. It's sad. I wish I wrote more when I was a kid. I feel like the world squeezes the "kid" out of me as it shoves responsibility down my throat. And what I did write at age six or seven is fascinating to me. I can't believe it's what I wrote. I mean, is it possible the younger version of yourself can teach the older version, that I actually was smarter in some senses back then than I am now? Some take pictures to remember, but it doesn't portray the moment. It's just a mirror image of what you saw. It doesn't explain, it doesn't make you feel or smell or remember at all. We also tend to shove our failures out of our remembrance, we try to forget. Sometimes we need to relive those failures to show us that we still make the same mistakes, or we've made progress.

It's embarrassing to read a passage when you were. . . stupid I guess. . . and you don't really want to believe that was once you. I feel that when I read over past years. I feel like I could just rip the pages out, but I don't, because I know I'll forget. As painful as it is to endure those stupid thoughts I wrote down once upon a time, if I didn't read them I wouldn't know that I'm ten times more of a person now than I was then, and that's important to me.

A journal is what strings all of the missing, odd-ball pieces together. The world as we see it may not make sense to anyone else, but your journal, see, that is what lays all of your life's impressions out on a big mat, and then you can see the big picture and find yourself.

Jack Kerouac: *On the Road*

"I woke up as the sun was reddening; and that was the one distinct time in my life, the strangest moment of all, when I didn't know who I was. . . and I looked at the cracked high ceiling and really didn't know who I was for about fifteen strange seconds."

This feeling is so familiar to me. I feel this way when there is change. I guess life throws it at you so suddenly you become flustered and don't know who you are for a moment.

"He was a real red-nosed young drunk of thirty and would have bored me ordinarily, except that my senses were sharp for any kind of human friendship."

This summer I flew out to Omaha, Nebraska by myself. A woman I tried to make light conversation with brushed me off like I was too young to talk to her and my opinion wasn't valued. She about made me cry right then and there. I was so scared, so desperate, so lonely. My home was someplace totally foreign to me with people I didn't know. I felt like I was just floating around. So when that woman turned her back to me I felt a harsh, hard, cold reality come over me. It told me, "Why should a stranger care? You're all alone. Deal with it." And that's what made me want to cry. I was just hysterical, desperate, but that's what traveling alone does to you.

It was extremely lonely. I realize now that I felt like I didn't know who I was then. I also felt like that when I moved here to Florida.

Why am I nobody
I'm not like me
I'm lost
What am I doing here
I ask through tears
I'm lost

I've lost myself 'cause you were what made me

I realized that we are in fact victims of circumstance. There are pieces of who we are or want to be in everyone. Our friends and ones closest to us hold the biggest pieces. So when you aren't around them anymore, when you're completely isolated, you panic. At least I panic. Suddenly you feel you've lost something, it's missing, and you feel totally alone. You're desperate to meet anyone, because they hold a piece of you somewhere. So maybe if you could just talk to someone you'd see the reflection of yourself and rest assured you are still here, you are still you, yourself, you're still alive.

Saturday, August 14, 2004 6:43 PM
To: tim

timtimtimtimtim I can't believe I made it through my first week of school.

So Friday Ryan kept on saying to his friend. . . "Oh my god, Rachel, I just cannot get over my shoes. Seriously, they are just so awesome! They were expensive mind you, they were REAL expensive. . . but you know I'm worth it. . ." I turned around to get something out of my bag and noticed his eraser. It was rectangle and white and written in pencil on it was "Ryan's bad eraser." I couldn't help but laugh to myself.

I'm reading On the Road by Jack Kerouac. It's for English; Nathan recommended it. It's good. You'd like it.

~kristenaciously kineticful kristen

Saturday, August 14, 2004 8:50 PM
From: tim
Subject: Tim's bad email. . .

Ryan sounds hilarious. There isn't anyone here like that. Not that I know of, anyway. I've never met a guy who "just can't get over his shoes." Haha. Alex is back and they're in a house now, so we're hoping he'll stay for all of our junior year. That'll be great because Melton says he's got some plays planned for next year, just for Alex and me.

Hoping the bad weather didn't destroy your beach house,

honorable judge flickersnitch presiding.

Monday, August 16, 2004 10:07 PM
From: tim

Hey, I guess you're too BUSY with Nazi math teachers to sit down long enough to write your best Sumter friend. Siiiigh.

Oh well. I'll have to keep writing on.

What's going on with you? Has your second week been as good as the first? Spent the weekend with any cool new friends, i.e. Hailey, Nathan, Ryan, etc.? I'm all interested; give me a story or two.

Feeling great and looking hot it is yours truly,

Tim 3+t

p.s. The gross face hair is coming along. I can tell it's going to be a goatee on the chin, a soul patch on the lower lip, and two massive side-burns and nothing that connects. Haha, can you imagine it? I'll have to take a picture for you once it's prominent.

Tuesday, August 17, 2004 6:52 PM
To: tim

I'm sorry, I'm sorry! I have interrupted our email system. Forgive me. Your theory was right. I'm too caught up with oppressive teachers to write. By golly! I had homework in every class except Dance, and I didn't get to do half of it. I really do have to pick which assignments are the most important and then hope I can do the rest between classes or at lunch. Ugh. It's insane. I can't believe I'm doing this. It KILLS ME!

I don't think I mentioned I'm talking Dance. I thought it'd help me out theatre-wise a little. I didn't know it was going to be ballet dance. And guess what we perform at the end of the year? The Nutcracker. (ugh. Please.) Can you imagine ME doing BALLET? I know, it's so weird. But

hey—it's actually fun. And it feels good to try something you might otherwise would've never tried in your life.

Ryan isn't my friend, Tim! I TOLD you that! I just OBSERVE him.

I sat next to Nathan at lunch Friday, and he says I'm part of the table
now (that felt nice). We talk about what we read in English class and joke
around and stuff. It's fun I guess, all the flip-flop preps and intellectuals
sit at that table. It's a really unique crowd. I like them. I don't like any of
the girls that sit at the table though. They act like accessories or something and interrupt the intellectual conversations with, "Hey, guess what
I did this weekend?" or, "OMG Kevin! You are so mean! I said hey to you
the other day. . . blah, blah, blah," but the only real reason I have to sit
at that table is Nathan.

Hailey is still the same, although I feel myself floating away from her a
tad, just because she is constantly surrounded with stupid freshman. I
like HER you know, not her friends.

gummy life savers in wild berries ~kristen

August 17, 2004

Wow. Nine days to be 15. I'm way too tired to be writing
this. I'm sad. School sucks. The homework is overwhelming.
Matthew Eldridge wrote me an email today. It made me laugh.
I'll shut up. That's sad.

Dear Nathan,

*You know some mornings I forget I live here and not
where I used to live. Sometimes I imagine conversations
we have and you ask me how I am. I mean, how I really
am. Sometimes I imagine you ask me about who I was,*

because that's who I want to be and I'm dying to tell you so you know who I really am. It's frustrating because the world is so small when you are alone. With every word you say to me I feel we grow closer to being real friends, but I know I blow things out of proportion because I'm so desperate, and I know this, so ultimately it just hurts because I'm trying to make you play the role of people I've lost. I feel like if you knew me—the real me—not the disheveled sorry lonely stranger girl I am to you, you might really like me. Because I don't. I used to, but I don't. I don't love myself because I'm not feeling loved.

I had everything. Everything. I was genuinely happy-go-lucky me. And everyone loved me. I'm down to rock bottom. It will take longer than I think I can bear to wait for people to know me. Do you know how scared I am? You know it takes every bit of courage I have to go up and talk to someone. And it hurts when I see they already have their 500 friends. It hurts to see them laugh out loud, because I used to laugh out loud. I used to have best friends. And I don't now.

I don't want you to feel sorry for me, or try to be nice or anything, I just want you to recognize what I go through. At the end of the day, after all that stress and pushing myself, I go home and cry. I ask myself for what purpose? Why am I even trying? But I keep trying and no one claps for me, gives me a good job, or understands. Life just passes right on by and expects you to deal. The fact that I'm actually writing you this letter that I will never send just shows how desperate I am.

What am I to you? Would you consider me someone to talk to or confide in? Am I just a face you recognize? Do you like to pull me out on a string or are you sincere? Am I a friend? Do you love me? Do you think I'm strange? Maybe it's the fact that I don't know what I am to you that is so disappointing to me. I wish you could grab me by both shoulders and make me realize who I am, where I am, and what I'm doing here. I miss it. I miss my friends. But maybe it's not so much that I miss them, it's that I miss having one. And so I substitute some stranger for someone I could spend forever with and pretend they are people who know and love me. It's frustrating because it's not real and I refuse to wait for it to be.

If I could just tell you. And why can't I? What is holding me back from spilling it out, from laying it all down? I don't know, but I don't. I try to, mind you, I try. It's all just a battle I fight within myself. And the problem is I can't let go of whatever is keeping me from finding myself again. I've lost it. I just know that if you were my friend, I'd find it.

Love, Kristen

August 18, 2004

It's unbelievable how much fate is determined by the small things like smiling at someone, or picking up a pencil, or eating pineapple with mashed potatoes, or any tiny random everyday thing you do.

Thursday, August 19, 2004 7:26 PM
To: tim
Subject: Tim tim cher roo!

Today was picture day. I stood in line with Nathan, and he asked me what I thought of On the Road so far, which brought me to mention you and how freaky it was we were reading the same book at the same time. I met this kid named Scott Smiley. He's best friends with Nathan and he's in my Improv class. He rocks at Improv.

Love, Charlie

Friday, August 20, 2004 9:20 PM
From: tim
Subject: A bit of you is the only substance I can't refuse

My first day of school was kind of. . . plain, I guess. I can tell my classes will be hard. In English 4, frickin AP, we were issued 14 TEXTBOOKS! (including Cracking the AP, Elements of Style, and Grammar with a Giggle (my favorite title of a book ever)).

Here's to homework-induced sleepless nights.

Like the shifting sands of the hourglass, so are the days of our lives,

Uncle Tim

p.s. OH OH! I almost forgot. I walked out to my car at some random place like Piggly Wiggly and THIS note is under my wipers: "Hi! Read your (cool) bumper stickers and thought that you may want to protest animal abuse? Call me at 972-0282 IF YOU'RE INTRESTED [smiley face]." The handwriting looks like a girl's, so I'm REALLY, REALLY intrigued by who this is. Some huge group of cool Sumter liberal vegetarians who will be my friends! So weird and cool. I stared at it forever. But seriously, THAT'S why I have those bumper stickers. It's all about the human connection. I like being the guy that causes heads to turn, brains to think, and hearts to laugh. I like being the guy that makes other drivers go, "What the hell?" and then have a story to tell their families over dinner.

Saturday, August 21, 2004 12:36 PM
To: tim
Subject: To threety bird

Seriously, reading your emails is like reading pages from a really, really good book. The story of your life, you know? You're so amazingly interesting, I wish everyone had the privilege of knowing you. 20 points.

So how 'bout Mom bought food the other day (like actual food. GOOD food, not like more mayonnaise. . . (why do we always have mayonnaise?)) and it totally rocks. I think I spent two hours this morning just eating. Everything in sight. You should have seen my face. I was just glowing.

~kristen

There are many instances in my entries where I mention that there is no food at home, that I have to obtain food myself, that I find food in other homes, or that I make food for other people. In wondering why I talked so much about food, my therapist and I recognized food as a representation of nourishment and nurturing.

It makes sense that there was never any food at my house.

In the letter I wrote to Sarah: "I miss your house. It's really weird I guess. . . but I miss the shed and the jam sessions, and I miss Katherine's bedroom where we used to play truth or dare all the time. I miss your fridge."

> *"I miss your fridge."* Sarah's house was a home where I felt taken care of and loved. I loved being fed, because it fed my soul. I made food for other people because I wanted them to feel loved too.
>
> *May 25, 2003*
> *Mom ate all the cherry Jell-O I made. I'm making onigiri for lunch.*
>
> Here is an example where not only do I nourish myself, but I'm feeding my mother. A slight indication that many times, I had to be the adult.

Monday, August 23, 2004 7:12 AM
From: tim

Please tell me that man's name can be something other than Scott Smiley, because I cannot picture him as a normal, non-muppet human being if you keep calling him Scott Smiley every time.

Yes, I'm completely loaded down with homework AL-FRICKIN-READY. I'm having to write you in the morning because I have no free time after school anymore EVER.

I've taken a picture of my car and then one of that darn cat saying hi to you, and tomorrow is Drama Club, so I'll get a picture of Mr. Melton's hideous face and then with the LAST picture I'll have my mom do an extreme National Geographic close up of my beard saying hi to you.

Love and hate, war and peace, sense and sensibility,

timbo medicine man jumbo

Monday, August 23, 2004 4:41 PM
To: tim
Subject: "Meet Threet" wins 8 Oscars including best picture and director.

Oh hey! Guess what I found out today? Mr. Urquhart is a vegetarian. Isn't that totally awesome?

Today Ryan said, "OMG Serena, I totally fell asleep in French class today, and I had like, 18 dreams. Seriously."

So guess whose birthday is this Thursday? I usually wear a nice skirt on my birthday, with chucks. In Sumter it was cool, but almost every girl in my school wears that every day, so it's way lame.

~southern krits

Monday, August 23, 2004 8:26 PM
From: tim
Subject: I had some funny titles with the name "Jex" but they were inappropriate. Hahaha.

That is a freakin' great name for a documentary of my life! I've always done the number thing, like: "One, Two, Threet: How to be Tim-larious in a few simple steps."

Mr. Urquhart sounds like the coolest teacher EVER. I wish I had a cool teacher like that. My Physics teacher shows no emotion. Well, she's very monotonous, and whenever she laughs it's like a cyborg. Like, "HA. HA.HA.HA." And she's very stiff. Totally weird.

It's really funny that you just talk to me about Ryan. How scary—like, what if people do that to us. He has ABSOLUTELY no idea who I am at all, but I think I could pick him out of a line-up, I know him so well. I'm going to choose someone from a class that sits near me and like stalk him and talk to you about him because it's so weird. I like to think about it. The big net of human lives that blows in the breeze, little electric

92

sparks jumping from this one to that one and sometimes it overlaps and mess. Really cool. NOT my best description, by far. Haha—I don't even think it makes sense, but whatever. I'm tired. Lol.

So for your birthday outfit. . . I say cowboy hat, giant prostitute earrings (prostihoops!), false beard, candy necklace, spaghetti strap tee-shirt over a shrimp torso costume, wedding dress skirt over jumbo purple 80s print pants, stiletto heels in the back, barefoot in front, and arm length black and white striped gloves. With rings OUTSIDE the gloves. Totally kick-A.

August 25, 2004

I guess when I wake up tomorrow I'll be 16. great.

Friday, August 27, 2004 8:10 PM
From: tim

Hey baby! Happy 16th! I've been working on your birthday present every night when I finally get to relax, and it'll be cool. I don't know if you'll like them or not; it's kind of a weird gift, so here's hoping for the best.

J'expedie le bonheur et des croquettes!

Remi boncouer

Sunday, August 29, 2004 3:30 PM
To: tim
Subject: Tim hundert percent baum wolle

My 16th birthday was awesome. In Improv class, everybody called me the birthday girl, and in every Improv game I was in they tied in my birthday to the scene. And then before class ended, Mrs. White came out with a chocolate muffin, and it had a lit candle in the middle of it and everyone crowded around me and sang "Happy Birthday," and I blew the candle out and was too excited to make a wish, and then all the guys mauled me for a piece of muffin afterwards. It was so unbelievably great. I felt really selfish. Here I was all boo hoo about not having friends, and look how many people did so much! It was a humbling experience.

I really cannot wait until I get your present. Really Tim, a piece of pocket lint from you would be enough to drive me completely insane with joy.

Wishing you a silent moment when all goes awry and crazy.

~kristen

August 31, 2004

People can't communicate if there is no common ground. They aren't interested if they can't relate. You need to know enough to understand. I guess that's really vague, but whatever. I know what I mean.

August 31, 2004

Lately I've been so tired I feel like I don't have time for anything. School is SO HARD! I'm unmotivated.

February 11, 2003
I've been kinda feeling kinda bad lately. I don't know why—I just do. I hope I'm better soon.

September 8, 2004
Sue Monk Kidd: *The Secret Life of Bees*

"It was a secret knowledge that would slip up and overwhelm me, and I would take off running—even if it was raining out, I ran—straight down the hill to my special place in the peach orchard."

The first day of eleventh grade for me was torture, pure misery. I don't know if you have ever had to move away and go to a new high school, but it's one of the hardest things I've ever had to deal with. I've often compared my pain with the pain someone would feel from their mother's death, because that is the only thing that comes close to what I go through when I move. No, my mom is still alive and I've never felt the pain that comes from that, but I do know what death means. The result is the same; you've been torn from someone you love. I've been torn from lots of people I love. Maybe it wouldn't seem so bad to you because you think, even though they're gone, they're alive. It's true, they are alive, and I could see them again or talk to them, but they are living a life without you and that creates a distance no one can travel. I don't mean to be disrespectful, losing a mother shouldn't be something you compare your loss to, but I do.

It's frustrating to me. People don't look at moving the way I do. I've moved nine times. Five of which I remember well. Five times I've been torn away from people I loved, and who loved me. I only have my mom and dad. They listen and they try to comfort, but really, how can I expect them to understand? They didn't move when they were kids. They don't have best friends who sleepover, or inside jokes, or anything!

My life has disappeared. I'm sure the kid who had to see his mother die had his life disappear also. My whole life has changed. . . What was that quote? Some Roman philosopher said something like, "With every thing that changes or alters itself comes the death of what it once was." So I had to start over. The most frustrating thing to me is people don't recognize that! I had a life. Any reputation or status or history I ever had has no bearing here. I keep looking for friends I once had in these strangers. Sure, people are usually friendly, for which I am grateful, but what am I to them? It's frustrating because they don't know. I mean, they don't know me. It's so obvious (duh? Of course they know me), but just think about it. I get tired of trying to show people who I am. So all of this, all the frustration and pain and the loss of moving, goes unrecognized by the world. I think to myself, they have no idea, no clue.

So this is my secret knowledge, like Lily's, and it slips up once in a while and overwhelms me, too.

It was the second week of school. I was sitting in class, just sitting. Watching, actually. I was sitting and watching. I saw this kid laughing. He was laughing really hard. It was the kind of laugh that made you sorry you didn't know what was funny. It was great. It was a genuine, all-out, gut-busting laugh. Just watching him made me smile. It was then my secret knowledge slipped out of nowhere, and suddenly I was on the verge of breaking into tears right then and there. Here's the lyrics I scrawled down when I got home:

I fight back the feeling of wanting to completely let go
I saw a kid laughing as hard as he could show
I barely recall the last time I'd ever laughed that hard
Ever laughed at all
I can't help feeling so inferior so insignificantly
small.

Of course. . . things get better. It takes time that's all.

August 23, 2001

I miss Sam. I miss her so much. I wish she were here right now. I hate it here. I HATE it! I tried to like it, I really did but I HATE IT! I need a friend. You don't know how much I need one. I HATE THIS PLACE!

July 15, 2001

Today Mom and I went to the mall. I took off the necklace Sam gave me and started crying. I miss her so much. I don't think a friend ever cared for me this much before. I smile every single time I think of her. She's great. Beyond adjectives.

Thursday, September 9, 2004 6:30 PM
To: tim

TIM! What a relief it is to write you! Okay, okay. Umm. . .

OMG! Today Ryan said THE MOST hilarious thing! He goes, "So I just solve this with the linear equation. . . like just get 'Y' on one side to find the soloosh? Right?"

He means solution, but he called it soloosh. Like you know, like Jack Black abbreviates stuff and makes up cool words, it was just like that. He was finding the "soloosh." This guy kills me!

How's work? How's life? Here's a hug from me to you. ~the K

Thursday, September 9, 2004 8:42 PM
From: tim
Subject: ALLELUIA!

I love you, I love you, I love you.

I've been pining. When I logged on and saw an email from you, I pumped my fist into the air and said, "Yes!"

Ryan sounds so funny! Matthew and I say delish (delicious) and condish (condition) and other stuff whenever it works. We laugh.

Work is as bad as it was before, but it is so nice to have money again. (God, I hate hearing those words come out of my mouth. Money's not everything, but I need gas in my car y'know?) Turns out, I will be VERY involved in Drama. I just can't say no, y'know? I love it too dang much! Good ol' Melto! I've decided though that work comes last. If there is a massiv-o conflict-o, I will totally quit my job before I quit a play.

Kristen Jex, tu es aussi jolie que les fleurs!

Yours to keep,

Yolanda Rick

Friday, September 10, 2004 12:21 AM
To: tim

Yeah, Ryan was totally serious when he said it. Lol! Omg! I hate to say this. . . but if there were to be a gay version of you. . . I think it'd be a lot like Ryan. . . I dunno. You slightly look alike. . . have the same personality. . . sorta. Like, he has this planner that's super organized like yours. And he takes French like you, and uses French phrases and terms all over the place like you. . . So he's a lot like you, except he's gay. Or maybe it's just that you act gay. . . lol! I'm so kidding! Don't be gay. You'd break my heart and I'd be very, very, very sorry.

~kristen

September 11, 2004
Caroline Bird: *College is a waste of time and money*

    I don't understand why college is the immediate step after high school. When Mr. Urquhart asked the class Friday why everyone wanted to go to college, I rolled my eyes. "To get a better job, because my parents want me to, because I don't want to be a bum. . . blah, blah, blah." Here's what I say to that: College is not a requirement, and if it is, it shouldn't be. I think college has BECOME a requirement and that's disappointing. I thought long and hard about what I wanted to do with my life this summer. A line from *Brighton Beach Memoirs* by Neil Simon (which I am doing right now) comes to mind.

pg. 89
EUGENE. (to audience) I guess there comes a time in everybody's life when you say, "This moment is the end of my childhood." When Stanley closed the door, I knew that moment had come to me. . . I was scared. I was lonely.

My grandma could very much be the epitome of a classic American. She is like a symbol of her time. She raised two boys and one girl in a nice home in Scarsdale, NY. She lights candles at the dinner table every night. She is the ultimate homemaker and mother. She wears red lipstick. Her life seems so perfect, like it came straight out of a 1940s film. She went to college because that was the thing to do, because her friends went, because that's where she knew she'd meet her husband. Those were the very reasons I don't want to go to college for. I don't want to follow this plan that holds everyone else's expectations. Why is college the only place to go after high school? So she asked, "If you don't go to college, where will you go, how will you be able to support yourself? Don't you want to marry someone smart with a good education?"

Monday, June 7, 2004 8:09 PM
From: alex

. . .Still have no clue what I want to do with my life. Just don't want to live that "normal" life, working all day behind a desk, living in the suburbs, wife and kids, 2 cars, working hard to earn things I see in a magazine, and it makes no sense. I mean when you "grow up" you only have fun when you're on "vacation." It's silly that you feel nothing? And then you just suddenly go out and have fun? Can't you have fun every day? Maybe not. I don't know. It's all so confusing, isn't it? It's rough being a kid. . .

The conversation went on, and the rest of the time I just cried and said it wasn't fair and that it shouldn't be the way it is. I offer no solution. I can't change society. It was good to talk to someone who was the extreme opposite of me, and just as stubborn. People like that aren't easily persuaded, so eventually you're just left to listen, and that's what I needed. The thought of having to face responsibility. . . no. The REALIZATION of having to face responsibility is totally horrifying. The question of what you want to do with your life feels like you're being shoved inward from every direction. Maybe life is finding what you want to do with your life.

Sunday, September 12, 2004 12:14 AM
From: tim
Subject: Here's some pancakes and coke

Yeah, about your duplicate friends, I'm totally convinced that everywhere you go there are a stock type of person that repeats itself. Like, all the states I've lived in there's been certain types of people that are SCARILY like each other. Kind of weird. We're all different, but not always by much.

Now I want to meet Ryan. I was laughing AT him and now he's the gay me? I think I need to see the facts here, Kristen. I'm just kidding of course. I think it's funny.

I finished your gift! I need to complete its decoration tomorrow and then it'll be in the mail Monday (fingers crossed). I seriously hope you like it because I've been building the tension for a month. Haha.

Hey, who killed. . .

Persimmony

September 12, 2004
Still reading: *The Secret Life of Bees*

It's peculiar how the night makes you feel so lonely and free. It's just a feeling that's hard to describe. But I like it. A lot. And it makes me feel like laughing.

"When I looked up through the web of trees, the night fell over me, and for a moment I lost my boundaries, feeling like the sky was my own skin and the moon was my heart beating up there in the dark. Lightning came, not jagged but in soft, golden licks across the sky."

If there was only one thing I was allowed to read for the rest of my life it'd totally be this paragraph. Nature is so soothing. It's not easy to go someplace where you can find nature—untouched and pure—and just let it take you away. It's like it erases your entire being, or maybe it's just that you melt into it and you can't tell one from the other, like how Lily said the sky was her own skin.

One Thursday in May, a few weeks before I left South Carolina, Alex, Tim, and I took a drive to nowhere outside of Sumter in Tim's red Geo Metro. It felt so good. I had my guitar with me in back and I serenaded Alex and Tim's conversations about Saudi Arabia. It was just us three in the Geo Metro down a dirt road. I can't remember who suggested we pull over, but we did and all three of us piled out while half laughing to ourselves. I stood in front of a huge wheat field, just 6 inches taller than me. As I stepped in, the dirt road and Tim's red Geo Metro disappeared. Luckily Tim and Alex are pretty tall, and they could peer over the wheat. Otherwise we'd have been lost forever. The wheat was so dense and fluffy, so I fell back onto it. It's the COOLEST THING EVER! They both laughed at me, but I convinced them to try it too, and so all three of us just lay there in a field of wheat. Nothing needed to be said. We were just there, silent. I looked up at the sky. It was perfect. It was so deep and blue and there were big white fluffy clouds and I could feel a breeze and the world seemed so far away. I lost my boundaries, and so did Tim and Alex. It almost seems unreal, but there is no doubt in my mind that it happened. Nature is such a beautiful, beautiful thing.

April 12, 2003

I'm in my attic listening to this band about 4 houses away from my backyard. I just came back from listening to them outside. They are great. Tonight is just one of those nights. The kind where you just go outside, look out at the stars, and hear the comforting beat of drums and faint guitar. (sigh)

Sunday, September 12, 2004 9:00 AM
To: tim

I've become obsessed with everything I do. We are supposed to keep journals in Mr. Urquhart's class, and the other day he mentioned we should have 7-8 pages written by now. I have fifty-five. There is definitely something very wrong with me. I've hinted that I've written a lot, but I don't think he really knows what I mean. And he has to read all fifty-five of my glorious pages. He's gunna die. (sigh) He's totally going to drop dead.

Did I tell you FWBHS Drama is building a 2 STORY SET for Brighton Beach Memoirs? Yeah! I'm totally serious. It looks a lot like the set that's on Noises Off. Which is totally cool and awesome. They made me sell three boxes of doughnuts Friday. It was horrible. I HATE selling things. I HATE it. Being popular is the only shred of hope you have of selling doughnuts. Anyhoo—I have to get ready for church. . . Write back soon
~kristen

September 14, 2004

We've been evacuated from hurricane Ivan, and I'm cooped up in a Best Western hotel room in Valdosta, Georgia. Mr. Urquhart was right. What else is there to do but read? Reading: *Catcher in the Rye*

Who else could have recommended this book to me but my friend Tim? Soon after I finished reading it the first time this summer, he sent me his copy of *The Perks of Being a Wallflower*. The inscription says, "To Kristen—because books make the best gifts and inscriptions increase their value." The two books are alike but I can't say what exactly makes them so, or makes them different from each other. I also can't decide which one I like better.

I told Tim I was reading *On the Road* last month and the neat thing was he was reading it too. I should've guessed though. Those books are kind of "beat-nik-ish." Tim seems to like those kind of books.

I hate Holden's character. I really do. BUT! I love the book. He is a walking contradiction, a hypocrite to what he wants. But maybe if I wrote down everything I did or said, I would find that I am contradicting too. Maybe that's just the way people are.

"And yet I still act sometimes like I was only about twelve . . . Sometimes I act a lot older than I am—I really do—but people never notice it. People never notice anything."

I once wrote an essay on how "adults don't understand." But what's the difference, where's the line between still being a kid and being immature?

Monday, September 20, 2004 9:56 PM
From: tim

I am so sorry. With all these hurricanes and me quitting my job (hurray!), I'm like, computer-deprived. I don't ever get on here (homework, the play's coming up, etc).

And snafus with the gift—not enough postage or misdirected or something, so I'm working on it. Is mail even running in Florida? Were you guys wiped off the face of the earth?

Geez, that set sounds cool, the journal sounds cool (it doesn't surprise me at all that you wrote that much. Writing is important.). Your life is rocking and flowing and ebbing with the tide; mine is stagnant, boring, and I'm going to hurt myself tomorrow if I don't do SOMETHING FRIGGIN INTERESTING. Quitting my job was liberating though. But it's tired and I'm late. . . wait, strike that—reverse it. . . and I'm off to bed.

I'm still alive my darling, if you'll have me!

paper mache

Tuesday, September 21, 2004 6:58 PM
From: sam lee

Dude! Are you ok? I know the weather has been completely awful down there. I'm just writing you to make sure you and your house didn't blow away. How's school treating you? I'm not doing too shabby. Made any cool friends this school year?

Hope to hear from you soon,

Samantha

September 23, 2004

Today was the first time in my life I cried for joy. Its unfamiliarity still lingers now.

No one knows how awful I have been.

Summer was great, but then school started and it's just awful! I'm crying right now just writing about it. I am alone. I have no voice, I'm just a bunch of complex emotions. Funny thing is, I had no idea how lonely and sad and tormented I truly was until I walked through the door, shifted through the mail, saw a letter from Robert, and whispered a small, "Oh my God. . ."

For so long I felt lost and unappreciated, unnoticed, ignored, stupid, worthless, WHATEVER, and then to read a, "Hey Kristen, I love you and I care," was just overwhelming. It felt like a waterfall just fell on top of me and I cried. My heart was so relieved to get that. It was something to hang on to.

September 28, 1998
We moved to Japan! There are friendly people, but I MISS BRITTANY. I HATE THIS PLACE.

September 29, 2004

Okay—so Urquhart said to bring journals tomorrow and I'm assuming we're turning them in to be read and graded. So before I hand this in, I want to write everything that's been in my system. He's asked for 10 pages; I've written 78. I figure a few more pages won't tip the scale.

Reading: *The Secret Life of Bees*

"It is the peculiar nature of the world to go on spinning no matter what sort of heartbreak is happening"

My dad is really smart. Because he is so smart he's a little lacking in emotion and sympathy, but I think that has come to serve me for the better. Last May my grades were slipping because I was spending so much time with friends. When he said something about it, I told him I had every right to spend as much time with them as possible before we moved, and that if anything, it was his fault we had to. I thought I had him, but what he said was really good. He said life doesn't wait for you to finish being sad or saying goodbye.

Life doesn't wait for anybody. And now that I think about it, I think if it did, we would never get over our sadness, or anger—we'd never overcome our circumstances. What I said before, a while back, how there are victims of circumstance? I lied. They don't exist. Life is to overcome our circumstances. It's the very point of living; it's to survive and endure to the end. Life doesn't wait for you. You can take a break and cry and shout a little, but eventually you've got to catch up and move on.

You have to allow change to be for the better.

One time when I was about 10, my parents said "no" to a plea to spend the night at a friend's house. I was upset. I remember this night clearly. I cried out in the hall outside their bedroom door, which was locked. I knew my parents would not change their minds, and it was too late at night to do so anyway. I cried because I was angry and frustrated and wanted to be with my best friend, someone who loved me. After half an hour, I was screaming because I was so mad my parents didn't care. How hard would I have to cry until they came out?

I wanted a hug. I wanted an "I'm sorry you can't have the things you want." But if I ever got one of them to come out, it was my dad to tell me to stop crying. This just made me more upset and frantic. He threw me on the bed, held me down, got really close to my face, and threatened me to calm down.

I was so scared I went silent.

It's stupid right? I don't know why I thought screaming and crying would croon him into giving me a hug.

I wanted empathy. I wanted acknowledgement that life affected me. His response to the hardest move I ever made in my life was to keep my grades up, because that was more important than crying.

All the more reason why Drama was such a haven for me. Because it was the one place where emotions did matter.

October 1, 2004

One— I'm not depressed anymore, two— I feel bottled up, and three— I have a crush on Scott Smiley.

So here's what I did wrong. I sat with the punks AND the preps (because those are the only two groups of people at my school) to try to figure out which one I fit into, and I now I can't decide because I've grown to like them both.

I went to the Homecoming Football game. We won 36 to 35!

I think I made a really good friend. Yeah! Her name is Ashley, but I call her Duffin 'cause that's her last name and there are two Ashleys, so yeah.

There's this foreign exchange student who was so hitting on me. He kissed my hand and I totally melted. I didn't SHOW it of course, I was like, whatever, but really inside I was totally mush. All I said was "nice." I'm so retarded. Agh! But that's okay because I don't like him much anyway. Scott Smiley has a girlfriend and she's. . . I dunno. She's nice though.

I'm disappointed Taylor wasn't at school today.

November 29, 2001

Tess wasn't here today, which really sucks. I think my worst days are those when my friends are gone. I've got a pretty lame life. I miss Sami more than anything right now. Well, I miss Dad, but I still miss her a lot. Bye!

Friday, October 1, 2004 12:31 AM
From: tim

You have to write from school? That sucks! Of course, I'm never on here to write back anyway. (Sorry about that.) Ummm. . .

School is hard (just for an update). My Physics teacher has gone scary robot-teacher on us. (*Monotonous Robocop voice* "DO YOUR WORK, WRITE A PAPER, COMPLETE A LAB, KILL THE PRESIDENT," etc.). It's past midnight and I'm still working on this paper that's due Monday. I've got book cards, I've got flashcards, I've got Sesame Street UNO cards (hey, how'd those get it here?). . .

I bought a new guitar. Go ahead and freak out.

YES, it's true. I've bought myself a Johnson travel acoustic and it is mine and it is my baby and I like it a whole lot. Very different from electric (and it's all tiny and cute). I know you're proud of me though. I play every night. Off to Homeworkville I go. They're open ALL friggin' night apparently.

Signed,

Eustice Jeffcoat Mulhalley.

October 5, 2004

So like, the 6th person (which was Russell) asked me if I was going out with Nathan. ???? It makes me feel kinda guilty because I like Scott.

I miss Alex. We haven't talked since this summer.

Tuesday, October 12, 2004 11:06 PM
From: tim
Subject: "Play it again, Kristen," Tim said slowly as the scene faded to black.

Your phone is working! yayyay. Je vais telephoner chez vous. I just don't know when! I swear, today was like, National Stress is Crippling Me Day, so I had to write you. You comfort me!

YOUR GIFT IS IN THE MAIL! You may already have it, I'm not quite sure. But you'll definitely be getting it ANY DAY NOW! And ONLY three or so months late! haha.

So the play went really well. The audience was, like, roaring with laughter and I just hurt my foot on the computer desk. Owie. Um. . . no, the play. I remembered all my words (ha.) and no one really messed up anything.

I can't tell you how glad I am I quit my job. I laugh to think that I ever tried to have time for one.

What if I went sky diving? I'm all afraid of heights, so I think it would be cool to do. Or like, became a pilot for a living. My story would be all, "I was afraid of heights and now look at me—independent pilot." I'd be a success story for PAX television to do an "it's a miracle" show on.

-yo yo ma

October 13, 2004

Today was so perfect. It was one of those days where you could SMELL winter/fall. Ugh! It was beautiful outside! I skipped school for a half hour with this girl April (she is totally kick-A)—She's a way cool tomboy—and she drove us out to a coffee shop. All we missed was homeroom, so it's not like it'll count against us. Anyway, it was fun.

I think I'm finally me now. Yes. Once again. Happiness.

Wednesday, October 13, 2004 8:35 AM
To: tim
Subject: Pages of you

I got your package yesterday. As soon as I saw it I jumped up and down and yelled out loud, "Today is the best day of my life!" and it echoed throughout the streets for like 3 minutes. The tape was atrocious. "Please don't cut this open with a saber"?! What was I supposed to open it with? I ended up using a pocketknife, but it took forever. But hey—better safe than sorry. So I guess the tape was good.

I read the entire thing in one sitting. You are a genius. It was incredible. It blows me away. Where do you come up with these people? I love each and every one of your characters. I love the little grey kitten that dances without music in moonlight. Gosh Tim, I'd end up rewriting the whole darn thing if I started to tell you what all my favorite parts were.

I put my hand against the print yours left behind. It felt so strange. Touching a remnant of you.

I really loved it, Tim. You are incredible. They are pages of you and I hold it as the number one possession I have.

September 1, 2001

I got a birthday package from Sami. I nearly cried. She gave me her favorite orange shirt. She LOVED that shirt, and she gave it to me. That's what I call sacrifice. That was so sweet of her. She got me a black belt with a glittery star buckle. I love it. She also got me a necklace, picture frame, lots of pictures, and some bracelets. That was like, the BEST birthday present ever! I am serious.

You truly have a talent for writing. I'd want the whole world to read it if I didn't feel like they don't deserve it. You came up with so many good characters and emotional and mental states. . . gosh! Take it somewhere. You have to. You are oozing with possibility and I feel there are too many kids out there like us who feel the same way and need to read it. It's worth wasting it all on the others as long as those who need to be reached are.

Everyone else is taking the PSAT's right now. I went to go sign up and they turned me down because my GPA is not in the top 20% of the school's highest.

February 6, 2003
I figured out this method of Algebra they haven't taught us yet (not until Alg. 2) by myself. I was so proud. So was Mrs. Johnson.

I feel really stupid. Almost everyone I know is taking it right now and I'm stuck here in homeroom. Oh well, that's fine.

Tim, I thank you muchly for my present. I wish there were more pages.

~kristen

Monday, October 18, 2004 7:40 PM
To: tim

I had a conference with my counselor today and I definitely have enough credits to graduate. But we decided against it. One, because I can't take another AP senior class next semester. . . I already have, like, 5 brain cells pop in there everyday. I'm afraid if I don't have at least one free period next semester my entire frontal lobe will collapse. That, and next year the high school will pay for college classes if I stay enrolled. So yay.

Keep it silky ~kristen

Monday, October 18, 2004 9:30 PM
From: tim
Subject: Orange marmalade on an ear

I'm the worst at emails anymore. But I have a legit excuse! My mom got rid of Road Runner, so to get online now we have to unplug our phone, drag this jumbo cord from the computer, across the room to the jack, connect and tie up our phone line, and then it's really slow. So it's hard. But that's no excuse, I should be willing to make the effort for my best friend ever. I'm SO glad you liked the present. I hope it was good enough to make up for the delay. I was afraid it might freak you out, because admittedly, it is a little frightening. All the death and roaches and. . . butchers and things. But that's how my brain works, I guess. I just try to keep the pen moving or the fingers flying.

All right, major life decision. I'm deciding to maybe be an actor. (Note the maybe—I can never 100% do anything.) I think I'm good at it and I've considered all these professions, but that is my passion, y'know. Acting can really move people—to laughter, to tears, whatever. I like it. I shouldn't chuck it out with the bath water just because, "Oh, well, I don't want to be a waiter my whole life." If I have that attitude, that's what I'll get. You take out what you put in. If I'm serious and study and whatever, it won't matter what I make because I'll be doing effing SOMETHING important. To me, to the audience, dare I say it—to the world.

After that long diatribe, I bid you

FAReWEll.

Tuesday, October 19, 2004 8:50 PM
From: alex

Hey Kristen! How's it going? There's almost too much going on here! I got a letter from my dad in the mail today. I keep having these weird flashbacks. . . I don't know, you probably know what I'm talking about. Like, I smell something or hear something and suddenly I have these feelings that I'm in Saudi. . . and a memory flashes by from Saudi.

I was looking over my yearbook the other day and you know normally you'll write in someone's yearbook, "Hope to see you next year!" and normally that means you'll be there the next year. . . It doesn't make me sad. . . I just accept it. . . like most things. . .

Oh, Happy Ramadan! I miss you kiddo. Hope to hear from you soon, peace out girl scout.

-Alex

Wednesday, October 20, 2004 6:52 PM
To: alex
Subject: The biggest baked potato. . .

Sometimes I'll get a whiff of something and it will smell like someone or a certain place and I go crazy. There's a few people who remind me of people in Sumter. The other day, Mrs. White was talking about mayonnaise and mustard and of course the first thing I thought of was Mayonnaise and Cheetos. And see that just sends me down this weird spiral of just. . . remembering. . . and memory itself is kind of sad, because you're being reminded of what once was. . . and isn't anymore. I still laugh at the inside jokes that lie there, that are between friends in Sumter. I swear, I took a bite out of someone's roll the other day at lunch and said, "Mmm. . . tart." and I burst out laughing. By myself. You guys would've died. It was just so funny. I felt awkward because nobody else got it and they think I'm weird. I don't think I can do much about that. I feel really socially retarded here. But anyway. . . I get the whole flashback thing.

The fact that you just accept it. . . I dunno. I mean it hurts me. I let myself feel. Sometimes it takes me to a truly dark and lonely place. . . but for me it's the only way I heal. I learned my lesson last year. I sucked it all up I didn't let anything faze me. . . and then right around March I came crashing down. I cried for you, for Robert, people who had left me. It was then I cried because I couldn't take the pressure of school and moving and not having anyone I could connect to because they were all worried about something stupid. I thought I was dealing, but I was just sweeping it under the rug. And then sooner or later it had to be lifted and it just wasn't pretty.

I feel. I've screamed for two hours straight some nights because of how sad I felt when I moved here. It really tore me. I had no leverage. It's hard to feel sane when people don't know you, or like you, or ignore you.

I miss you guys. I miss Melton! Will you, Tim, and I ever be the great trio again? I sure hope so.

~kristen

October 21, 2004

You ever write on something without ink or lead? I mean with your finger? I wonder what kind of messages, thoughts, pictures, drawings, images the walls, desks, floors, the surfaces would reveal if they shone. Can you imagine? Millions of feelings glowing through the room. Through the entire space.

Agh.

It'd be so interesting.

Wednesday, October 27, 2004 10:12 PM
To: tim

Today I learned that Mr. Urquhart brushes his teeth at school every day after lunch in the bathroom. Who does that? Amazing.

Here's what I've been thinking about all day. Okay, now think: It takes like a trillionth of a millisecond for your brain to react and reflex, to process picture and sound and movement. So really everything we experience has already happened. What we think is "live" really happened just a trillionth of a millisecond ago. And you know deja vu? Yeah, well Mr. Urquhart said that the only good explanation people have recently come up with is that one side of the brain processed the information faster than the other, so when you think, "Oh my gosh, I swear this feels so familiar, like I saw it happen before," it's because you DID. You just saw it happen and it just reprocessed.

Isn't that crazy?

We're living LIES! TIM! LIES! All lies! What we think is the present is really the past! (cue Twilight Zone music here)

I'm hoping you'll find time this week to rewire your plumbing, switch telephone companies, reposition the satellite dish, buy the Starz On Demand movie package, plug the phone wire to the stereo, and jump-start the modem on your computer to check your email. I understand it takes some effort. I just hope you read this soon. I'm missing some threetness.

~the dancing Ritz chip. . . ten

Saturday, October 30, 2004 2:21 PM
From: tim
Subject: I effing love that dancing Ritz chip

You really got me thinking about that deja vu thing. Very Twilight Zone, I admit. What if you trained your brain to react instantly, cutting out that split second so that you can react a lot quicker than everyone else. Like, you say "phone" and THEN the phone rings immediately. To you, you hear it start and say phone but it's the other way around to other folks. You would win every fight, dodge bullets, be a fantastic juggler. . . effing cool.

The Haunted House is going pretty well. Last night, while two groups were taking the tour and our side was just sort of hanging out, all of the sudden the fire alarm goes off, effing screaming, echoing, lights flashing . . . we run out of the building (all 30 of us) in Halloween costumes, me in a cloak and barefoot, across the street to wait for 40 minutes while the Fire Dept. shows up, walks through the building and determines it was our fog machine.

I know that was a really long sentence. Sumter is sometimes cool.

I can NOT believe how fast this year is flying. Time goes by so fast (seconds drop like rain, too).

I'm thirsty. I have to be at the Haunted House at five, so I'm going to go drink water for. . . let's see, three hours, I guess.

Au revoir,

jumbo scotch mcnally

Sunday, October 31, 2004 8:54 AM
To: tim

So last night was our designated "Trick or Treat" night because I guess the base didn't want Halloween on a Sunday. Somehow I got shoved out the door with a bowl of candy and ended up passing it out to the little kids. I took out my little cat ears and tail just to be festive, and my AP American Government book to do homework in between kids.

There was this little 2-year-old whose brother was dressed up as a butterfly; he was dressed up as a spider and had eyeballs painted on his face. It was the funniest thing! His mom was video-taping the whole thing though, which is weird. Just think, I'm going to be on their home videos. Someday 20 years from now his parents are going to turn to his fiancé and go, "Would you like to see John's first Halloween?" and they'll be watching and there I'll be smiling and panicking because his butterfly brother put his hand in the bowl and I had a hard time getting those sticky fingers OUT! And his brother will probably be really embarrassed because his mom made him dress up as a butterfly.

Three witches about 9 or 10 years old came, and as they're walking away I heard one of them go, "She's like, a NICE teenager." It definitely made my night.

~kris10 and 10 3 8, 4ever

November 17, 2004

Feeling lonely lately, on top of being stressed. I'm just looking for a best friend and I can't find one and that's really depressing. Agr! I miss SARAH! I miss having someone to talk to. It's eating me up inside.

July 5, 2001
(sigh) I miss Sami. I need some friends. I need them bad.

The deadline for wishes
was way past written
She doesn't have much left
to hang on to
On the verge of wanting to
completely let go
She tried yet again and again
another attempt that failed so

I'm sick of trying to make you understand
just who I am
My life has disappeared
shot and smeared.
So would you like to meet a lonely stranger girl?

chapter four

the art of rumination

"I sink into myself, afraid of the fall that never ends...
The panic begins."
- Motion City Soundtrack

November 28, 2004

I hate myself for being so lazy. I procrastinated all the work I had to do (and believe me, it's a whole lot) over Thanksgiving break, and now I'm stuck with it. I'm exhausted. From doing absolutely nothing. OH MY GOODNESS. It's such a long list. I'll die. I'm dead! I exploded!

I'm such a horrible person.

I'm overwhelmed. I hate the way this feels. Grrrrrr. I'm so tired! So much to do! Slam. I failed. Squished. I hate myself for being so lazy.

December 7, 2004

I find the older I become, the harder it is for me to find a middle ground with boys.

Not that I don't—because I do and it is loads easier than trying to find middle ground with girls—but it's just been harder these days. Probably because as we grow older we start to like each other, and then all of the sudden we're, like, scared.

January 16, 2003

Sometimes—just sometimes I get the feeling I am the way I am because I could never get along with kids. Girls didn't like me as the geek that I was, and the boys certainly couldn't look at me as a girl, so I thought (boys are stupid!) maybe they'll accept me as a boy.

So here I am today, evolved, but never really fully recovered from it. I feel like such a loser. Sometimes (only sometimes) I almost wish I was a NORMAL GIRL. I know. Scary. But nevertheless true.

You know every one of my guy friends have asked me what to get for their girlfriends for Valentine's Day. I'm like, "I DON'T KNOW!" I'm not a girl! Wait. No I am. Sorry I still can't help you.

Like every time I write Zach a set list or give him song lyrics he thinks it is a note and one time he said, "I thought you didn't write notes," and I said, "I don't—this is the list of songs we're doing."

I told you I'm such a guy. I'm like a freaky girly guy.

Isn't it stupid how you can be a tomboy until you're 12, and then if you're a tomboy any longer, something's wrong with you and people ask if you're a lesbian. The transition is frustrating. I went through this awkward state from being just "one of the guys" to being "one of the guys" as a girl. First I didn't want anyone to acknowledge that I was a girl, then I wanted to be recognized as a girl.

One time I was carrying this really heavy box and my friend Fred asked if he could carry it for me. I said "What? You think I can't carry it because I'm a girl?" and he shocked me by saying, "No, I was trying to be POLITE and a GENTLEMAN because you're a girl." It was then I realized I couldn't have it both ways.

Thing is, I was kind of raised as a boy. Yeah I had Barbies, but my dad always played with me outside. Riding bikes, playing catch, rough housing in the pool. Girls do those things too, but my dad didn't do things with me that didn't interest him.

When I was 14, I told him I needed a razor to shave. He defensively asked, "Why? To shave what?" I was too embarrassed to tell him I wanted to shave my legs, so in a nice save, I told him it was to shave my arm pits. (Which was not a lie.)

My parents didn't know at what age it was appropriate for me to wear makeup. It wasn't until I was engaged that I bought my first pair of adult underwear. I was buying them in the little girls' section at Target until then. Size 14. I once babysat a 5-year-old girl and discovered we were wearing the same kind of panties.

I'm positive my dad and my Japanese mom didn't know what a modern, American teenage girl should look like.

I hit puberty early, before it was cool, and everyone made fun of my boobs. I was embarrassed of my sexuality, something I never discussed with my parents, save the time I got my period at age 10. So throughout this stage I wore boy clothes. I never wanted to carry a purse. I had a wallet and a wallet chain.

(P.S. That one time Alex, Tim, and I went to Shoney's I complained about how girl's pants had such tiny pockets, I couldn't carry anything in them. I wanted bigger pockets. Tim then stated he hated the pockets on all his button downs, so he ripped off the one on the shirt he was wearing and handed it to me.)

No question I was attracted to boys. But I didn't embrace being girl. It felt safe to be one of the boys.

December 9, 2004

It's weird. How people change. The stages that we go through. I look back; when I was 12, I could never imagine myself being the way I am now. I didn't know what talents I'd learn, what style I'd have. It's creepy to think that maybe three years from now I'll be someone I'd never imagine to be or worse—someone I hate.

It's scary. I feel like I'm a totally different person than I was this summer. Isn't it amazing how in just a couple months we change our lives. I've thought through this a thousand times, this change thing, and I still can't get over it. It still surprises me. Sometimes I think, "Aren't my parents sad? That they're adults?" It's kind of unfair that we won't know what it's like when we're older until we get older. It's unfair ignorance is bliss. That people can't appreciate things until they're gone. But on the other hand, if I knew what was coming I couldn't enjoy the time I have. I'm not sure which is worse. Worrying about the future, or not knowing and feeling like you're wasting opportunity. Sometimes I just think that I'm not living life to the fullest. . . that I'm not filling all the pages I could.

I have a hard time taking one step at a time. It makes me a fast learner, but things overwhelm me because I can't break it down.

December 13, 2004

Finally. School is out. On my way out of 5th period I asked Taylor for a ride home. We ended up going to Kraig's place. Kraig locked his keys in the car, and anyway to make a long story short, Kraig, Taylor, Scott, and I hung out at Kraig's place. I really like them. They are fun. Maybe I'm actually starting to make. . . no. . . can it be? FRIENDS?!

Anyhoo—I washed and waxed the car today. It looks nice.

December 25, 2004

One day we'll be able to drive beyond our limits
     late   at   night
I hope we can write far beyond

                            our mar-

gins
Our favorite things will never end
One day we'll discover a color
See beyond our judgement

We will be happy without dreams and wishes or hopes
Maybe we will just enjoy
    the   ride
Live our lives toward something beyond this life, for the next. Live beyond ourselves for others
One day our memories won't make us sad anymore
and we will smile
                Could it be?
One day we won't have to reach
Stars will be among us
One day change will change
and we won't be afraid to tell the people we love that we love them.

January 11, 2005

The hallways smell nice in my high school, instead of urine and weed like the last one. The boy next to me gets out of his seat. He wants to drop the class—I think, "I'll miss him, won't he miss me?" I feel that it's over, he wants me out the door. Was it my fault? I had to take the exam too, but I survived. It's all because of his music.

Last night I laughed. I wonder what my friend thinks of me. I like him—we're both nervous around each other.

The latch on my lunchbox fell apart and my lunch was strewn along the locker hallways. A nice girl picked up my water bottle for me. Simple. And yet she gave no thought to how this would change my life, my outlook on human kind.

I am waiting mostly.

July 9, 1997
I can't wait until August when I turn 9 and school starts.

May 28, 2000
I can't wait until I'm 12.

July 24, 2001
I can't wait for school to start. I can't decide on what to wear. Anyway, love, me. p.s. I am bored, I am bored, I am repetitive, I am bored. . . I am.

February 17, 2001
I can't wait until Monday. I miss Sam and Jeff!

January 2, 2002
I can't wait until tomorrow! I get to see Ted and Kayla!

January 5, 2002
I can't wait to see Sarah and Meagan.

June 18, 2002
I can't wait to know what Alex says.

September 16, 2002
Can't wait for Drama Club tomorrow!

February 26, 2003
I can't wait until PDA.

August 22, 2004
I can't wait for Alex to come home.

Most of my life is spent waiting. I am impatient. Waiting for what? I am impatient.

I wait for it to be over and then I am sad when it is over. Perhaps because I was waiting the whole time. Waiting instead of living, holding on to this belief that it will be best when it's over. And so I wait instead of live, and when that finish line comes I rejoice! For the wait is over.

I was waiting for nothing.

A teacher from Louisiana asks me what I am so "bummed about." He's quick to make the joke, and I sit there staring back, to which he adds, "What were you thinking?" and I say, "I am always thinking."

"Scary," he says, and everyone is happy because he finally met the joke. So I am burdened with a mind that is constantly thinking. A nightmare.

I had a nightmare. I was in a room, with an urgency to get out that I cannot explain. I felt warm hands from the being behind me on my arms. I ran out into the living room, relieved to run to my mother, but she was dead on the couch staring blankly into the red ceiling. I have never experienced such fear, and as my last breath was fast coming I cried unto my Heavenly Father.

I woke gasping for air. My room was dark and quiet and I could hear Mom in the kitchen. Later she told me this sometimes happens, a nightmare you cannot wake from, a nightmare you are trapped in. "Your body falls asleep, but your mind is still awake, so you're trapped in a lifeless body." Trapped in your mind. Though my mother assured me it was just a dream, it had been a long time since I was afraid of the dark. So for the past few nights I've been bitter toward myself, not sure whether to blame my body or my mind for the scare.

But I am grateful somewhat for the way I constantly think. It's what I do when I wait. I am hopelessly flawed in doing things like dropping my lunch in the hall, but I quietly like that part about me. It reminds me of a time when that kind of stuff didn't embarrass me, that my pride is more ridiculous and embarrassing than the simple mistake of dropping a lunchbox, and yet somehow at that moment the world (my world) laughs and points at me from such a simple thing. That in itself is ridiculous! My lunchbox mishaps remind me of how ridiculous life is and should be.

Funny how everything was wonderful between me and the boy I like before each of us considered the possibility of us liking each other, that we're both scared out of our minds to tell the other how we feel, too scared to even move, even hint at any emotion. It has crossed my mind, my dangerous mind, to just ask, but it's not sensible. I am waiting. I have waited before until the chance was gone and that was much worse. I don't want that, but my sensibility won't give me what I want.

January 17, 2005

I did nothing today but sleep. I felt I kinda wasted the day, but not really 'cause I slept and I needed that.

I've gotten really close to Scott, Taylor, and Kraig. Oh! In fact Thursday Taylor, Scott, and I hung out at Taylor's and had dinner. Then Saturday night, Kraig and I drove to Scott's place for just a few minutes. So I've spent a lot of time with them.

January 25, 2005

Scott Smiley wrote me a note in Japanese today. He said (translated), "To my angel Kiyomi, your eyes are really pretty."

Agghhh! I really like him! I hope he likes me, too. Ugh. No, Kristen! You can't worry about it.

April 1, 2003
Alex gave me a button. He gave me his Foo Fighters button. Isn't that so nice? It made me so happy.

Alex is so sweet and irresistible, and even though it's going nowhere, I'm hopelessly attracted to him. I mean, I WROTE him a SONG for goodness sake. So it's like this dramatic love plot with him.

January 28, 2005

When I get married, which will be like, AGES from now, I need to marry someone who will make me laugh every day. You know, that's what Scott is missing. He doesn't make me laugh every day. Alex did.

February 10, 2005

April didn't show today. Again.

I'm getting closer—no. I'm there. They like me. 10 miles of notebook paper for a life yet to be written. They all ask incessantly. . . I DON'T KNOW. And should I? I honestly want to run in every which decision. I'm indecisive. That's for sure.

The girl in my economics class says I curl my letters. So I'm curly. And contagious. Curly and contagious am I.

I don't fancy adults much. Now I'm British. Today was what makes yesterday not so bad, but Algebra 2 makes me feel guilty. . . I don't do my homework.

For some reason, I just thought of Sam.

February 12, 2005

This morning, Mom and I had root beer floats for breakfast. It was the coolest thing.

February 14, 2005

Pahpy Lavenstines Yad!

Taylor at lunch: "Things you would not normally give your Valentine—a tire!" (so I ripped the punch hole from some notebook paper and gave him a tire—he laughed!)

To April: you help make my life make sense

Ryan King: "How can you automatically assume they were skipping?"

Lord Shapiero: "Guilty until proven innocent."

From 6th period today, I thought: There's a lake in the lane.

Mrs. Fister: "It was a Segway."

Ryan King: "Oh I wish I had one of those. Have you seen one before? Oh my gosh they're amazing!"

Blame. If only it did not make her so guilty. She had a tendency to be too hard on herself. She was a little odd. Quiet and hopelessly flawed and clumsy, apologetic and even pathetic. Yet confident, loud, dramatic, smart-mouthed. She runs after the rambunctious half, apologizing, regretting.

Yet happy? Complicated, shy and not. . .

Was she not sincere? She wasn't. That was the truth.

I'm talking about myself here.

When I wasn't around people, I felt very serious. I think it was a side of me that did grow up too fast, a side that required me to take care of myself, that was unsure of things, that lacked confidence. I needed to be accepted, though, and I was willing to be anything you wanted me to be so that I was.

I had to make you fall in love with me. I'd reciprocate the energy you exuded. I'd magnify whatever we had in common. You had my loyalty, my heart. But I'd be someone totally different to someone else, and they would have all my devotion too. In my mind, this was possible. I just compartmentalized my life. I was a blank slate. I'd create a different reality than the one that really existed, because anything was better than that, and the more realities I'd make, the more attention I reaped.

But sometimes in the moment to feel accepted I would do things I would regret later.

March 6, 2004
I fool myself sometimes. I forget myself in a world I try to create, but only to really fool others. Yet in doing so, I ultimately forget and fool myself.

My chameleon ways were just a way to hide. They were a defense mechanism. A skin I could pretend to be happy in, like I was playing an award-winning role in a movie that didn't exist. I was vulnerable, insecure. Afraid of discovering what really lay beneath was someone I would hate. Some monster I could never love.

I think it's why I never formed an identity structure. I was just a mirror of who was around me, and the people I loved the most held the biggest pieces of who I was. I just assimilated my soul until I couldn't tell where I ended and you began.

February 15, 2005

Amazing how song will speak to you before you even know what you're saying. So you should write even when it doesn't make much sense because you might not understand where it came from, but later on your subconscious will speak. Your mind will speak to you.

Shanna had guitar earrings today. That means she can PLAY BY EAR.

They have one tortoise too many for it to be an endangered species, for it to make the list. They're running them over.

We just need to kill more so they can make the list, then we can start saving them.

pg. 538: "A black hole is believed to be formed when a star's core collapses. The gravitational pull becomes so strong that even the star's light cannot escape."

February 16, 2005

I cried today. I was frustrated, I procrastinated
I wonder what he'll say
I asked him today. Was it wrong?
I was wondering. . .
I'm just being honest
I honestly think I'm hopeless. New page.

If you could have one memory
What would you forget
If there were words to fill these empty emotions
Syllables I haven't met
Leaving here is a place I haven't reached yet
Today I fell off the hinges that swing me

back into reality
Life made me look the other way
when it took my soul away
Bending possibility

Sometimes when I'm at a loss for words, words will just flow out, words I don't understand. I'll write it down and go, "Where in the world did that come from?"

Then a week later, a month later, sometimes even a year later, I'll be writing down emotions and thoughts and somehow I have the perfect song for the situation, like the lyrics now make sense. I had one of those moments today.

Kelsey said, "But why can't she just move on?" and you said, "She hasn't quite gotten there yet," and it made sense. Leaving here is a place I haven't reached yet. Before I left South Carolina I remember writing, "Leaving here is a concept I can't grasp," But now I've left. I grasp it alright, but I haven't let go.

It's all very confusing when you feel your identity slipping.

One memory. If I could have one memory. The other night I was listening to Oasis and I thought about the day Tim, Alex, and I lay in the wheat field. This memory has been so perfectly etched and glorified in my mind. The best day of my life. The smallest hinge on which my life was so acutely and heavily swung like a massive pendulum. I was so freely elated. Feeling my heart pound for the first time as I dropped from a reality I wanted to forget forever. I will never feel that way again. From: *Perks of Being a Wallflower*

"When we got out of the tunnel, Sam screamed this really fun scream, and there it was. Downtown. Lights on buildings and everything that makes you wonder. Sam sat down and started laughing. Patrick started laughing. I started laughing.

And in that moment, I swear we were infinite."

February 19, 2005

I babysat today.

I have these weird flashbacks and daydreams when I do. It's fascinating how small but real a child's world is. I have a hard time putting this into words.

I just remember making up stories to go with pictures and pretending and not knowing how anything is made or where it comes from, why things were funny and made people laugh. I didn't know that all the stories and movies and toys came from real life. I thought they were just pretend. But they're not. They reflect real emotions and real things.

It's like as soon as I enter their house I forget about my world. . . I realize how tiny it is. . . high school. It's unbelievable how consequential and inconsequential it is. When I'm in their house, I think about things. I think about the future and past. It makes me feel guilty because I feel like I haven't DONE anything with my time. I can't catch up! It's overwhelming.

I feel I'm drifting a little bit.

New page.

I miss Tim and Alex and the way it used to be. I listened to Joanne's CD the other day, and it killed me. Why can't I let go? Talking to Tim on the phone is depressing because he knows and I know it's not the same. Haven't spoken to Alex since the summer. It's all very confusing. . .

Somehow I can't let go of who I used to be. I still AM, but I can't let go of the perception they held—is that prideful?

I can't stand it when Scott types on this little phone. I hate cell phones. DEATH to electronic devices when there's life to live and see. Pay attention to me and don't text the rest. Then maybe I'll be happy.

I hate how he lives a "second" life apart from the one he shares with me. That reminds me of Alex. I hated Alex for that too.

April 12, 2003

I'm having doubts about Alex. Gosh. I dunno.

I saw a bunch of girls last night and tonight who came— actually it was Emily Chance and some other chicks. Man—last year I didn't even give a crap about them. I didn't worry about them at all. Now all the sudden Emily is Miss Perfect (she is. It's nauseating), and I know she had a crush on Alex last year. But she wasn't pretty then and she was just annoying.

Emily asked Alex to go to the choir ball with her. He did. It seems like he's always hangin' out with older, prettier, nicer, well-dressed, all-round-pink-and-pretty girls.

And then there's me. I've got the worst haircut ever. I'm a tomboy. I'm punk. I've got glasses. I feel so UNWORTHY of being with Alex. I can't help but think Alex likes them and just looks at me as something else. But I can't tell. I don't know how he acts around all the other girls. But, no matter what—I swore to myself I'd sing him the song I wrote for him, so yeah. Gosh. I can't get over him.

I hate it when I'm like this.

Why I am still searching? I thought I already found myself. Tim wrote, "don't ever stop searching for answers"—

I guess that's why I don't ever know, why I won't ever know anything— I'm forever searching. I am and it drives me crazy. Just WHAT am I looking for? I'm searching for a reason to find what I'm looking for. I'm looking for an answer to what I'm looking for. I'm getting confused.

I wish there were more colors. There just aren't enough. I wish I could paint colors people can't even imagine, or play notes our ears can't fathom; come up with an idea never thought before, or have a feeling no one else has ever felt.

I wish there was more time, more time to get to know people.

I don't like this. I don't like being a kid and not, at the same time. It's stressful. It's depressing, really. Somehow I just can't let go of this want to be something more, bigger, better, something. It's this anxious yet free, truly free feeling I get when I'm infinite.

February 24, 2005
Physics Textbook pg.252
Laws of Thermodynamics:
1) You cannot win
2) You cannot break even
3) You cannot get out of the game

February 26, 2005
The radio is playing in the weight room, and the door is open. Switchfoot is playing, and all of the sudden I feel infinite. I get the notion that my music could be playing in some high school's gym room—that it's possible.

I wonder if they know that some crazy kid in Florida feels infinite in 6th period because of their song that just happens to be playing. That I'm not doing homework right now because I feel compelled to write, that it reminds me of Brandon Orr* and how I want to marry him when I'm older and how the feeling immediately disappears when the song ends.

* A nice Mormon boy I met once in Utah

March 2, 2005

I don't think we look up enough. I walked past this kid who was lying on his back looking up at the ceiling. I realized I don't ever notice the ceiling.

I loved what Urquhart said today. His little lecture he gave today was so moving—I'm skipping Gym class just to write about it. I realize how much time I waste. I'm just trying to understand life. I thought I did—I thought I got a pretty good hold of it. . . shows how much I really know. Just starting to realize my actions, however small, good or bad, will haunt me, that I am the same person I was no matter where I go and who I want to be. It's overwhelming, but I am at the point where I know the gospel will make me happy. I don't feel that I'm living it as well as I could, and so I'm living it as well as I can, and so I'm disappointed.

I get confused. I just want to live life. I think of April. There's so many things I want to do in life.

I think of Brandon.

I know what Tim meant when he said I was the ever-present symbol of his life. It's still confusing though. I have a hard time letting go. I spend a lot of time thinking about it.

I wonder what Sam is doing. Is she looking up at the sky like I am right now?

Sam. . .

January 10, 2002
I still miss Sam. I wish she was right here next to me. I miss
her so much. I wish I could move far away. Away from every-
thing.

I think if I were to have met myself, I mean the me two
years ago, I would've been annoyed.

March 3, 2005
I truly believe what we read finds its way into who we are
and what we write. You know how people ask, "If your life
was a book, would it be interesting?" Well I think if your life
is boring, your writing will be boring also. A simple realization
I guess.

I think I remember things in my life better than they were
really.

I don't read enough. At all. Watching people read thick
novels makes me feel extremely idle.

The finalists' question for "Miss F-Dub" (that's what I call
it—it's too much to write out Miss Fort Walton Beach, but
hey, I just did) was, "Pick an event that has occurred within
the past 1000 years that has changed the course of history and
describe its significance to you." I hesitated to share my first
thought but couldn't think straight because this is what I feel
is the most significant to me. So I said when Joseph Smith
received his first vision. I did a brief explanation of how much
my religion means to me and the connection between his First
Vision and the Church as it exists today.

It took everything I had to say what I truly believe and
it was exhilarating. . . afterwards. I felt so vulnerable because
most people don't know anything about The Church of Jesus

Christ of Latter-day Saints. It's awkward for me to introduce my faith, try to untwist set notions, cliches, and stereotypes associated with Mormons to my friends. I really think I made them feel uncomfortable because Monday they didn't mention it at all, and my friend Scott said he didn't know what to say. I just now realized that every kid that's said I did a great job was there to hear me stand as a member of the LDS church also. That's cool.

Anyway, so after the show, I felt uneasy about my response until I noticed the whole entire Young Women's Presidency (4 of my Youth leaders) were there—all of them beaming, and my dad was so proud of me; I have never ever seen him so proud of me ever in my life. It was then I felt the audience didn't matter. I didn't care. I was just so glad I said it. And I won 2nd runner up, AND Miss Congeniality!

Copied from my *Untitled Notebook of Mad Composition*

"Just starting to realize my actions, however small, good or bad, will haunt me."

I kinda knew this—but I see the effects of my decisions more clearly now. MUCH more clearly. For example, I had given Mrs. Britt a bad attitude for taking my cell phone one day, especially because I NEVER have a cell phone with me and I was just using it to call my dad, and now she won't let me into Leadership—which is what I've wanted since I found out about it—because of this small incident. I was mad, thought that was pretty dumb, and complained to Dad.

He laughed. I laughed. I said it wasn't funny. He said there wasn't a more perfect example of justice served, that he couldn't help but laugh. Then I realized how my actions, however small, would haunt me.

My dad gave me the "college" speech yesterday. . . kind of the climax to this feeling I've nursed for a while now. I mean, it's not the question of what I want to do with my life, it's the little annoying ones like what college to go to. I promised myself last year that it wouldn't matter, but it does. I mean, even the classes I take next year are choices that bring opportunities to meet people, learn things, do things.

It's like choosing a cup. You don't know what is underneath, and there's really no point in guessing, so it shouldn't matter what cup you choose. . . right? But you know as well as I do people will spend FOREVER trying to decide which cup to pick, trying to look for some variable that will lead them to control or predict their fate. But you can never tell!

Life dishes out great things as well as horrible things.

March 7, 2005

Sam ran away. Gone.

I can't write this. Sorry, I can't. I can't write this. I can't live in this house knowing Sam doesn't have one to come home to. I can't do my homework knowing Sam dropped out of school. I can't face my friends knowing she left hers. I can't sleep in my bed, I can't eat, I can't do anything. The worst thing is that I can't do anything about it.

I used to look at those flyers and think, that just doesn't happen, kids shouldn't have to feel so unloved they run away. Kids shouldn't have to feel like they don't have a home. It just doesn't happen.

I hate not knowing who she was before she left. What could've happened that she threw her life away? This is depressing. I can't do this.

Maybe one day I'll get over my fear of writing, of always being reminded, knowing someone will read what I write. One day I won't be afraid of an audience and I'll know exactly what words I mean.

I'm tired of feeling bogged down. I'm stressed, I worry. I worry about having a boyfriend, embarrassing as that is. . . I worry about the school I'm going to. It all sounds so cliché, and I hate that. When did I end up cliché?

I've always wanted something more. I have big dreams, big ones. It's sick how I feel that I'm forced to forget them for now. I hate that. There just isn't enough time, yet I waste a lot just dreaming. . . WAITING. I spend a lot of time waiting and I don't know what for. I'm feeling out of place. Sometimes I feel I'm better than everyone else, then other times I feel just plain stupid.

I like it when the light shines through the window. When all the lights are off and this cool dark glow comes through, and you notice your pencil's shadow across the page. It's very quiet now and I like that.

It's still overwhelming. Everything. Life. All the things I think about. I can't keep up; it's everywhere. I'm everywhere. Sometimes I think I'm spread too thin, but I'm not.

I shouldn't feel that way. There's work to do, and it needs to be done.

March 16, 2005

Sometimes I feel like every truth has been explored and mapped and read and explained already. Like my own discoveries really belong to someone else just because they were born before me. This is from Tim. He sent me 30 pages of pure Tim Threet on my 16th birthday. It's the best gift I have ever received in my life.

"It really is a double-edged sword though, isn't it? Kids have no cars, no money, no real social life like I know now. But are those things better than bliss? Kids don't know how mediocre those things make you feel. I remember thinking 100 dollars was the most in the world. . . I remember thinking, 'I wonder what I'll look like when I'm older.' I mean, obsessing on it, how cool it would to be old and in college, but now I really don't care. I hate to use a cliché and consider myself 'jaded,' but that's really what it feels like, the world has lost its shine, a little."

I hate that we have clichés. They're mined words. Brilliant ideas once, then someone photocopied them into fakes, and now no one can use them without being phony, and no one can recognize the real thing. They are unavoidable.

The Things They Carried has changed me. I was so upset Wednesday.

I told Kraig exactly how I felt about everything, but he didn't feel the same way. Not even close. That made me feel even more down about how I felt, and I was beginning to get depressed even. I don't know how to pin my emotions, I was almost angry. He said, "I don't mean to be insensitive, but I think it's neat that you can be so affected by a book. It's cool that you're getting so upset over it."

When I read the first chapter of *The Things They Carried*, I was shocked to read the f-word. Not to say I haven't read it before, I mean it's all over the place really—It was just because

I had no idea what I was getting myself into, and because you had assigned it. For a school assignment. At one point I was bitter. I was mad at you for making me read the book. (Obviously you didn't make me.) There is definitely something to be learned of war, and I've been sheltered in plenty of ways. That book had broken a window in my mind. All the sudden I felt scared, and at the same time, I'm better than I was before, but I felt so much safer behind the glass. I had a smidge of ignorance leave me. Understanding the book makes me click. I understand people differently than I had before. I understand now that every story has its truth. I mean I really get it. I see it now in my songs, in my writing, it's all me. I mean, Tim O'Brien's stories were the only way he could get at his memory. The only way to relieve his pain—every emotion expressible, and the emotions that aren't.

I have never read anything more honest than Tim (Threet)'s writings. The majority of them are these bizarre free verse sections about roaches and grey kittens and weird names like Georgiana but they are all so. . . TIM. Anyway, I guess it seems silly to rant about art expressing feeling, how art has meaning (duh?) but like I said—who's to say my discoveries don't mean anything because I haven't had the chance to live life yet?

In fact, there's nothing more real than fantasy. I guess you could say that our pretending is just extreme exaggeration of the truth.

Back to *The Things They Carried*. So I'm at Kraig's house. Pawing through his infinite collection of DVDs and I spot *Eternal Sunshine of the Spotless Mind*. I pick it up and put it back. Kraig was like, "Whoa! Whoa! I know you've told me you don't watch R rated movies and I respect that—the only problem is that I watched your eyes light up for a brief moment before you saw the rating and then you looked all disappointed."

Then we talked about it. How the rating system is faulty, why things are rated for what reasons, what I try to avoid, the specifics and general rules I have. I mean, how are we to know?

Well it doesn't matter what rating—if it makes me feel uncomfortable, or isn't spiritually uplifting, I don't watch it. And see, this worked fine for me. I held strong to my resolve. Until *The Things They Carried*. This book would definitely be rated R, but I walked away with something valuable. Kraig was telling me about all these movies that are just like that, that aren't all about the sleeze, just raw life. And so I'm left to rethink this line I've drawn myself.

First, will what I walk away with compensate for whatever "harsh" stuff I experience? Am I being ignorant by banning all R movies?

As I left Kraig's house, he handed me *Eternal Sunshine*. I didn't take it, but I haven't decided if I ever will.

Kraig and I also talked about "movie inflation." Kraig told me his parents didn't like him watching movies like *Kill Bill* because they're afraid that if someone were shot right in front of him, Kraig would brush it off like it was nothing, because he's seen so much of it.

We laughed about it, but it kinda happens to people. I kind of felt like the "Lemon Tree" story made a cut so much deeper because I was never exposed to anything like it. Some kids just brushed it off, didn't care, were totally numb to it. Nothing's enough anymore because we've already spent what we were supposed to save. I guess I don't want to watch R movies unless I've learned enough about life to understand? I sound stupid, but it's not.

You know, Kraig Kelsey is such a smart kid. I'm so glad we've become friends.

You remember how hard last semester was for me. Things didn't change until the last day before Christmas break. I couldn't get a ride home, and I didn't want to wait 2 hours for the detention bus, and it was by pure chance I caught Taylor in the hallway, and because I really didn't want to stay stuck at school, I got the guts to ask if he could take me home. He really didn't want to but he said, "I guess."

Before we left, he needed to stop by the Drama room, and while we were there, Kraig invited Taylor to his place, and I asked to come along, and they said sure and were all nice and stuff. So we arrived at Kraig's house, and then he locked his keys in the car so all three of us were locked out of his house. Then Scott stopped by and we played soccer outside until Kraig's mom came home and we went inside.

Anyway, I remember feeling like I finally belonged, like things were getting back to normal, that I was starting to actually make friends. Those are my friends now. Scott, Taylor, and Krage. And April. She is so cool. I have so much respect for her. I was surprised to find we have the same values and ideas. Anyway—I felt like I needed to write this because my last journal felt sort of incomplete. This is kind of like a happy ending.

I started keeping another journal since February. It's called *The Untitled Notebook of Mad Composition*. I keep everything in there. Weird things that happen, lyrics, stand-up material, thoughts and ideas, everything. A good portion of it is things people say. Sometimes I write out the whole sentence, sometimes I just write what I like. They're just fragments but they sound cool. Usually they're words that have meaning, but sometimes it's just words that sound cool. Like 'purely persuasive'.

I wanted to share a page I wrote because I think it's neat how I came across the same idea but fell short and now after *The Things They Carried* I understand.

From: *The Untitled Notebook of Mad Composition*

"I didn't know that all the stories and movies and toys came from real life. I thought they were just pretend. But they're not. They reflect real emotions and real things."

See, on Wednesday you asked the class if anyone was getting upset because the stories weren't real. I was upset because they were. April said when she was little she had a hard time realizing movies weren't real, that it was just pretend. I was the opposite. I knew it wasn't real. It's pretend. I knew. It wasn't until I was older and lived life a bit that I recognized the emotion and appreciated the humor. This is what I was talking about, waiting until I can appreciate. It seems like I'm saying there's no such thing as fantasy, and that's not true either. I mean, sometimes we just need to play and that's totally separate from expression.

Ah, that's what I wanted to say. Is that I can recognize expression. I can recognize expression in art now. And that's the most important thing! It's the only thing that gives art substance. It's not just watching colors and hearing funny noises—now I can get the jokes and follow the story. It's more than entertaining because it represents so much more.

Yes, that's what I was trying to say. I can recognize expression.

March 17, 2005

This morning I made the Physics class laugh: ". . . metal expands. . . do humans expand in heat too?"

With Scott and Taylor: "crazy, POPCORN, regulations, rules, directions, hazards, cautions, warnings, *precautions*! That's the word I was looking for."

Ryan King: "Thanks Nick. Stop hitting me with your dumb textbooks!"

March 18, 2005

Sitting here on the marina, the sand. I decided I'd stop by on the way home. I got to thinking. . . What is my biggest fear? I would hate for my future husband to die. I love how it's always windy here. No matter what. Man I have to pee.

March 23, 2005

Maybe life's not so sad after all. I like how the ink shines in the sun before it dries as I write.

The Things They Carried has put me in a bad mood all day. Like, I felt I'd never be happy again, and that's when he walked up and kissed me on the hand. Never lose faith in the little things you do for people. Never.

I always save the last Tic-tac for when I'm really depressed, but I ate it anyway because I figured I wouldn't need it later.

March 30, 2005

I've decided not to watch R rated movies. I thought about it. I mean, I really did. I think *The Things They Carried* is well written, it's neat. I did gain from it, but I had to read about the "Lemon Tree" to get there.

You saw me cry in class.

The things I read in that book were awful. What's worse is that I can't get them out of my mind. Though I gained from the book as a whole, I gained nothing from the "Lemon Tree." I can read tons of history books on the Vietnam war. I can read lots of books with literary value. There isn't anything in that book I can't get anywhere else. Presentation counts. It's something I learned from your class.

I felt discouraged at Kraig's house because I felt like my reasons weren't good enough. Because if they weren't good enough to convince him, well maybe they weren't good enough for me either.

That's stupid. Just because the world agrees with you doesn't make it right! (sigh) This is hard because I don't want to be mean about it or offensive. I want to be firm without being hard-headed. We can't label everything art and think it's okay. That's really what I'm trying to get at.

I also know that my sense of right and wrong isn't everyone's, and so I'm not forcing my own sense of integrity on anyone. I don't hold it against them either. But I do have my own integrity, I know for myself, and this is why I can't finish *The Things They Carried.*

Throughout Mr. Urquhart's English class, I pondered the value of art.

For a sociopath, murder can be a form of expression. Does that make it art? Could be. Then murder is an art whose audience we surely do not want to cultivate. But what art should and shouldn't be shared is up to society, I suppose.

As a teenager I had a very low tolerance for anything sexual or violent or that had bad language. I censored the information and media I viewed.

The themes we read in my Junior and Senior English classes included abortion, rape, murder, insanity, and so on. I hated it. I didn't want to feel or experience those things. I already felt the maximum amount I could feel for my own painful problems.

That said, the girl next to me was pregnant, so the topic of abortion was part of her reality; she did relate to it, because that was her life. Different works of art speak to different people at different stages.

Later on, in my Senior year, we read *The Yellow Wallpaper* for class. I related to the woman in the story who was going mentally insane, probably much more than my classmates. The emotions it drew from me overshadowed the literary lessons we were supposed to learn. While the class casually discussed the prose, I was forced to secretly relive my own trauma.

As a deeply saddened, anxiety ridden, 16-year-old with religious innocence, I already felt I was growing up too fast. I wanted to be a kid a little longer.

I was not ready to be in an audience exposed to the graphic nature of the Vietnam war discussed in *The Things They Carried*. It made me too sad. I didn't want to analyze writing style. I wanted to cry.

That said, just months before, I wrote this:

January 27, 2005
"I'm through with the greater-than symbols," Claude said as she fixed her mechanical high heeled shoe-muppet.

Her friend has been working for the penguin-infested work-shop for three and a half years now, and she grew impatient with Baxter. "And what is that painting doing by my car? I was late for work this morning; it wouldn't stop looking at me."

Baxter hid his feeling of disappointment. All he ever wanted was to learn the language and what; his impatient sister had sent him to this horrid place where everything is metal and cold and hard. It is a place where he sits by the window at night and listens to the orange echoes and thinks about his dear Sharlene. Sharlene, with her soft caramel hair and quiet sense of humor. How Baxter sat and thought in numb composition before that accusing canvas. And so he replied with orange color, deprived of the light brown he was yearning to paint instead, and yet it didn't hold his sister long enough. Why did it not torture and pull at Claude's very existence as it did his? "I never wanted to work with those penguins, you know. Maybe if you would stop—"

"Maybe if you could tell me how operation Amber is going."

"I'm not a liar, Claude!" Baxter slammed his spoon at the chair across from him. He hated cereal anyway. It reminded him of Ted. He was the first person to talk to Baxter when he got here, and they were best friends for almost a year until he was promoted.

August 6, 2001
"So uh. . . you're in this class?" A boy I noticed today in homeroom with blonde, spiked hair and red suspend-

ers was leaning against the wall. "Cause uh. . . then we'd be in the same class, you know?" He is unnaturally skinny and tall with translucent freckles on each cheek. Although he had been the first to speak, he seemed just as shy as I was.

The door opened. "Yes?" A young, blonde teacher appeared in the doorway.

The boy went first. "Um, I think I'm in your class." He showed the lady his schedule. "Ummm. . . Yep! Sure thing! Come right in!"

November 27, 2001
Ted and I are like best buds.

Ted killed himself last week.

"Well, what are you going to do about the painting, Baxter. Why don't you sell it?"

"I wish I could sell you."

"A psycho might think it was good enough to burn."

"A psycho might try to shove knives down red-headed children because she thinks they are pretty."

"They didn't deserve to live, Baxter." Claude picked up his spoon and tossed it in the sink. The smell of cheap citrus and blood filled her mind as she followed the crimson lines run down the pipe. It was Baxter's fault she had gone insane, because he was stupid. He couldn't work a decent job. She had to kill those red-headed children.

"The spoon is washed already. Go upstairs. I have to practice reading."

"You won't ever get better, Baxter. You're stupid, okay?"

"No. I think with my mind. Minds are not stupid."

"That's the very reason we have to regulate the use of paper, Baxter. It's people like you who use paper to paint and read and think! You can never be normal, Baxter. You will never be able to hold a decent, normal conversation with anyone, and you will never learn to read."

"She means to read like everyone else," Baxter thought. It was his stupid mind! He hated the fact it was constantly thinking, withholding him from actually living. Once Sharlene had given him a flower, a tiny little yellow flower. It was mid-fall when the air was still warm and still cool. It was when her hair somehow seemed richer.

It's ironic that things I secretly created were the sorts of things I'd reject in public. They weren't pretty and uplifting. I drew pictures of skeletal emaciated naked women. I drew blood and knives. I drew pictures of myself crying. I drew these things because I had to get them out of me. And they're all images that are graphic and inappropriate to the standard I set for myself.

This short story, or whatever it is, is how I felt. Suppressed hate, and anger, and loss. That I made Ted a character who killed himself because we weren't friends in real life anymore, that I had images of shoving knives down someone's throat because I was frustrated life wasn't fair, that I horribly missed someone who once loved me—those themes were just a metaphor for my life. These are real feelings and emotions. It's not my fault that's how I felt. You can't censor life.

April 3, 2005

Still thinking about *The Things They Carried*.

You can say you liked a book because it affected you, because it made you feel something, but effectiveness is different from value. I literally cried for an hour after reading that "Lemon Tree" bit until my mom finally came into my room to calm me down. I was so depressed after reading the book and it made me feel guilty.

Perhaps your liking of a book shouldn't be based solely on the fact it made you feel something, but on what it made you feel. It's all about what you remember, something you've learned, it's what you take with you. I just want to do the right thing. So I'm going with what I feel deep down is correct.

The summer before I turned twelve was the summer I moved from Yokota Air Base, Japan, to Prattville, Alabama. That summer sucked. Someone shot my pet PJ, I had to leave my best friend, Robin Godfrey, I didn't know anyone, and I spent all summer in my room hoping for school to start. I just sat there in my room doing nothing. Hoping some kid my age would ring the door bell and invite me to a movie or a game of basketball. I hoped so hard I pretended the door bell rang, opened the door and took a good look around, only to come back inside. I would get so frustrated with myself I'd cry. You could call me insane, but loneliness can do that to you.

I was really nervous about going to school there, so I prayed for a best friend. I spent all summer thinking of the perfect best friend. I hoped she'd have red hair, and she'd be pretty. I hoped she and I would be best buds. I hoped she moved from North or South Dakota, so she would know what a prairie dog was and help me get over PJ's death. I hoped she'd live in Alabama for ten months just like me. I hoped she could act silly like me, and that when I saw her, I'd know. Maybe we'd meet on the first day of school in gym class or something. I just hoped.

Then, on the first day of school, I walked into the Gym looking for red heads and a place to sit.

There she was, sitting up on the bleachers.

It seemed like she was squished in every direction but one: there was an opening to her left. And I knew she was the one.

I met Sam exactly how I imagined to meet her. And she was everything I wanted her to be, red head and everything. To some extent, it was creepy, but that didn't faze me much.

I remember when the bell rang, I wished P.E. would never end. She dropped her hair clip, and I insisted on getting it for her.

Sam is amazing. She is a year older than me. She is athletic and pretty and funny. She makes all As, she's popular, she has a German shepherd named Jake. I remember one day she dragged me to audition for the middle school play. We were asked to read a script and sing "Happy Birthday" if we wanted a singing part. Before I went on stage, I remember wanting to back down and bail last minute. Sam said to me, "Don't be afraid of what others think," and she meant it too. She is extremely fun loving.

People tell me I'm fun loving; they've got no clue.

All the guys fawn over Sam. Sam has never been snub about it. She's just as interested and nice to everyone. That's why she has so many friends. I feel like she is my sister. Sam was forever saying perfect things like, "Don't be afraid of what others think." Never met a more sincere person.

I've been friends with Sam for four years now. I have pictures of her in my room. Tons of pictures. We used to send each other packages; we filled shoeboxes with stuff. One time she sent me her favorite orange t-shirt. It was all soft and worn. It smelled just like her. In the shoebox I sent her in return, I made sure to give up all of my very favorite things.

One night this summer at her place, her friend called and said he had to leave town because he had gotten caught up with the wrong crowd at the wrong time or something like that. He was running away from the police. She was crying. She said it wasn't fair. She didn't understand why she had to deal with stuff like that. He stopped by in the middle of the night to say goodbye.

I think Sam would've liked Tim and Alex.

One day we were watching VH1 or something, and this girl was singing. I thought it was lame and said I could probably write better music. Why wasn't I on MTV? I really wasn't serious but Sam said, "You will." She was so sincere it nearly killed me. She believes in me so much. She thinks I'm beautiful and talented.

When we were in the airport before I left Omaha for Fort Walton, she took one of the baggage tags while I was checking in and wrote, "I love you!"

Last February, I called to tell Sam all about the Miss Fort Walton Beach pageant. Her mother picked up, I asked for Sam, and she sighed and said she hadn't seen Sam in three weeks.

I asked if she was at a camp or something or on a trip. She said, "Kristen, we don't know where she is." I think she had to repeat it three times.

I asked stupid questions like, "Have you called the police?"
"Of course, Kristen," she said. I didn't know what to say.

Eventually we hung up. I stood there for a minute then burst into tears. I completely broke down. I was crying because I felt sorry for the people she left. I was crying because I knew she must've been hurt and sad and really unhappy to leave home. I was crying because she dropped out of school. I was crying because I didn't know if she'd ever contact me, if I'd ever speak to her again.

It's been two months and she's still gone. It sucks. I told my friend Sarah about it, and it's like my story went flat. What did I expect? All she could say was that she felt sorry. Which horribly is the exact same thing I said to Sam's mother. What else is there to say? She didn't know Sam. She wasn't Sam's friend, and I'm not Sam's mother.

I just don't understand. It's stupid. I either feel angry at Sam for giving up and running away like a coward, or I feel awful that she had to escape a life she couldn't bear. I guess it's a little bit of both. I'm caught between sympathy and blame.

Anyway, the point is that I miss her. I was just sitting here thinking about *The Things They Carried*, writing in here, and when I looked up to sort my thoughts, I fell upon her picture and kind of became overwhelmed.

I talked to Alex on the phone yesterday. Tim is going to Argentina for a year in August, and Alex is planning on living with his dad over in the middle east by Saudi Arabia.

Maybe once or twice I've thought about what would happen if I ran away—but I never thought about one of my friends running away. Nothing is the way I imagined it.

Kids make a lot of promises to their friends. So do promises mean anything if you don't know any better? As kids we don't know what forever is. We don't know what it means. Or is it us who forget as we get old? I wonder if she ever thinks about it. I wonder if she ever thinks about her promises.

April 4, 2005

I wrote this song two years ago. Sadly, it is one of the few songs I can still relate to. I mean, it's sad that this is a song I still feel passionate about. I feel just as strongly about it today as I did when I first wrote it.

My 8th grade English class was first period. Alex, Ted, and I were in that class. I didn't know Alex very well—Ted was pretty much my only friend for a long time.

Tim and Ted were really close, but I didn't know Tim back then. Ted moved away after 8th grade. He'd call me and we talked, but only a couple times.

One night he told me he was taking crystal meth. It's strange, but I guess that's how Tim and I become friends. Tim was at the table talking about Ted and we both shared our disappointment.

In that 8th grade English class there was a kid named Dallen. He had two best friends, Grayson and Trevor. They were always joking around and being obnoxious in that class. Dallen moved away after 8th grade. I wrote this song the day I found out he had hanged himself in the bathroom.

I thought of Grayson's face all wet and pink. How horrible it was to see this guy cry for his best friend. I understand how helpless you feel. Helpless.

If I

Makes me think of how you used to laugh and smile
Things are different, things have changed,
and it's been a while
But I remember a you, that's not you right now
What has happened, or should I be asking

You have lost your best interest;
there's no longer this glow
About your presence that you rarely ever show
Where do you go, what do you do,
what do you see in this?
What do you say, what do you think,
is there anything you miss?

And I ask myself could I have made
The slightest impact, the slightest change
I ask myself could I have done
Something to make it all the same?

I can't go in, I press my face against the glass
They – as in people I recognize –
smile and wave as they pass
I could never be understood.
I don't even understand myself like I should.

They don't know what
I can feel

What kind of ignorance I steal
What's wrong with me? Will someone please
Make it stop.
Please.

This is not an easy thing.
I wish so badly I could bring
you back to me, go back in time
to see you being happy

And I remember how we used to smile.

April 4, 2005

What always made Sarah laugh: "It's a baby!"
I had almost forgotten.

April 5, 2005

I do not understand guys.

June 20, 2003
Friday.
So Alex isn't that bad when he isn't around Emily. Today
I went to Alex's house to read through Scott's playwright and it
was Alex, Scott, Kelly, and I. Then Kelly left and I stayed. Scott
was nice and said I should stay 'cause he'd take me home. So we
three just hung out in Alex's room. . . Then Scott left, leaving me
and Alex alone.
You know, so many people have said Alex and I are alike,
that we have good chemistry together. Maybe that's why Alex
treats me different than other girls. Because I'm like him. Maybe
that's why we have so many inside jokes. You know what he said

to me while he was rearranging his picture board? (see? I have one too!) "Kristen, you're so much fun to hang out with," and he told Scott, "Scott, she's like my new Tim, my new partner in crime."

That just feels good. And I'm glad I'm his best friend and I get to make fun of him and laugh and make inside jokes with him.

I remember one night before Big Cheese Awards or REACH or something, we were sitting on the hood of Scott's truck (we do that a lot) just me and him. He goes and looks at me and says, "I think it's funny you're the only one who knows my exact emotion."

June 28, 2003
I saw Alex and Emily hold hands today. I know. I need to get a life.

I hate being led on, but I guess I do the same thing to other guys.

I hate guys. I swear I hate them. They make me feel stupid. Yeah, so what if they tell me I'm cool. Lasts for two seconds before they find some other chick who's better than me.

I'm arrogant.

This is arrogant, but above all I'm impatient.

April 6, 2005
We all try too hard
then we stumble and we fall
and stutter and our life is a clutter
we all color inside the line
It's hard to fit in but harder to be different.

Too many of us feel with our minds.

Could I change my mind?

Could I change anyone else's?

We see places, fill spaces, hit faces.

April 7, 2005

Can I be honest? The only reason I like Scott Smiley is because of his looks and status.

I've been trying to block this out, but it's true. I just want to know I can get a guy like Scott Smiley. I'm not happy with myself unless I know I can. Which is dumb because there's so much more to life than boys.

January 31, 2002

Gosh I'm tired. I'm just sad. I'm just tired of being this way and I wish I wasn't. I feel so unpretty. I really do. I feel like I look like crap. I prolly do. I just wish someone would tell me that I'm pretty.

Urgghr! Screw it. Whatever. Bye.

January 17, 2003

Can I kill myself? PLEEEAASSE? pretty please?

Why. Why do I have to be the way I am? Why do I have to be all tough and manly? (lol) Why is it, that it is me who gets left behind?

I've never held a guy's hand before. Never. Couple of times at a dance (DUH!), but that doesn't count. See Kayla complains all the time about being rejected by guys. But she's been KISSED before, and there are some guys who hit on her and flirt with her. It just sucks. All of it.

I don't know why I like Scott, but I get very uneasy if he is with other girls. I want to know that he thinks I'm special. That I'm unique and different from all the other girls. I need to know that. And I want him to love me for it. I don't know how I want him to act or what he should say around me, I don't know. I just hate that he isn't Tim or Alex and that no one here is.

There. I said it. That's what it is.

I want him to be Alex, and I want Ryan King to be Tim, 'cept he's gay and he'll never be Tim even though sometimes he's so close it makes me sad. Because all of the sudden I remember Tim. I remember I'm in Florida and that I haven't talked to him in 5 months and that we're growing apart. Ryan isn't Tim, and I'm frustrated with myself for tricking me into thinking he was—just for a moment. What a cruel joke.

It all comes down to my mind. It's lonely.

I took advantage of Joanne and Sarah and Robert and Tim and Alex. Their minds are gone and I'm stuck here with these weird people.

It's not bad or anything, I just miss it.

June 16, 2000
Today's the last time I'll ever be in that school + last time to see my friends. My heart hurts sooo bad. I will miss them.

Wednesday, April 13, 2005 7:34 PM
From: sam lee

Hey babe. I got home today. I was okay while I was gone. I love you too. I miss you so much. Today has been an extremely emotional day.

I don't want to be home, but I know that my family loves me and I have the support of my boyfriend. Hopefully I will get to hear from you soon.

Samantha

Thursday, May 8, 2003 6:51 PM
From: sam lee

Hey cutie, what's goin' on? I can't wait for summer to come. I'm kinda in a bad mood right now. I hate being around my family. They are completely driving me nuts. I can't stand it. When I'm home I am COMPLETELY miserable unless I'm talking to someone on the computer or phone or if I'm asleep. I spend more time sleeping at home then I do up and doin' stuff. I'm so pissed off right now.

I dunno. . . I'll talk to you later babe, Sammy

Tuesday, April 19, 2005 6:08 PM
From: sam lee

Hey Kristen. How are you? I'm not so good. Things aren't going so well for me. Living here is really difficult. I love my family; I just can't stand to be here. I'm so unhappy.

I had to go to a psychiatrist today. I didn't talk to anyone; I just had to fill out a bunch of paperwork that I've already filled out before. I don't know if I can go through all this again. Sometimes it seems like everything is too much for me to handle. I'm starting to feel like I did before I left. I don't know why I hate it here so much. I feel trapped. I feel like I don't have anything that's worthwhile.

The only good thing in my life right now is Phil, and even that's being threatened. If I don't "behave" like I should, then my mom is threatening to cut me off from him. I wouldn't be able to handle that. I just need

162

you to pray for me and be there for me. I don't have anyone here who understands.

I love you and hope to hear from you really soon,

Samantha

April 20, 2005

Don't you hate it when you can't think of the right word
Jamming concepts into corners still not heard.
Can't remember how I got here but I'm here.
Do you know what I mean?
I can't stand hearing you listen to me.

April 21, 2005

I can't relax at all. I've gotten really lazy lately, and I don't know what to do to push myself.

April 28, 2005

Reading: *The Chronicles of Narnia – The Magician's Nephew* by C.S. Lewis

I had read these in 6th grade—which seems like forever ago. I appreciate them more now. And they're funny! His writing is so clean and neat.

The ending, though, is bittersweet because Digory's mother lives, but only because of the magic apple Digory gave her. It's bittersweet because people can't go to other worlds and bring back magic fruit to save their dying mothers. It was just a twinge of bitter—but maybe that's how he wants you to feel.

March 30, 2005

What I like about Sis. Church: 1, Knows the gospel. 2,

Fun. Takes me places like the mall! 3, wasn't mad at me when I couldn't finish the bags. New page.

I worry about things. I worry about college. If Sarah Brown and I will both go to SVU. I wonder if I'll ever get to see Brandon Orr again.

There's this weight I carry around. Sort of like guilt. It's not guilt, but it overwhelms and haunts me in very much the same way. It drives me crazy.

I wonder if I'll ever get to see Tim and Alex again. If it will ever be the same. But most of all, I worry about Sam.

I can never stay up too late because late at night you start thinking; you start to feel lonely, and that's when I remember. It makes me sad.

The art of rumination is truly an exhausting, cyclical, fruitless endeavor.

In high school Kraig's impersonation of me was to cock his head to the side and, with both hands, frantically stroke a lock of hair. That's me.

I used to count myself to sleep back then. Or recite the alphabet backward under my breath. Sometimes I practiced addition. Most nights I would pick the worst part of my day and dwell on it. I'd play it over and over again, wistfully thinking, "I'd should've said this, and then they would've said that, and then I could've done this."

I picked my face, I'd pull out my hair, I'd copy the alphabet in a hundred different ways in the margins of my class notes. I hated talking on the phone because I always thought I was being judged on what I said, like they were going to rewind and replay some recording of the conversation. Which is stupid because words on paper is about as permanent as it gets, and that's what I was comfortable with.

But my anxiety was never rational. It was always excessive, and in any given situation it was usually the result of Black and White thinking. My worries were always tied to the thought that I would fail horribly if I wasn't a raging success, and the pressure usually ended me in tears.

I'm hard on myself. It has to be perfect the first time or else I'm not doing it at all. I still worry about stupid stuff like that.

I overthink things, and I can never really stop thinking. I pick apart every thought and action and reaction. Sometimes I wish so desperately I could just unplug my brain.

May 7, 2005

I hate guys. They scare me a lot.

Driving scares me a lot. I'm horrible at it, and it depresses me.

I feel crunched for time. How am I going to be a good wife? Like, secretly deep inside everything I do is so I can become a good wife. Guys are awful. I'm horrified of every one of them.

Sex scares me. A lot.

I'm terrified of everything! It's just too much! I'm exploding and my heart is overwhelmed and it sucks. I'm pathetic and I'm scared. I'm scared because I don't want to be an adult! I have one more blasted year and then I'm going to college! I'm going to college and I'll never live with Mom and Dad again. I'll be on my own, and that's scary. I can't bear it.

Life is really terrifying. How long ago was it when I was a kid? Just a child? How old am I? 16? It's sad to me. Is that right? I mean, should I be sad? I'm so scared. I'm scared of the future. I'm scared to have kids, to be married, to buy a home, to live with a man. How will I ever do it? I'm TERRIFIED. I'm really, really worried.

You know when we were taking the English AP Exam, I realized I was the only one sitting the way I was. I felt like a kid. I was kind of slouching with my folded leg up against the edge of the table.

Like, I'm NOT MEANT to be an ADULT. I'm too hyper, too crazy, too wild, too anything. I don't know what! I'm different. Not just because I'm LDS. I'm different. And I'm yearning to do something with it. I'm worried.

Ugh. I'm sick of boys. Sick. I can't see how people do it. I don't see how people survive life.

May 14, 2005

Mom and Dad and I went kayaking in the sound, and it was fun. Dad and I made a sandcastle. My eyes are sore from the sun and from the crying I did earlier today. I was so overwhelmed by and worried about everything. I was very anxious about the future. I mean, really I have no idea what the future holds, no matter how much I imagine it. . . It's just very nerve racking because I have to make big decisions, and that bites.

I'm so tired of my friends here. I mean, I appreciate them, but they don't understand.

Like last night, Russell invited me to a movie—of course it was rated R—and asked why I wouldn't go. I told him it was 'cause I don't watch rated R movies and then he's like, "You've never seen an R rated movie before? You gotta be kidding. It's 'cause your parents won't let you right?"

I hate that the most. I feel like they're discrediting me, like I can't choose for myself. Like that kind of standard is so obnoxious it has to be enforced by my parents. I mean, I know they don't know and I can't blame them, but it's so frustrating. It's just frustrating.

May 16, 2005

Kate Weathers and I went to Duffin's house today. We hung out and talked and listened to music until Nathan showed up with some other girl I didn't care for. She had a see through white mini skirt that was untied and unbuttoned. I mean she had a bikini on or whatever but it was stupid.

Scott showed up and it was then the real party started. Krage showed up later and we ordered pizza and Duffin brought down a painting she painted for Scott and then more video games like forever. Nathan finally said we should go swim in the pool and I was bummed out 'cause I didn't bring a suit because I was on my period. It was Scott who made me feel better. He was like, well at least come outside. I'm glad he didn't make me feel left out.

So I went outside and Scott and Nathan threw pool balls at me. I got soaked anyway once they got me with the water gun. Then Kraig made me mad over something stupid so I went inside. He thought he had hurt my feelings but I just went inside to grab his clothes. I threw them in the pool. It was the best come-back ever, until Kraig pushed me in. I changed into Duffin's PJ bottoms and a t-shirt. We put my clothes in the dryer. Scott and I played Super Smash Brothers again and he beat me again. We're about to leave and my clothes aren't dry so I steal a pair of Duffin's jeans. Nathan and I jump in Scott's car and before we leave Scott notices that his hair sucks 'cause it dried funny and mine did too, so we dash out of the car, sneak through the gate, dip our heads in the water and split. We drop off Nathan and Scott is still wearing my sunglasses. We go to his house and I see his room and we play this weird block killing game with these pill looking people. Then we pick up Russell, and Scott makes fun of his haircut. We go to Hurricane Lanes in Destin, where they try to teach me pool. We see they have air hockey but it's too expensive. So we drive all the way back to Fort Walton to play air hockey in the mall arcade where it's cheaper. We play. I lose. Scott and Russ play 4 games and I swear I've never seen Scott so grave and serious in his life. Best game I've ever seen, best 50 cents ever spent. When I got home I realized left my wet clothes in Scott's car. I called and he said he'd wash them. I thanked him and thought that was a really nice thing to do. But I left my panties in there and I'm so embarrassed!

Ugh!!!! I'm so embarrassed!

May 21, 2005

Mike Boyd and I went to the beach today. It was a lot of fun. Then we went to Tropical Smoothie. Mike is such a tease. I like hanging out with him a lot.

Then I called Scott and we went Putt-Putt golfing.

Tuesday, May 24, 2005 5:32 PM
From: sam

Hey girlie. I'm back home. I was picked up on the 5th of May. I just now got out of Juvi today. I'm starting all over. This time I actually want to do better. I've decided that I want better for myself.

While I was locked up, I went to church twice a week, and I want to get my life straight. I'm gonna go the righteous path. God has a plan for me and I know it. I know that since I want it this time, it will happen. I love you!

Love always, Sammy

p.s. I graduated and walked with my class and everything!

May 29, 2005

I'm sitting in the airport waiting for my flight. It's been a long day and it's only 4:10 p.m. I just barely finished all of the books in *Chronicles of Narnia*.

It's all been very hectic and crazy. I haven't spoken to Sarah in a while. My life is falling fast into place. I try not to worry too much, otherwise I become very overwhelmed.

I'm excited. I can't explain this joy and anxiety that comes over me from knowing I am alive, that I'm still young and good people are out there, and how the future is so uncertain and unwritten, and how I want to keep in touch with the hundred-something people I know.

I've gotta keep going. That's all that matters really. Keep going.

June 5, 2005

I'm at a really crazy point in my life now, like twilight— I'm in the middle, you know? It's frightening. I'm trying not to think I'm going to be an adult and that I'll be leaving Mom and Dad. I'm trying not to be too sad I'm growing up. I'm trying not to be too sad about turning 17. I'm talking one step at a time, you know?

10 miles of notebook paper for a life yet to be written.
I'm still not fascinated, I'm still not smitten.
Not to say life isn't life or that it's not exciting,
but I believe that those pages are worth writing.

May 19, 2003

There's something about free notebook paper that is generous and open, almost inviting. It's like infinite space for a pen to just flow, as words do in music. Of course sometimes you make mistakes, but even so, there's room for them. It just feels good.

It keeps your mind off of things. It's like I'm transforming all my worries though the pencil onto the sheet of paper.

Sometimes I'll just write for pages about absolutely nothing. I just write whatever comes to mind.

I love this pen. I used to write notes to Sami with this pen.

June 10, 2005

When I die, I want to feel really close to God.

I want to be the same person I feel like I've always been. I want the people I care about to know I care and I remember. And then I want them to grow closer to their God too.

This is what I want in life.

I wonder how I will see myself five years from now. Maybe I'll grin and sigh and think, "Oh, Kristen." There are things

I have written that I had forgotten, important things, things that are especially important because I wrote them as a kid, I wrote them when I was growing, and those things we should never forget.

It's frightening. Life. It's very frightening.

You know as a kid you think every adult's life is the same. I mean, basically. You're a kid, you get married, and have kids until they have kids. There's a pattern, so that's what we expect out of life. I watch my friends. Robert Brown, Sarah Brown, Alex Kyger, Tim Threet, Joanne Peverill, Sam. I stand in awe of the life they're living and are choosing to live. It's amazing.

I'm excited too, but a bit uneasy. It's the uncertainty, but it's also the POSSIBILITIES I am blessed with. There is just so much ripe opportunity. Do I have any idea what my Father in Heaven has in store for me? Can I even fathom the question?

Leaving Mom and Dad makes me sad. Real sad. I hope that even when I leave, I'll come home and things will be the same.

I have been so blessed. Truly blessed. I think of all the people I've met in my life. They've all been blessings. I have so much to be grateful for. I really do.

I get discouraged when I see individuals who are really good at something. I feel like there is so much pressure on what we DO in life, and then there's the pressure of being good at it, and being better than everyone else. Competition always gets me. But that's a form of pride, isn't it? It's part ambition and drive. I shouldn't feel down about it.

I like Fender and Twinkie. I love how human they are.

I feel like I'm just beginning to understand. I'm 16. I'll soon be 17. But I hate that we have to count.

June 15, 2005

Today was my first day working at Target! When I'm not working, I've been babysitting.

I just realized how lonely I've been lately. I feel like I need to talk to Sarah and have a sleepover or something. I need a best friend. If I stop and think about it, I'll get depressed.

Like, the other day I was staring at something and then all the sudden I thought of Tim. And then I felt really, really sad. I mean, just as sad as I felt when I first moved here.

I remembered I'm still here and not there with my best friends.

June 25, 2005

I worked from 2:00-5:00 and had part of my lunch break with Kraig today. He works there too. He told me Scott said hi, AND that Scott's college brother Matt said I was hot and that Scott should go out with me. Kraig laughed because I was blushing so badly. It was a total surprise. . . agh. To think MATT SMILEY thinks I'M hot. I smile every time I think about it.

June 26, 2005

My days seem so LONG.

June 27, 2005

Black and White

I see your face just like you
see the colors in a book
All the words are black and white
and all of them are spelling hurt

You let direction lead you
and now the needle says you're lost
Time keeps spinning on a clock
where all the hands keep falling off

I will guide you
I'm right beside you
I'll take your tendency to hide
I'll put it in the pocket you sent

The walls stare blankly at you
so look away I'm right beside you
and can't you see what life could be
At any given moment
when I felt my light was broken
I realized I closed my eyes so please

I stole. . . "I see your face just like you see the colors in a book, where all the words are black and white and all of them are spelling hurt" from Patrick. That's his line. I feel guilty, but it's such a good song!

The last night on the cruise, I remember Patrick whining to all us kids to hurry it up with the pictures 'cause he wanted to go buy a beer and the bar was closing. . . lol. He gave everyone a hug before he left and then he turned to me and said, "Kristen, you get the last hug 'cause you're such a cute girl," and then he gave me a kiss on the forehead.

!

Isn't that sweet? That just made me feel really good. Even

better than finding out Scott's college brother Matt thought I was hot.

I'm listening to Third Eye Blind right now. I'd listen to them for the rest of my life and be happy.

Fender lay in my lap while I shared some Ritz Chips with her. Tim said, "I effing love that Dancing Ritz Chip," as one of his email subjects once.

June 28, 2005

I just finished looking through my Sumter High Yearbook, and I've grown so much since then. I can't really pin point exactly what—I know I've grown spiritually, and I've gotten prettier. . . lol.

This upcoming year is going to be fun. I can't wait!

No never mind. I can definitely wait. Summer is good.

chapter five

the things i like about life

"Every line is about who I don't wanna write about anymore."
- Brand New

I am **sixteen** thinking it over **enjoying the view** I have from my shoulder **a ride in a car** air rushing past the music is loud and we're going **fast random meeting** what are the chances **chance meant to be** and LDS dances a Tropical Smoothie with someone I **like** someone who is fun someone like Mike **layin' some soul** wherever I can a **passion** a **love** my **guitar** in hand a well written letter from my best friend **sticking** the postage on letters I send the **feeling I get** when

I choose the right when I read a good book when it's **quiet**
at night

an infinite moment

In a field of tall **grass** the sky is so blue time doesn't pass
inside jokes that never get old and ones that just happen
and can't be told spending time with **Mom and Dad** my dog
Fender and when **Twinkie** is glad an invitation a whole day
planned **the beach** where it's **warm** and there's lots of sand
growing up a good **cry** learning and stuff **saying goodbye**
knowing I am loved knowing I am liked

these are the things I like about life.

June 30, 2005

I had lunch with Krage today at Target. We laughed a lot.

July 1, 2005

I worked cashier today. It's really interesting to see the
things people buy.

Maggie broke up with Kraig. He's. . . well, upset I guess. I
couldn't really picture them together anyway.

I feel like my body has changed. . . like all of the sudden
I'm beautiful. Isn't that horrible? I've been spending hours in
front of the mirror. I've been buying make up. I need to stop!

July 2, 2005

Kraig was feeling down all day and yesterday, so today
I'm like, "Hey Kraig, let's go do something!" so we planned to
see a movie. We ate at Johnny Rockets and it was cool. Kraig

talked for 30 minutes straight, which was the longest time I've ever paid attention to someone ever—and some stranger from the table next to ours came up to Kraig and told him next time he goes on a date he should let the other do some talking . . . that was funny.

Kraig was offended, mostly because we weren't on a date. But the coolest part was when Kraig took us to Scott's house. I really wanted to see Scott. I was so excited when I saw him, I got a running start and knocked him over on the front lawn and bit his neck. He was like, "Did you just bite me? You should do that more often." I got to play them that new song "Black and White." It was perfect. Like, I was impressed with myself. And if I'm not, I'm disappointed, so I did awesome.

I came home at 1:00, and that's the latest I've ever come home. Dad was really mad at me. Yikes, I know.

Monday, July 4, 2005 1:27 AM
From: tim

I saw War of the Worlds last night too! It was freaky. I kept wondering how it would be to feel like that. Like, the sheer panic. All the actors did a good job of making me frightened. Okay, ummm, I'm going to figure out how to get down to Fort Walton Beach to see you. Because I'm serious, there is no way I'm leaving the country for eleven months without saying goodbye in person. I'll get a hotel room and wake up early every morning and you can show me all around your town. Don't worry. I'll get it together. Because. . . yeah, okay. Not much to say, just wanted to write back immediately. My heart lifts whenever I see an email from you because I KNOW it will make me smile. I love reading your words. Anyway, enough crapping around. Love you muchly,

Six Flags Over Timothy

July 4, 2005

I had a dream last night where I'm trying to tell Scott about my church on a t-shirt, but I can't write it out and I'm ashamed to show him.

So I wrote this down.

Convictions

I am standing here trying to convince myself 'cause
You don't think my convictions are enough
I don't have half the courage it takes to confess
So as I'm speaking I'm creating a bigger mess

I'm writing it down, I'm tearing it up
I'm starting all over, I'm drawing the line
I'm telling you now, I'm not moving

The only thing in between
me and your questions is why
Sometimes faith is a reason to try

At least I can say that I know who I am
Say that I know I still can
I'm not letting go I'm not giving up

Standing here trying, convincing 'cause
my convictions just aren't enough to tell you why

July 5, 2005

I lent Kraig my *Perks of Being a Wallflower* book. I hope he reads it.

Did I tell you? I'm going back to Sumter! I didn't think I was, but I am! ugh! I'm so excited. I'm going right after Girls Camp. I won't get to see Scott until the first day of school. I told Kraig this, and he said, "Don't tell Scott that, he'll be really upset," and that made me feel good.

I'm so happy right now. I feel like everything is in place. Everything is good. LIFE is good. Tonight I watched Kraig read the directions on his frozen dinner box to himself out loud and it cracked me up!

I dunno. I feel like a new person. That anxious yearning feeling is gone. I feel like I reached it. I'm here.

Summer is always weird for me. It's what I wait for all year. It's the pinnacle of the seasons. There is this apprehensive feeling creeping up. It's just this curiosity of what next year holds. It's knowing things will change. Lots already has. I just hope Kraig and Scott are the ones who stay with me next year, and I have a feeling they will. I wish Tim and Alex could meet Scott and Kraig.

July 6, 2005

I can't believe I'm really going back to Sumter. I've never come back to the same place before.

I'm trying to bury my anxiousness to see Alex and Sarah and Rob and Tim again. It's weird 'cause I have 10,000 times that anxiousness at the thought of them coming down here. If I could fuse old and new best friends. . . I mean, that's been my dream forever.

Fender fell asleep in my lap tonight. She was so cute.

September 1, 2002

I miss Ted. I wish I lived in a city with Ted, Sami, Kayla, Sarah, Meagan, Tim, and Alex.

July 10, 2005

Mom and I are in Tallahassee right now being evacuated from hurricane Dennis, cooped up in this little el cheapo hotel. I'm exhausted. It's been so stressful.

I just can't wait to go home and have things back to normal again. This isn't fun at all.

July 11, 2005

Dad finally gave us the okay, and Mom and I are going home tomorrow. What a relief that Dennis wasn't nearly as bad as Ivan. Things have definitely calmed down around here. Most of my time has been spent reading.

I have to drive tomorrow, so I have to get some rest. The drive up here was neat 'cause I got to talk with Mom. Twinkie has been cranky this entire time, and I want to strangle her! We watched E!'s *Top 10 Bachelors*, none of whom were cute or attractive in any way, then we watched women's body building, which makes you feel a little better about being unfit. Then we watched a men's ice skating championship, which is like the exact opposite. Instead of watching bulky women, we're watching graceful men. I'm sorry I wasted a page on TV.

Anyhoo, so I'm glad I calmed down. I'm not freaking out. My life is still intact, though it scared me. Made me realize how much I love Florida and value my friends. Also made me realize how much I value things, my goodness!

Hotels are awful. Dreadful places. Ugh.

July 12, 2005

That's what art is, isn't it? Bits of odds and ends strung together that make no sense at all, but they make sense to you. They are the impressions, the words, the smiles that have made an impact on your life. You know and understand their meaning. And if they search deep enough, others can find pieces of their life in the work also.

And when you step back and look at it all, it's undoubtedly a representation of you. It is truth beneath the fiction we write. It is raw, real and bold, and it is beautiful.

It is also misunderstood and misinterpreted.

It's all about relating to people, finding a piece of who you are in their expression, discovering that touch of common ground. Something you can relate to, that gives you comfort. So really, the art we paint and the media we choose tell us the people we are, and are to become.

July 14, 2005

Kraig called me this morning. He's in Alabama. Turns out HE's the one I won't see til school starts 'cause I talked to Scott today, and he's taking me on what he called an ULTIMATE DATE! He was like, "There's no time for a first date, no time for a second date, or a third. This is an ultimate date. It'll be Scott Smiley and Kristen Jex's ultimate date. Kristen Jex will be so tired she'll be falling asleep at work."

March 9, 2003

I've been thinking a lot about Alex lately. I wish we were moving to the same place so I could date him when I turn 16. I really do. He's such a sweet guy. Such a GOOD guy. Darn it.

July 16, 2005

OH MY GOODNESS!

Today was one of the best days ever! Scott picked me up at 7:00 a.m., and we went to Waffle House and played video games and watched *Madagascar* in the theatre, which was awesome.

I met his family too, all of them, and his brother Matt loves me, and I like his sister, and his mother is so sweet. I played a song for Matt and his girlfriend, AJ, and all his college friends. It was cool. And on the way home, Nathan was on the phone with Scott, and Scott said, "No, I'm not asking her that," all embarrassed. Anyway I think, THINK Scott likes me and I hope, HOPE he still does when school starts 'cause I totally like him and I wish we could try going out. Today was incredible. Oh yeah! And Mrs. Smiley invited me over for dinner!

Okay, and I totally thought I'd be tired and cranky at work today, but I wasn't. I was really focused tonight. I was so twitterpated over Scott, I was actually hyper. And I am right now as well, so I got some snacks and I'm going to read.

April 19, 2003

Today I went over to Alex's house to work on this Drama thing. I went over there @ noon, and I stayed til 5:00. lol. We had the funnest time. We played with foil. He makes me feel like a kid. He makes me feel like a best friend. And it feels good. We did all these stupid things.

He sculpted the letters of my name out of aluminum foil and made it into a name plate. lol One of the greatest moments was when we covered his cat Tinkerbell in foil and she looked like a giant baked potato. Putting foil through the paper shredder was fun too. When I'm with him it's like it makes me feel like life's not going by too fast, but that I'm alive. And I'm making the most of it. After 2 years of swooning, I feel like Alex and I have finally come to a point.

July 17, 2005

I've been thinking about Sumter, how weird it will be to see them all again and my friends. . . I can't believe Ted and I used to be best friends. Everything is spiraling out of my control. I feel like, I dunno. It's crazy.

And I've SO been stressing out on which college to go to. Not FSU, not SVU, not BYU, not U of U. BYU-Idaho. That's what I decided on tonight. I don't know what it'll be tomorrow.

One week. One more week and I'll get to see Sarah again. This year has been the LONGEST year of my life. Hands down.

Friday, July 22, 2005 5:41 AM
From: tim
Subject: EXCIIIITTTED!

Hey, don't know if you'll get this before I see you, but here's hoping you do. I'm going to Sumter tomorrow. I'll be with Matt Eldridge pretty much the whole time, but ANYTIME you need to talk to me so that we can get together, I'll have my cell phone. I will give up sleep to spend time with you! I want to play songs and talk and. . . flipping eat your face. Gah! It'll be hard to say goodbye A-FLIPPING-GAIN. Anyway, can't way-yait.

Timothy

July 23, 2005

I made a 2 on the AP English exam. Urquhart let me down! I was so upset over it.

July 26, 2005

I'm here! I'm finally here in South Carolina, safe and sound. I feel at peace.

I'm here. I'm here.

It's awesome to be reunited with Sarah. I don't even want to think about saying goodbye again, but I do have friends in Florida.

July 27, 2005

I saw Matt Eldridge and Tim today! Tim has an eyebrow piercing, which totally fits his personality. Tim is a nice friend, but it drives me half-crazy that he is such a genius. He made a 5 on the English AP. He's amazing at guitar now, and I LOVE his songs.

Sometimes I feel I can't handle it. It's weird. I feel like the treasure I left here has turned to dust. It's all very strange and hard to make sense of. It's just. I dunno.

When I look at Tim, I sort of marvel at how handsome he is, but I really do like Scott. I really, really do.

I feel so sad because I know the Alex, Tim, and Kristen in a wheat field, I know that moment has passed and never will be again.

It's so sad. Saying goodbye. I think I finally understand and accept the bitter beauty of saying goodbye. People change and there is nothing I can do about it. I feel like crying. It's all crumbling down so fast.

Tomorrow I will see Ted. I'm surprised to find how much I miss Scott and Krage. I just want to hug Scott for a long time, and I feel like I'll be utterly heartbroken if he doesn't feel the same way.

July 28, 2005

Tonight was the worst night of my life.

While Kristel, Kayla, and I were getting ready in Kayla's room to see the boys, I made some comment about how Kayla could have Ted, but Tim was mine. And then Kristel was like, "except. . . Tim's gay. You know that right?" I mean, Kristel is a gossip anyway; she doesn't know what she's talking about. And then when we met up with the group, they just talked about crazy parties and drugs and tattoos and piercings and having sex, and a bunch of them were smoking and I don't even know what to feel.

I want to go home. I want to go home and break a window, scream, and cry. I feel betrayed somehow. Hanging out with everybody was awful. It was totally disgusting. I hate thinking about it. I can't even relate to them anymore. I'm so upset.

I can't process gray area very well.

You can't do that with people, though. People are complex. You can't rationalize them down into one simple, clean category. But I did. Because like every component in my life, things had to be one way or the other. No in-between.

As children, our simple minds can only identify "good guys" and "bad guys." It's how we play games, and know who to trust. Kind of like how we idolize our parents as heroes, until we're older and realize they're just people too. As we grow up, we learn how to process the variables.

I just couldn't. My crazy, unstable life already had infinite variables. I needed to know who I could love, who loved me, who could continue to define who I was.

I worshipped my friends. They were perfect. If there was anything they wanted, I would find a way to get it for them. Conversely, if they disappointed me, it broke my heart. I would feel a deep betrayal and sorrow. They were dead to me.

In psychology this is called Idealization and Devaluation. One moment your BPD friend loves the life out of you, another moment she hates your guts. The hate is just a defense. I was scared of losing my friends.

I held myself to uniquely strict standards, and I hated my friends when they made choices I couldn't relate to. As they grew up, I felt increasingly abandoned.

I demanded swift and mighty justice upon those who crossed me. I wanted contrition. (That's not a BPD thing, it's a Kristen thing.) And I wanted the assurance they still loved me.

My emotional swings exacerbated this black and white thinking. I felt only in extremes, and all my feelings were a result of my circumstances. Someone said I had a great outfit: best day ever. Hours later, bad grade on a quiz: I should just give up on life. Next period, cute guy flirts with me: I'm the most awesome being in the entire universe.

Side note: People think this is what it means to be Bipolar, but it's not. Mood variation in Borderlines is instantaneous, a result of a constantly changing environment, not broken chemicals in your brain that cause the longer-lasting high and low mood cycles of Bipolar.

Back then I was always feeling something. It was exhausting. I felt either alarmingly happy and excited or angry and despondent. There was no zen, no mere existence. My mind was always thinking, my interactions always changing, my emotions inextricably tied to situations I perceived were out of my control.

July 31, 2005

It's so nice right now. I'm sitting on the couch with Sarah.

I hate that my other friends are going in a direction I can't follow. My appreciation and love for Sarah is inexpressible. That she would stay true to the faith, set the example for me, that in fact she has proved to be the only one still standing by me. I am so grateful that God had us meet four years ago.

I have grown so close to Mom and Dad over this past year. I trust them completely, as I hope they do me. I want to be totally and completely honest with them.

August 1, 2005

On the plane going home to FWB. I guess I'll be 17 in 25 days.

I just finished reading Tim's "Tim'cerpts" and Sarah's novel. They are both talented writers. I'm jealous of their incredible talent, for spilling it all out on paper. Tim is a genius, I tell you. I'm just glad to be running in the same circles as these young, talented, fresh-minded people. I am a little sad that I didn't get to see Alex Kyger, but I know we will meet again.

Tim is not gay. Kristel is just mean and Kayla is just deceived by her.

Tim is how he's always been.

The sky is so beautiful. On the way up here I thought, I don't care what pleasure awaits me when I die, as long as I get to sink into a cloud before I have to do anything else.

Tim is amazing. He really is.

I am so happy right now. I'm happy. I feel like happiness is just this delicious chocolate my soul delights in consuming. Ugh! I don't know why I'm so HAPPY!

She sat there fascinated by how the road shimmered like the sea. How could solid concrete possibly resemble the sparkling sea?

I wish I could spill paint on the carpet floor, but paint doesn't dry like you want it to. They don't sell plush paint. If they do, it's not what you want to think it is. I wish changing color were easier than it is. It seems like if you wanted to change something's color, the effort wouldn't be worth it.

I feel jealous Tim and Sarah can write freely and beautifully and I cannot. I can only hope my songs will touch people like their writing does.

July 30, 2005

Dear Kristen,

There are so many things I want to write to you, so many things I imagine you reading. I don't exactly know how to express it all, but I communicate best through writing, so I'll give a letter a shot. I know I will write many songs and poems and emails, etc., to you and about you in the future, but this will have to do for the time being.

Leaving you cuts a big hole inside of me. In my stomach, in my heart. I just love you in a way unique to all others.

Perhaps I love you more than you know. We may never be a couple, but that love will remain.

I want you to know what tremendous respect I have for you—your musical and writing ability, your passion for life, your desire to live a pure life, your outlook. I know I've said it before, but your voice is so unique and so awe-inspiring. I look up to you.

Kristen, your laugh delights me. That may sound random, but I'm just trying to communicate these emotions to you, so bear with me. I love the fact that you crack up at Matt's sound effects, my stupid jokes, a movie line. You have such an intense reaction—the tears, the doubling over.

I adore talking to you because we are always running parallel. Same page, same wavelength, whatever you want to call it—it's fantastic.

You make me nervous. It is very strange because you also make me feel very relaxed. I know I can be honest around you and speak my mind, whatever, whatever, but I also put so much value in your opinions that I'm a little afraid of looking stupid. Maybe that's love, I don't know. Don't take this paragraph the wrong way. It's just one more jumbled up feeling.

I imagine you savoring this letter. I see you smiling as you read it, feeling fuzzy. You save it, in my head, and pull it out occasionally while I'm gone on nights like this when you feel separate—you don't have to do that if you don't like. I just imagine it. Just know that it makes me very happy to think of you reading what I pour down on paper, touching the words that I wrote. It connects me to you. And believe me, I'll be taking everything you've ever given me to Argentina—I know I'll need it. The ugly purple t-shirt, your music on my iPod, your letters and guitar picks and stickers and picture. I cherish it all.

I love your handwriting. I love how you think. I love you incredibly—INCREDIBLY—and always will.

A big bear hug,

Timothy Threet

Tuesday, August 2, 2005 11:22 AM
To: tim

Oh, Tim. Your writing is so genius. It made me smile and laugh out loud and think it over. It made me sad and it made me imagine things. I love it. I love your songs. I love "Red Geo Metro." It hit the spot, if you know what I mean.

I respect you and admire you so much. I'm so glad you're still here as my friend and didn't wind up making stupid decisions.

Thank you so much for everything. I do savor each page of your writing. It made me laugh when you're like, "I can imagine you reading this. . ." because I was doing exactly what you thought I would. And I laughed exactly how you described me laughing, which just brought in more peals of laughter.

I really am glad we became friends. I hope I never stop being with you, talking to you, sitting with you. I loved everything! I love you, Tim. ~Kristen

Tuesday, August 2, 2005 2:17 PM

From : tim
Subject: Incredibly happy

Ahhh! You are so awesome.

I think I need a grin-ectomy.

Tim

August 2, 2005

The second worst night of my life.

I called Kraig and he was on his way to the beach. He was like, "Do you wanna come? I'll pick you up." and so I did and we pulled over to this random, secluded patch of beach hidden by all this foliage. As soon as we meet up with the crew, Kraig starts whining about how he chipped in for the beer, and it was almost all gone.

Kraig helped buy beer that was in SCOTT's cooler. Everyone else besides Maggie was smoking and/or drinking. Yeah. On the way back Scott was honest with me and told me he had 2 ½ beers. Great. I could smell it.

I was about to flipping break someone's face. Nightmare. I'm so mad. So, right after I come from Sumter where everyone let me down, I come back and my ONLY TWO FRIENDS, Scott and Kraig, are buying/drinking alcohol? WHAT? Not

Scott and Kraig, please. Not Scott. Not Alex. Not Ted. Not Ray. Not Kraig. Not Kayla. Not Carter. Not Tim. Not Sam. Please. No, not Sam. Don't let me down, don't let me down.

August 3, 2005

The damage is done. You've left a hole I can see though. DON'T AVOID YOUR FAULT. It very much was.

Sweet dreams and other things, what will they mean tomorrow? You're chicken and you know it, but I can't stay this way with you. I know you understand, but I can't stand to see you do nothing about it. Don't even try to let me down. Don't butter your way through the holes you've left in my heart. Thanks for the ride. Thanks for while it lasted.

August 5, 2005

Scott seemed guilty about that night, and I'm happy about it. Kraig formally apologized. Good ol' Krage. And I told Dad about the whole night. So I felt much better. I've been extremely happy lately.

Danny cut my finger on the first day of school by hitting me with a binder, so I've had a band-aid on me. Today during 7th period No Class in the library, I was hanging out with a couple of the cool underclassmen, and one guy sat on the couch, and it broke. It totally made my day.

I thought, "This year is gunna be a great year," PLUS I gave Urquhart a copy of my new CD! He said he was really excited to listen to it this weekend, so I can't wait!

Music Theory is so interesting. I really like that class. That's the rundown. Goodnight!

August 6, 2005

I guess I turn 17 in 20 days.

It's weird. 16 seemed to go by fast even though last year took forever. I can't believe I'll be seventeen!

This year is going to be the best ever! I got to work hard lines today at Target, and Kraig had a section right next to mine, which was awesome 'cause he could help out when I needed him. AND we had lunch together and we talked about Tuesday, and I feel much better about the whole thing.

I feel like I just keep on being blessed in so many ways! I totally feel closer to Mom and Dad, I feel happy all the time, and I am so grateful for everything!

August 8, 2005

I'm totally bored out of my mind.

One of the sisters in our ward has terminal cancer and has only 2 months to live. They say they are paying like, $18 per hour to keep her alive. It made me think—is every hour of my life worth $18? I dunno. I'm being really idle right now, and I feel bad about it.

Idle Page.

8 Letters.

I'm really frustrated with Scott, and now the old puzzle comes out again. Why guys like me but never make a move. I'm so impatient! I hate when everything is luke-warm. I want to know black or white.

Saturday, January 10, 2004 7:45 PM
To: alex

I read your email. I noticed you put 'love' at the end. Why? Like, I don't understand. What is it supposed to mean, if it means anything at all. Look, remember that time I asked you if you even liked me, and you said something like sorta? Well, honestly, I didn't understand that either.

I think you either like someone or you don't. It's black and white. You can't just say "sorta" and leave it to the interpretation of how much sorta, or maybe I didn't want to tell the truth sorta, or ANYTHING sorta.

Whenever I make the move, I ALWAYS muck things up.

August 9, 2005

Mr. Urquhart said I sound like The Sundays and some Canadian chick.

I hope tomorrow I'm a better person. I dunno. In general. Oh! And April is in my Music Theory class. Everyone got their Senior Pictures back. I'm jealous! I don't know when I'm taking mine. Goodnight.

August 10, 2005

Today was the best school day ever!

So everybody totally loved my Snoopy shirt.

Danny totally flirted with me in Improv today.

Then in 3rd, which is my No Class, I went to the library. I always want to sit on the couch, and I saw Stephen sitting there. I didn't know him and I got a lot of wrong impressions about him. Turns out he's like the COOLEST KID EVER! I thought he was 19 still in 12th grade, smoked (both of these wrong impressions came from Kraig, by the way), and at one point I thought he was gay. (I'm still having trouble dealing with that kind of stuff. . . I mean you never know who is and I don't want to be rude. . .)

Anyway, It's so exciting to find a new cool kid! Man, and it's only the very beginning of the year. I have NO IDEA what this year holds and I can't wait.

I totally cannot wait!

August 11, 2005

I will be brief 'cause I only have like 5 hours to sleep. I failed my driving test today.*

* Note: Always stop at a Yield sign.

August 13, 2005

Saturday. I hung out with Kraig at the mall, and then we went back to his house and watched Eddie Izzard. I helped him with Physics homework. Then I went to work and I loved it 'cause I finished early and helped Kraig with his zone. Then Stephen showed up, and it was way fun with him there. They invited me to hang out afterwards, but it was too late (10:00) and Dad said no. I almost got Kraig to come with me to church tomorrow, but his mom wouldn't let him.

August 15, 2005

I just avoided a really awkward existence. At least I hope I did. Stephen asked me out. I told him no.

What? I didn't want to date him. Half because I really don't like him, and half because I still like Scott. Everything is so complicated! I kinda know Scott is already over me, and it's sad, but I still like him a lot. I don't know what my problem is. I want to stay in control, and somehow whenever a guy makes the move, I lose it.

It may be because of my bad experience that I am unable to take a chance. I don't know. I think I'm just like this because I don't have Tim. I do—but he's not here and I never feel like he loves me when I'm with him. This is half because Alex Kyger was a disaster too, you know? He kind of scarred me for life.

May 19, 2003

Alex is dead. Sad to say. Yeah. I know I said Alex would be different, that I'd make something happen. He's going out with Emily Chance, he told me. She held up her wrist in the hallway, and was like, "Your watch is so cool!" today.

I'm cool though. Alex is still my best bud. He calls me his "Partner in Crime." I'm a little frustrated, and appalled by the fact he'd be attracted to HER, but yeah whatever. You know what though? I don't think she really likes Alex. You would think that was GOOD news. But it's not. Because Alex is in love with Emily. And that's way worse than Emily being crazy for Alex. It's kind of annoying because I haven't talked to Alex, well, I don't get to talk with Alex as much because he's around her. He's constantly looking at her and it drives me CRAZY!

I love Alex. It's so pathetic. Will somebody shoot me or something?

Today at lunch he made Emily this heart made out of foil and she totally brushed it off. I hate that. I mean, the little things are what count! Alex was totally crushed. I dunno. Plus foil is OUR thing. I know Alex still thinks I'm cool. . . It's just, this week man, he spends all his attention on Emily. . . It's like there's no partner in crime time. Yeah. But whatever.

I wish I could hurry up and get to BYU-Idaho so I can date all the guys there. I don't know. I feel like May is a long, long, long, long, LONG flipping time from now. I hope then I'm still friends with Alex Kyger, Tim, Scott, Kraig, Nathan, and Stephen.

Anyway, this year is going to be crazy. It hasn't even begun yet. I can feel it and it hasn't even begun. One day it's just going to erupt and all mayhem will break loose.

I can feel it coming on already.

August 16, 2005

I PASSED MY DRIVING TEST! That means I have my license! It's so awesome driving by myself. I absolutely love it. So, so, so much.

August 17, 2005

My new amp came today! I'm so HAPPY. It is amazing. I'm happy. There is nothing amiss in my life now. Nothing. I'm reading *Harry Potter 6* now and I'm loving it, 'cept I'm really tired. I should've taken a nap. Anyway, driving is fun.

August 18, 2005

After work before driving home, I just sat in my car and looked up at the moon. Immediately I felt a desire to pray, so I did.

I'm so happy in my life right now and I know that it is all because of Heavenly Father's love for me. I don't know. . . I had a flashback to Sumter Sophomore year when I was 15 and scared of everything. I remember thinking how 17 would be, and it's a lot better than I imagined.

I am repeatedly blown away at how much I take for granted in church. In AP Lit. the other day, talking on religion, some girl honestly asked, "I want to know why we're here," and my soul ached! To think that she doesn't know she's a daughter of God, that she doesn't know she has a Heavenly Father who loves her, that there is greater joy here on earth! It made me very, very sad. No, it really did. We know so much more on a much grander scale! I don't know, I mean, that's everything to me. And I know the big picture. I have no fear. I have no doubt. I am sound. I am faithful. I feel love and peace and I'm so happy!

I just have a feeling this year is going to be crazy fun. Things are going to change.

I believe in Jesus Christ. I know God is real. I KNOW for sure he lives. I know.

Friday, August 19, 2005 2:20 AM
From: tim
Subject: Hey.

I wrote you awhile ago about school, but I haven't heard back from you. I leave for Argentina in a day and a half.

I think, well. . . I. . . rrgh

Um, lately there has sort of been this explosion in my inbox; I've been receiving tons of mail about this, so it sort of prompted my telling you. I'm gay.

I'll write it again because I know you'll want to reread that to make sure you weren't mistaken: I'm gay.

All of the sudden, Matthew Eldridge found out from somebody else and Jessie Ali found out from somebody else and. . . I just, I wanted to sort of neutralize the situation—I mean, not that it's this big, dire thing, I just really, really did not want you to hear it from someone else. I really, really hope you have not heard this from someone else already.

I guess I need to explain, right? I mean, there isn't that much to explain, but. . . talking is. . . good? Nothing I've ever said to you has been a lie, nothing I've ever written—I've just sort of had to skirt the truth. And the reason I say that is because I really don't want the honesty of our relationship to suffer or die or something. I don't want you to think of me as untrustworthy or even as a liar. I never meant to be.

When I said I love you unlike anyone else, I meant it. When I say I'm in love with you, I mean it. I just could never tell you I was gay, too.

How could I have told you after your September 9th, 2004 email? I quote:

"I hate to say this. . . but if there were to be a gay version of you. . . I think it'd be a lot like Ryan. . . I dunno. You slightly look alike. . . have the same personality. . . sorta. Like, he has this planner that's super organized like yours. And he takes French like you, and uses French phrases and terms all over the place like you. . . so he's a lot like you, except he's gay. Or maybe it's just that you act gay. . . lol! I'm so kidding! Don't be gay! You'd break my heart and I'd be very, very sorry."

I'd break your heart?! I mean, my God, what can I say? I'm not trying to!

I hope you write back and want to talk about this because, even as freaking hard as that will be for me, it would be better than never hearing from you again.

So. . . hmmm. . .

I think it would insulting for me to tack some "How's the weather?" comment on the end of this, so I guess I should just go. Lemme know . . . something, anything. A'ight, talk to you later.

Timothy

Friday, August 19, 2005 5:16 PM
To: tim

Why was I the last to know? I'm supposed to be Tim's best friend, for goodness sake. I had to hear it from Kristel?!

Is this what you meant by, "we may never be a couple"? Tim. I don't know what to say. I have to go to work, I honestly do, but I'll write later, I promise. ~Kristen

August 19, 2005

Today was awesome.

October 25, 2001

I'm in total shock. I'm still in a daze. I hide from reality, I really do. When I don't want something to be the way it is, I pretend it's not. I'm really lost. I am.

Overall, it was way awesome. The Foo Fighters were playing on the radio this morning! Scott put his arm around me today. ♥ And Stephen spilled coke on my arm/shirt today on purpose, which was wild, but not really fun. Um. . .

I was really upset before work, but work made it better and my paycheck was $200-something.

Tim wrote me an email telling me he is gay. Yeah. Tim is gay. I cried. I was so upset. I'm let down. I don't know. I am very disappointed though. It makes me desperate. Anyway, I don't want to think or write about it right now or I'll go crazy. I wish I could talk to Kraig or Scott, but I know they went to the game and I don't want to dampen their spirits.

Anyway, I'm all right now. The issue hasn't been confronted, but at least for now by some miracle it is suppressed.

Sunday, August 21, 2005 12:54 AM
To: tim

I cried and cried, Tim. I really did. The thing that hurts the most is that I still love you. I mean, like in the boyfriend sense. I was so embarrassed at Kayla's house. Here I was trying to set up a double date and stuff with you and gushing to Kayla about how much I liked you, and you're gay.

I don't understand! I thought you liked me too! Didn't you like me last summer?! You said you adored me and loved me, and I don't know what that effing means anymore. Did you ever love me? Ever? Maybe? I mean in the girlfriend way? Didn't you ever want to be with me and hold me and gosh, I don't know, whatever! Didn't you?

It was just such a letdown, you know? You did break my heart. It hurts to know you don't feel the same way, and never will I guess.

Tim, you're the only guy who tells me I'm beautiful and brilliant, the only one who adores me. And I know it's not fair, but now that I know you're gay I feel like that stuff is insincere. Like it was just fluff. And I took you seriously. I feel cheated. I feel really stupid.

Nevertheless Tim, you are my best friend. You are still that. And even though it hurt, I value your friendship so, so, so much. I really don't care that you are gay. I just. . . didn't know. But now I do, and it's okay. I do appreciate you telling me like you did.

I know you are leaving very soon and you will no doubt be very busy, but write when you can

~Kristen

August 20, 2005

Well really August 21st 3:28 a.m.

Wrote Sarah and Tim today. I'm still upset about Tim being gay. I'm also upset about Scott. Or really just guys in general.

Anyway, I hate lies.

You Lost and It Died

I need to sit down. I need to reflect on your words,
divide them in thirds
and collect them. Put them in frames and believe
all three.

How you can't stand the honesty heat.
Truth is a game that no one can beat so you lied.
You lost and it died;
the person that I used to know

When I think of it all,
I could take down the walls
Oh the walls of my mind hang on every word
that you hung

I need to sit up. I need to breathe in.
My sympathy's thin
but it's mending as we keep on pretending.
This world isn't perfect, but I don't deserve this

And when I think of it all
I could take down the walls.
The walls of my mind hang on every word
They remember

So you lied. You lost and it died.
The person that I used to know.

Monday, August 22, 2005 2:48 PM
From: tim

I'm so glad you're still my best friend. I was not shocked by your response. I guess if I had told everybody a whole lot sooner, then things would be better. But that's high school, I guess. That's adolescence. Figuring yourself out is hard to do in public. That sounds like some strange lyric to a song, but for me it was so internal that I never told anyone. So I know it seems like I misled you for years, etc. etc., but that wasn't my intention. I'm just sorry all my attention. . . got your hopes up? I don't know, that sounds extremely insensitive. I honestly don't know how to apologize, y'know? Because I feel like I never really did anything wrong, but then I feel like I did. Whatever, I'm insane and trying to figure all this out in another flipping country.

We'll work through it.

The only thing that kept me from totally crying in all the airports was listening to your CD over and over and knowing I was the first to get one. I cherish you so much. Can't wait to hear from you again.

Big bear hugs and an Englishly accented Adios!

Timothy

August 22, 2005

FIRST DAY OF COLLEGE! I switched 6th period AP Lit. to 3rd so I'd have time to get to class. It all worked out well. I am so grateful Heavenly Father is watching over me; I've been so blessed lately.

Sis. Church is back! I am so happy—I'm going over there to talk and say hey. And I want to give her my CD! I totally like my Seminary Class. Sis. Cowart is such a good teacher!

Tuesday, August 23, 2005 10:52 PM
To: alex

Alex I don't know whether you heard or not, you probably have, but Tim is gay.

Tim is gay.

I don't understand. It's really hard for me to deal with. Tim knows it's hard for me, but he doesn't. Does that make sense?

Alex, this is crazy. Going back to Sumter was awful for me. Really, really awful. I hated to see all my closest friends doing stupid stuff like smoking and drinking, and I dunno, they've just grown so far from the things I associate myself with. . . so near to the things I don't. . .

Why are we all falling apart?

Sometimes I think I might've been better off not knowing the truth. Not knowing any of it.

I really wanted to see you this summer, Alex. I really, really, really wanted to. I have to admit though, I was reluctant to call you the day before I left 'cause I didn't want to see that you had changed too. Everyone had changed since I left. Everyone. I didn't think Tim had changed either

. . . but. . .

I mean, it's not like he isn't the same person, it's just. . . I dunno!

I feel betrayed a little and mislead, fooled. All of the sudden I feel like I can't talk to Tim anymore. I don't trust him.

I've long since gotten over the fact that things will never be the way they were again. But it's bittersweet, you know? Things move on, you learn. Friends are not the number one thing in life.

I want to know what you think. . . anything. Anything at all

~kristen

August 23, 2005

Pretty unproductive day. Did some Algebra this morning, but not enough. And I have college tomorrow, which I didn't prepare for. Went to the mall and fawned over jeans and a shirt I really want for my birthday.

Wednesday, August 24, 2005
From: alex
Subject: The sad truth

Hey Kristen, how are you? Yeah. . . reading your email made me remember how I never manage to let myself down. Maybe I've learned to lower my standards for a lot of people? I don't know, it's just really frustrating.

I really wish I could have seen you this summer. . . bring back old times . . . just hang out, not smoke or any of that, just end up in some aban- doned field. It makes me sad to think about how people tend to not get "better", if you will, as time goes by. People seem to only sink into some "reality" that they think they live in. It's so stupid. Look at Scott. . . he's fat. . . He drinks a lot. . . He seems to miss out on a lot of little things, you know?

Being in Bahrain, the "Party Island" is cool, I guess. But last night, I climbed onto the roof and watched the sun set over the ocean. It was so beautiful. And tonight while most of the people in my class go get stoned, I'll watch the sun disappear over the sea and then hang out with Tucker and tell him how one day I want to walk the entire world. See everything, just walking from place to place. . . I want to do it so bad, roam the earth. Maybe it's stupid, maybe it is better to get drunk and pass the J around. . . nah, I'd rather walk the world or tell you about how I strap myself into bed every night.

Yea, Tim's changed. More than I thought. He's still Tim. . . but. . . What I'm saying is, yeah people change. . . but true friends never change deep down inside. No matter what happens, they're still true to themselves, some things about them may be better, some things may be worse, but they still smile, they don't change what makes them who they are. And you love them because they are who you knew when they first became your friend. Those things that made you want to be their friend in the first place are still true. I'm not saying Tim has changed like that, I'm just . . . I'm saying what I've learned. I like to think that Chocolate Milk and acting crazy are still the things that keep me going. I don't know. . . and I'm happy we still email each other even though so much has changed around both of us, we're still us, and we're still friends. . .

I wish I could have seen you this summer. . . I'm so sorry, I wasn't trying to distance myself from people. . . you wanna know the truth? I hate "bye." I'm no good. I just like being around people and then, no big deal . . . leaving. Maybe that's bad, but I've always been like that; I mean, "bye"s are nice, but. . . I just don't like the process. I was glad to hear from you. Have a great day Kristen, I'll talk to you later. . . peace out girl scout!

Love, Alex.

August 25, 2005

I'm sorry I didn't get a chance to write yesterday. I was so tired and it was crazy, so I brought this to school and I'm now in 1st period No Class in the library writing you. Dad woke me up yesterday morning and told me Grandpa had died. He left this morning. I'm really not upset about it. It's sad, but I know he's in a better place. I mean, I haven't really even gotten a moment's silence to think about it until now.

School was insane 'cause I had college classes yesterday. My Earth Science teacher is old and he stutters. He really wears my patience. I try to remember Hemingway's *A Clean, Well-Lighted Place*, though, and try to hold it in, 'cause I feel sorry for him you know?

I got home and was able to talk to Alex Kyger. I mean he wrote me an email. He somehow has the great capacity to be in the exact same point as I am in my life, or at least, even though he isn't, he can know and understand it very well. He is a really good friend. I am thankful for him.

On a less serious note, my birthday is tomorrow! Duffin has been really nice in planning me a birthday dinner at T.G.I. Friday's Saturday at 5:00 or something. Well, today is the last day I'll be 16 so I'm making it good. I've gotta do some homework now so. . . bye!

August 25, 2005

Today was a bad/good day. I was feeling up because Scott was being especially affectionate today but then down x10,000,000,000 because I saw him with another girl. He kissed her bye. On the lips. I heard her yelling to her friend they weren't going out though. But I was way depressed and went to the mall and got those jeans I wanted. I was down.

I called tonight and told him I wanted to go out with him. It was terrifying but I feel much better. I'm glad I asked him when I did, 'cause he can drop the other girl. I don't know.

He likes me. I know he does. He's just afraid 'cause if we broke up blah, blah, blah, you know. I asked him, "Can you ever imagine yourself hating me?" and he said, "I can't imagine myself not liking you." So I'm holding on to that.

We'll see. I hate thinking about the conversation though. I was so nervous!

May 13, 2003

Man. What a day. What a flipping day. It's crazy. I played the song! Alex didn't say a WHOLE lot (maybe he was tired or in shock), but it was still an awesome feeling.

His brother Scott seemed to be more happy and appreciative of me than Alex. . . but I think Alex didn't know what to say. Scott and Alex are really close. They've got a good family.

Man. I'm all. . . my head is all racy thinking about Alex. Earlier today was pretty bad 'cause Alex mentioned he traded my watch with Emily Chance's (yeah, her.) and that he "made out" with her. It's always hard to tell when Alex is joking or not though. Then I was reading in the Cock's Quill Senior "Last Wills and Testaments" section and Emily's Senior sister wrote: "To Alex, I leave you Emily. You're the only one I trust with her." So that struck me down pretty fast. But I just had to suck it up and try to be cool about it.

I almost wasn't gunna play it, but I'm glad now I did. It just expressed everything I wanted to in his yearbook. . . so yeah. Here. I'll write the lyrics for you.

Starbucks

If only I could buy, the world's best egg roll
Take you to snowman heaven
Or race a toilet bowl

Then maybe you'll see and maybe we'll be
and maybe one day I'll say

Maybe I'll sing real loud and off key
Maybe you'll laugh one more time for me
And maybe one day I'll
tell coffee bean boy
My doughnut has dawned

I'll stay away from the flagpole
I'll let you bust my lip
I'll carry you through puddles
On every PDA trip

Stupid things remind me of
How wonderful you are
I wouldn't change it for nothing
'Cause nothing's wrong so far

You could be my Norman
I'd write a different end
I can't care what happens
As long as you'll still be my friend

Maybe I'll sing real loud and off key
Maybe you'll laugh one more time for me
And maybe one day I'll
Tell coffee bean boy
My doughnut has dawned.

I'm sure none of this makes sense to you. . . The whole song is just filled with a bunch of inside jokes Alex and I have made over the past two years.

What a day. I can't stop thinking about Alex. I wanna know what he's thinking right now. I don't think I'll be able to sleep tonight.

August 26, 2005

Seventeen.

Sixteen is over.

Another page,

To put in my folder.

Kraig was so thoughtful and gave me flowers and *Nine Stories* by J.D. Salinger. He was such a sweetheart about it! Scott worries me 'cause. . . I dunno. I'm excited for Saturday.

August 28, 2005

Me and Mom are in base housing 'cause there's ANOTHER hurricane. Katrina. I just found out about it, well today really, since we have no TV. Ugh. It's a pain. I hate having to live in a hotel.

August 30, 2005

Gave Stephen a copy of *The Book of Mormon*. Got Duffin's number. Voted for homecoming court. Did absolutely nothing else today. Totally unproductive and it feels awful.

Thursday, September 1, 2005 5:12 PM
From: tim

Do I listen to Kristen Jex because I'm homesick, or am I homesick because I listen to Kristen Jex? I don't know, but I know that while it hurts my heart a little, it also fills me with hope, courage, happiness, joy. This isn't hollow and it isn't fake. As an artist, I thought this would be something you'd like to hear.

Your music matters. A hell of a lot. My Top 25 Most Played list on my iPod is Further Lacking, Miss Maybe One Day, Losing Sam, Lucky Save, etc. I can listen to these songs again and again, and they always affect me. The writing is gritty, clever, and really speaks to me. Your music matters.

I didn't bring my guitar, but so much for that. I'm already looking to buy one here. And also, there are some guys here who want me in their band because I can sing really well. And in English, which they like. Believe me, you'll be the first to know if anything comes of it. I'll teach them your stuff.

Jeez, I wish I had a Kristen Jex Fakebook. Seriously, I wish you'd taught me your stuff, haha. It's hard to pick out. I had a dream that I saw Aerosmith performing Further Lacking and I started arguing that they didn't write it, like, rallying thousands of people that my friend Kristen wrote it.

Alright, I gotta get off here. I hope I'm not too far from making sense. Your music matters.

Chau, chica!
Tim con queso

September 1, 2005

Today at school was awful. I was crying when I woke up from my nap after school. I mean, if it's pain that won't even go away after a nap, it's bad. But work helped me forget and I got two compliment cards. Two in one night!

I finally was able to access my email, and the emails I got from Tim totally erased any negative feelings I had left toward him. I love Tim. He is my friend, and I care a lot about him. He has been really supportive and understanding, when he could've easily been offended or angry. Anyway, I feel better. Thank you, God, for the little things you send in life.

chapter six

letters to tim

*"But now I've got to crawl, to get anywhere at all.
I'm not as strong as I thought."*
- Bright Eyes

When I started school in Florida, I wrote Nathan a letter about how lonely I was. "The fact that I'm actually writing you this letter that I will never send just shows how desperate I am."

During my Depression, I started writing handwritten letters to Tim. I never sent those either.

My most meaningful and honest entries during my Depression aren't in my journal at all. They're in Tim's letters.

I couldn't write them in my journal.

February 3, 2004
Would you think I'm crazy? Or disgusting? If I. . .
Maybe you'd understand. Maybe I'm being plain stupid.
Am I wrong to think this will make me happy? Should I
trust you? Would you think I was sad, could you under-
stand? I trust no one. . . It's lonely that way. So lonely.

What I was ashamed of feeling was wanting to cut myself. I couldn't bring myself to write the words. I didn't want to admit I felt that way.

So in my need to express all the ugly feelings I had during Depression, I wanted my audience to singularly be Tim. I wanted it to be Tim because he made me feel loved more than any person ever had, because I trusted him, because I knew even years later he wouldn't be embarrassed or ashamed of how I saw the world in those letters and drawings.

I didn't want to see myself. I didn't want to reflect back on an image of me being broken. (It's why I broke the largest mirror in our house when my depression was at its worst.)

Like the letter to Nathan, I think merely addressing my letters to Tim allowed me to believe we were communicating, though I didn't need him to say anything at all. I just needed him to be there for me. And he was.

September 2, 2005
Dear Tim,

One day is three weeks. It's not as cool as it was the past few days, but it is cooler.

I wish life wasn't a competition. I feel like I'm losing the race, badly. Class starts in five minutes. This is the fifth day. And the juice has already worn out. I'm sick of boys, guys, men, whatever you call them. I hate girls also. Am I just jealous of the world? I always feel like the person in front of me has it better; has it better because I have it worse. I am grateful, don't get me wrong, but it's this panicky feeling, the sensation you get when you have one last chance to make it or break it, but you're totally unprepared.

Friday, September 2, 2005 12:09 AM
To: tim
Subject: K is ME!

Ahhh! Thank you for being the most amazing person in the world! My day totally sucked and it's all better. Really.

My music is yours for the keeping. You have the unfailing ability to make me smile. I listened to "Red Geo Metro" during Katrina and it TOTALLY made me pine away for a jam session with you. We need to jam like bad traffic! Ahh SNAP! "Red Geo Metro" is my favorite song by the way. I was giving these girls a ride to school from Seminary one morning and was like, "Listen, when he gets to the part where he says, 'hangin' out with A and K, the 'K' is me, okay? The 'K' is me! I'm IN THE SONG! It's ME!"

We're constantly reminded of how horrible Katrina is here. There are donation boxes everywhere, and I already have kids in two class periods from New Orleans who transferred. Our high school expects some 100 kids or so from Louisiana and Mississippi. It's crazy.

Love you, love you, thank you for being the best friend ever ~Kristen

Friday, September 2, 2005 6:42 PM
From: tim

Target sounds like so much fun. If I were there, I would pretend to shop for hours and hours just to make eye contact with you over and over holding different objects. Get you in trouble for laughing. Haha. I seriously would. I'd see you totally friggin' across the store and hold up a bag of diapers and you'd crack up, for real!

Hasta luego!

Yolanda porridge nostrils

September 3, 2005

Let's be honest.

Where to start?

I'm almost in tears! I've been so tired. So stressed. So hopeless, so useless. Don't get me wrong, I've been reading my scriptures, I've even done a ton of scripture mastery. But it's not enough. Can I just list out my problems? Please?

School: Homework, OWC classes, time driving there, gas.*

* Because of Katrina, buying and saving gas was stressful as prices and availability were unpredictable.

Katrina: The devastation overwhelms me. I haven't even seen the worst because we have no TV. Just glimpses and I haven't got the time to think about it: donations, latest news, world problems.

Friends: Scott, Kraig, mostly. But everyone else too. I'm just working through a lot of problems. High school stuff. Confidence issues.

My room: I hate it. It's a mess. I just want to rip down all my posters and collages.

ME: I'm losing control! I'm crying. I keep forgetting the Savior loves me, watches over me.

Maybe I thought I could. . . that this year would be easy?

Trust me. There are temptations in the most unsuspecting places. And it's scary. I'm just scared right now.

I'm getting physically sick, I'm getting exhausted. I have a lot—

There is a lot of pressure.

I've been so concentrated on vain things. How I look, my clothes, spending money, getting a BOYFRIEND. It sounds stupid, but it's not. Not when you're the only one. In fact NOTHING is easy. My standards are getting so much harder to keep!

I have nothing to look forward to each day. What kind of life is that?

God help me. I'm so scared.

I don't know what I'm doing! All the sudden the world is up to me, and I'm not a kid and I have to do adult things and it's scary and I hate it sometimes and there's so much pressure, and I can't wait until I go to BYU-Idaho 'cause I'm finished with this daily struggle.

The world is so far from where I want to be. I can't believe how far I have veered. And it's 'cause I'm all ALONE.

This is so scary! This is awful. Every day is so dark. It hurts. I can't even explain. It's awful. It's so extreme! I'm ashamed to say I've been so focused on the worldly things. Like it's a race I have to win. Man! I can't believe how far off my focus has been.

If they only KNEW. If they only knew how hard I'm trying.

I need to be better. I need to do more searching, and sincere prayer.

There needs to be time for that.

I've become kind of like a robot. I haven't felt much. Just empty.

There needs to be change. Yes. Change.

One of the saddest things about teenage Kristen is how strongly she believed that if only she were more righteous she would be happy.

It breaks my heart.

I couldn't feel God's love, and it made me very frustrated. I was doing everything I could. I was being grateful. I was reading God's word. I was following his commandments. I should've felt God's grace and love. But I didn't, so that probably meant I wasn't trying hard enough. I was wrong. Turns out, my brain was broken.

Our brain is the most important part of who we are. You can think about the spirit and soul all you want but you can't do that without a brain. You can't move, think, or feel emotion without your brain.

This is where I tell you what it means to be depressed,

and what it means to be Depressed.

A normal, emotionally healthy mind can relax; it can feel at peace, zen. It doesn't really feel like an emotion at all—you just are. Day to day, you feel positive or negative, but these feelings undulate over a steady baseline of normal.

Sometimes traumatic things happen. Foreclosure, divorce, death, etc. You are sad. Day to day you feel positive or negative, but instead of going back and forth to normal, you have a steady baseline of sad. Doesn't matter what you do, or how momentarily happy you feel, at the end of the day, you're still sad. This happens to everyone. This is what it means to be depressed.

Through whatever therapeutic means, over time we overcome these tragedies and our baselines rise back up to normal.

If we don't, over a lengthy period our bodies can literally adjust the chemicals in our brain to think that this sad baseline is now our normal baseline. Which means no matter what we do, or how much therapeutic process we undertake, our brains are unable to allow us to feel happy. Modern medicine is the only way to correct these chemicals. This is what it means to be Depressed.

But if you take medication without undergoing some sort of therapy to help you overcome what made you sink so low to begin with, you will never find peace. Numbness maybe. Feeling sort of blank. But that's not the same as peace.

When I said I wanted to be happy in these entries, I was not talking about my general satisfaction in life, because no one is happy all the time. I meant I was actively sad.

My unrelenting devotion to God did not make me happy, because I was Depressed. I needed medication and therapy.

However in the end, I do believe God made my recovery possible.

September 6, 2005

I cut my hair really short today. I don't really care. This year is entirely impulse.

I also bought a pair of jeans today at the mall because they were on sale. I tried doing my homework today but I was distracted. I did some laundry though. I hope this week will be great. I'm going to get some rest now.

September 11, 2005

I haven't been writing like I should. I've been really depressed lately, but I keep trying, and right now I'm hopeful that I'm starting to get better. I love my parents is all I can say.

September 13, 2005

Fender is on my bed. She's usually never in my room. I like her lying beside me. It comforts me. After work today, I drove to the beach where it was really dark and totally silent 'cept for the waves and the moonlight. I kept telling myself I was going to be all right.

It's been non-stop. Tomorrow is when I stop working at Target, when I take my Algebra test, and when this will all be over. I hope. I've tried my best at this. Pray I'll be fixed!

I want to be HAPPY again!

Gosh. Life has been pretty bleak lately.

September 14, 2005

April's birthday is tomorrow. I bought *Chronicles of Narnia* for her. Today was Duffin's birthday! I made her a birthday card that said,

HAPPY

DUFFING

BIRTHDAY

She and Kate Weathers both thought it was funny. I can't quit Target for another two weeks. :(Bleh. But it's okay. I'm gaining more control of my life. . . I mean, I'm not breaking down into tears every day.

Oh! Guess what? I really AM getting "better" because today I wrote the first lyric since my last CD. I haven't played any yet, but hey, it won't be long. Here goes—

the tension that is tangible

the tangles

that you tie

you can't pretend

the truth will bend

just because

you

LIE.

Not exactly happy but I like it.

September 15, 2005

Today was good. Spending time with April was so great. We watched *Pride and Prejudice* (which is close to eight hours long), and it's so AMAZING. I have to make pancakes tomorrow for Seminary so I gotta go.

September 17, 2005

"F" on the research paper

58 (oh I'm sorry) 48 on my math test.

I finished all my math homework this time, but I don't understand Music Theory, and I'm not feeling any better. I'm going to make a list about all the things I'm grateful for.

Mom and Dad, Fender and Twinkie, The Scriptures, The Gospel, prayer. . .

I give up.

Tim's emails are the only things that bring me joy.

I hate my music.

I hate listening to punk 'cause it's too peppy.

I hate my hair. I hate school. I hate everyone AT school.

I hate life. Pretty much.

There's just not enough, I dunno, to make me happy.

I'm not ME.

What am I living for? I can't stand it. One year is too long. How can I live day-by-day wishing, knowing I have to live like this ONE WHOLE YEAR.

I hate Scott. You can die.

Duffin has a cute boyfriend, so I don't like her right now.

I hope I can hang out with April soon. 'Cause that was the last time I ever felt a glimpse of happiness.

Look at me. Yuck.

Yuck.

September 18, 2005

Talked to Dad.

How silly I have been. I mean, gosh, nothing matters in this world—nothing except love and service and living the gospel and Heavenly Father's plan. What's important in life is having a strong mind.

I'm so glad Dad is my dad. I'm so glad he knows the gospel. I must move on—press forward, keep perfecting myself.

I was telling Sis. Church how bad I couldn't wait to go to BYU-Idaho and she said, "Kristen, Life is a waiting game." All it is, is endurance and patience and I need that.

Buck up. That's what Sis. Church always says.

Buck up.

September 19, 2005

I feel overwhelmed by tremendous responsibility. Progress, Kristen! Don't be lazy!

September 21, 2005

I   am
seven and teen
        a   picture
            a   frame
                a   portrait of me
                    going   insane
The darkest color
I've   ever   seen.
I am three and four then
a   little   behind
    while I battle my mind
                    I   am   Kristen
I am sad and that's sad
    a   fact

that   I   hate
   I can't bear to wait
that's definitely trad
   GIC (k)
tick,   tick
   as I'm wasting my life
      sinking,
hey.
   I   am
    Kristen.

I have an Earth Science test tomorrow. I have to rewrite the paper I spent 6 hours on when I could've been studying for this test. I have three pages of Music Theory homework. I have umpteen number of odd circle graphs and general equations to write for Algebra. I have however many pages to write for stand-up on "toys." I hate stand-up. I have to look up a—something or whatever—for AP English because *Hills Like White Elephants* is the worst story in the world. Ernest Hemingway can fall asleep reading *The Old Man and the Sea* for all I care.

I'm always late to Seminary; I lost my keys this morning; Erik, our president, isn't here and has been gone for three weeks; but I can't complain much because I love Seminary. I still have Personal Progress to do but I haven't been, because I feel like I have no time. (Yeah, I "feel" like I have no time.) But that's horrible because it should be a top priority—but since everything is a top priority in Kristen's life right now—the priorities attached to failing grades are taken care of first, so I'll fail anyway in addition to failing spiritually and just failing in life.

I now hate Scott, Kraig, AND Nathan. I'm just sorry I don't have the opportunity to hang out with Taylor, who was nice enough to lend me *Spies Like Us* because he thought I'd really like it, but OF COURSE I haven't had time to watch it, and oh yeah our TV is broken; and April, because April is cool and has always been cool, and I feel happy with her and in her home. Because I really wish we could just watch *The Importance of Being Earnest* one weekend because I've decided today while watching it in Drama (which is the only reason I stayed, trust me), and because she was nice enough to let me watch *Pride and Prejudice* on HER birthday, and because it reminds me of Sarah.

But today in Drama, this girl kept complaining about how different it was from the play (and I didn't read the play because I don't care and because I went and ate at Osaka's (a cool Japanese restaurant I want to take Mom to—just me and her one day) for April's birthday, the day we were reading it in Drama), and it drove me insane, and I hate how someone says something negative about something you absolutely adore and ruins it for you.

Anyway, I tried playing guitar and it's dumb because I can't think straight and I'm not inspired at all, and I feel like no one will listen but Tim—and I can only talk to Tim through email. Tim is my very best friend and I love him with all of my heart, as much as a person can love another.

But so anyway, this whole thing has been seriously ridiculous, and I just feel I keep messing up and falling into the same hole OVER and OVER again and it's exhausting! I'm so flipping worried about failing. I'm not studying, which is pathetic. I know!

I just don't know when this will ever stop. When will I finally see the end? Learn the lesson?

I'm really rather upset with Target, even more let down because quitting Target did not solve all my problems, I knew it wouldn't, but I had hoped.

I hate formal settings. I hate business, I hate grades, evaluations, formal anything. Sometimes I drive myself so mad with the pressure to be polite that I come off very rude. I'm really insecure in this sense.

So I had to work last Saturday and this Saturday too, which is Homecoming. I'm not that upset about not being able to go to Homecoming, but still at least there could've been a chance? But most likely I wouldn't have gone because no one asked and I feel very separate from the people who are going.

But!

The TRUE reason why I'm unhappy is because I'm lazy and spend 3 hours writing stuff like this instead of doing my homework. So while I was writing you, I just failed a test, failed to have an experience, failed life, wasted TIME.

But what can you do? You're so overwhelmed you need time off because you don't have the endurance to keep going because in the back of your mind you've already lost the race. Yeah, there's hope. But hope has lost you so many races—hope is nothing.

Belief in yourself is something, but what's that with no chances of winning? So you're already behind—next goal is not to finish last. So reevaluate, get it together. While you're working so hard the chances are getting slimmer, and finally you feel you need a drink of water or you'll die, and while you're drinking water—you've lost, and that's just as bad as dying.

The depressing thing is, I feel like the older I get the less I APPRECIATE life. I don't appreciate the fun things, but I don't appreciate hard work either.

Isn't this awful?

And honestly.

Truthfully.

I'm just going around and around in circles and what I'm saying is pointless. And what I'm saying is pointless because I'm not pushing myself.

And more importantly, it's because I'm not living the gospel as fully as I could. I can honestly say that.

I am strong. I am tolerant. But I want to be myself again. I am stronger than strong. I'm stronger than tolerant. I'm loving and cheerful and happy and I am filled with light.

That's who I am.

I am Kristen.

September 23, 2005

ugh.

The only thing left to do is my restoration paper and my personal essay on *The Importance of Being Earnest*. It's almost 6:20 and I have a couple hours left. I really, really wanted to watch *Spies Like Us* with Dad tonight, but he had a dinner for work in Niceville. I didn't go to the football game tonight, so I could finish my homework. I didn't go to the pep-rally either, and Kraig refused to talk to me because of this, even though I knew he was kidding. . . kind of. It hurt my feelings, especially since we've had such scarce contact with each other—I mean, I think today was the first time this week we exchanged any conversation and the only thing he said to me was, "Did you go to the pep rally?" and then very rudely ignored me when I said I didn't. This is like murder! I hate high school! When I said hey to Scott he said, "I haven't seen you all day," and walked off.

???????

I hate feeling sour toward them, but I do. I mean, any normal* person would. I'm just trying to be. . . no, not really. I just don't have any other friends to fall back on, and there isn't anyone. Any guys at least. Grr. This is so hard to put into words.

* Ha.

I'm trying to be grateful. But I'm so unhappy! I'm left out of everything, I hate school, and I keep trying to convince myself, "Hey—friends don't matter," but it's so much easier, NICER having friends. Being "cool."

I don't know what's wrong with me and my guitar. It feels like the more I need it, the worse I suck.

So I didn't go to the pep-rally, the game, OR homecoming, and I don't think I mentioned I have to take the ACT tomorrow morning then work a EIGHT and a HALF HOUR SHIFT from flipping 1:30—10:00 at Target. I'll be missing Anastasia's baptism.

I have also been called as the YW Laurel President, and Sis. Cowart is giving me a lot of responsibility as Seminary Vice President.

We're reading a story in AP English about abortion. That's what *Hills Like White Elephants* is about. I don't care if the couple wants the baby or not, I DON'T CARE. I just wish we could read *The Chronicles of Narnia* or something and analyze that.

And Duffin has this romance going on now with this boy from Choctaw, and it doesn't make me jealous or anything, but I find it really disappointing 'cause that's just one thing less we have in common, one more difference to wedge our friendship apart.

I can't relate to anybody.

I wish I could spend time with April.

September 24, 2005

Today after talking it over with Dad, and praying, I realized I have no reason to be unhappy.

The fact is—It isn't really all about me.

I have a responsibility, the Lord's work to do, and before I give up, I truly need to do ALL I can. I need to be more obedient. I need to strive. I need to grow. I need to FOCUS. I need to just DO IT. That's all I'm going to concentrate my efforts on.

My mind is full, WAY full of junk I'm still pondering over, and my spirit is mending, but the hour is way late and I want to be alert for Seminary tomorrow.

Saturday, September 24, 2005 3:06 PM
From: tim

Dear Target,

You, coupled with homework, are stealing the love of my life from me. Give Kristen a break, homework and Target! Or I will kill you.

Friends Forever,

Timothy Threet.

September 25, 2005

I have GOT to be the QUEEN of PROCRASTINATION. I didn't do ANY of my homework today. But just because I was procrastinating DOES NOT mean I was idle. I spent all afternoon organizing my stuff; my piles and binders and folders chock full of PAPERS. I'm out!

September 28, 2005

This week is going so SLOW! I haven't gotten anything done. While I was emailing Tim I thought, wow it's really sad it's taken me a whole week to respond, and Dad immediately reprimanded me for spending so much time on the computer. Then I complained to myself about not playing guitar in over 2 weeks, so I picked it up today (and I totally blow), and then Mom complained I was spending all my time playing guitar.

BUT

While I was at OWC, a 20-something from Panama walked into the Library from outside to tell me I had beautiful eyes.

So I win 10,000 points today.

Other than that life is boring.

October 2, 2005

It's been a long up and down day for me. It's exhausting. I only half-finished my homework, but I tried my hardest and best. I'm so physically and emotionally exhausted. I have a slight headache and my back hurts.

I'm so confused. My state of emotions goes up and down and I hate it. But I am determined to do my best at everything, especially in the gospel. And I really want to read *The Book of Mormon* by the end of the year.

I hope I can survive tomorrow.

I miss Sarah.

For Tim:

When we survive this mess

and they'll all talk about your success

I can say

I had the brain

but never had the rhythm to write that way

I think it's nice

You are never the same person twice

And it makes me laugh

How impossible we are to graph

and you'll see

the world won't love you more than me.

Melancholy heightened my attention to the very small, unnoticed on-goings in life. The chip in the paint, the sound of shoes on pavement, the number of red cars in the lot, the hair stuck to her sweater.

It was a way to cope with a life I hated to dwell on. I absolutely hated life, so I focused on everything around me. I narrated other people's lives, conversing with them in my mind, where things happen the way they were supposed to.

When I no longer felt I existed, when I couldn't feel anything at all anymore, I coveted the feelings around me. I imagined what it was like for them. I was a vapor, floating around like a recording angel, writing down life's mundane details.

Interaction is the only tether I have when I'm like that. But even the perfunctory "hello"s and "how are you"s back then sounded far away. Like the sensation you get when you realize someone was actually waving to the person behind you.

A fly on the wall, the sense of omnipotence. I was just a machine. A hollow, broken shard.

October 3, 2005
Dear Tim,

It is 1:55 and my Algebra teacher rolls past me with her rolly bag thing, the sort of luggage an executive tugs at the Dallas Airport, and says, "Doing your homework?" and gives a polite laugh. I still can't believe what an amazing day it is. I wasn't sure whether I wanted to do everything or nothing, but just so I'd have the option I brought everything.

This time it's a girl with a black shirt that reads "Metallica" in red-orange letters. She's got Chuck Taylors on like me, simple black ones, but mine are a lot dirtier. She has thick, dark brown hair that looks frizzy but the tight little curls work for her I think. I hope that book she's reading is really amazing because it would be a shame to read anything boring on a day like this. Then again a day like this just might make practically any nonsense enjoyable to read. Ah, the girl is stifling some laughter. I can tell it's a good book. I'm glad.

It's too bad you couldn't get a room this temperature. The air is too harsh in buildings. The air I'm breathing is soft and open and smells like October.

On second thought, I might have been confusing her facial expression for a look of concentration. She looks mighty occupied now. She rearranged herself Indian style on the lunch table. I caught a quick glance at her eyes, but I don't know what ethnicity she is.

Her forehead rests on her forearm and she's definitely not enjoying her book. Rats. That's so disappointing. I don't enjoy writing about a girl who doesn't enjoy her reading— particularly a girl with an unidentified ethnicity.

She might be grateful if I struck up a conversation, but you never can tell. I'm really not in the mood to try it. Oh! She's lying down now! Definitely a sign of literary distress.

I can see the title. It's called The Last Hours of Ancient Sunlight. *I'm going to the library now to find out if this is an interesting book.*

The library didn't have it. The man there exclaimed, "Happy Monday!" before I left. A clean, handsome guy listens indifferently to a girl who thinks her stories and issues are worth his time.

Two men stand silently when a woman smoking a cig and chugging a Coke yaps out some little complaint with her raspy voice.

Women have the notion that they are the most important thing.

The clean, handsome one says, "All I do is study," and the woman smoking talks like she's 11. She probably has a kid who is 15.

The clean, handsome guy all of the sudden squeals, "Thank you. I've heard enough. I'm good. Okay stop!" and the whole troop then makes their way inside.

I didn't bring a watch today. My phone begs me to mandatory arrangements but otherwise I didn't bring the time.

It would be really nice to go bike riding. Or go to the beach. I feel like I need to eat, but anything seems like it would be bland in this weather if it weren't a picnic egg salad sandwich.

Was this the weather that brought us to the wheat field?

No, It was springtime then.

A different change.

A different year.

It rained a little too. Did I exclaim, "April Showers!"? Maybe it was you who reminded me it was May. The best month of our lives.

October 3, 2005

I'm really behind on my Music Theory. (wince) Fender has been sleeping in my room lately, and it's been a comfort.

I love Tim. He's been such a friend to me.

I'm working hard and trying to stay optimistic while trusting in the Lord. At least I can say I'm happier than yesterday.

October 4, 2005
Dear Tim,

Did I tell you? When Sam stopped at the gas station on our way to the Old Market she told me I could get something since she'd be using her parent's gas card to pay.

When I couldn't decide, she handed me a bag of Peach Rings and said, "Here. Get these. They're Tim's fav', right?" So I got them. I think they tasted better in Ray's van.

October 6, 2005
Dear Tim,

He hit the pointer on the chalkboard, and I almost fell apart. I felt like crying. Don't hit please. Don't be violent. Stop it! Don't slap me! I'll shove it down the old man's throat. It's not fair. Your voice gives me a headache. So does the perfume from the girl next to me. She dyed her hair red. She has pretty eyes but her face is so ugly I wish I could fix it. I want to cry without having to. You'd think I'd run out of tears. I'm tired of it. Crying is tiresome. Oh man. If I could have a confetti cupcake.

October 7, 2005
I feel awful. I feel so, so, so awful. (sigh) It's a really long story.

So this morning it was me, Danny, and Ben at his house playing video games. Then Matt came over, then their extremely gorgeous friend Caleb came over, and he was so good looking. He goes to Choctaw. We threw marshmallows at each other, and that was the only cool part of the night. Then we started watching stand-up and it was so low and dirty and awful. I'm so sorry now that I sat through that.

Matt and Danny and all them are really cool, but they have potty mouths and say bad things sometimes and I hate that. Danny flirts with me so bad though, and I really, really like the attention. But I know that's low. I failed today, okay? I'm ashamed of myself and wish I could press rewind, make these past few days disappear like they never happened.

I'm pathetic. I guess I'm that desperate for approval. I hate myself. I've been lacking some serious self-confidence lately. I'm awful! It stinks. I wish I could change people.

And here's the worst part: Caleb's girlfriend kept calling him on his cell phone and it was really annoying, and they all took turns answering and saying mean things, and I said it'd be horrible if I answered and Matt said, "DO IT," and everyone egged me on, so I did and I said I was Sharlene and I was really mean to her, like her voice was shaking in tears, and I totally did not care and was very rude and mean.

I did that to another DAUGHTER OF GOD. It's awful. I feel so bad. I got a high five and that was it. She could have been me. I'm awful. No girl should ever have to be mean to another. I don't even KNOW her. I'm sorry, Laurie. I'm awful for it. I am so sorry.

I am so ashamed.

August 1, 2002

I was really mean to this one girl today. I feel really bad. I can't believe some of the things I said to her. It's scary. I really wish I hadn't said those things to her. I have to be careful once school starts. I WISH I hadn't said those things! I don't know if Heavenly Father will forgive me. I was yeah. Really bad.

It's so tricky. It's one of those things where it doesn't really start anywhere, but you weren't strong enough to say you weren't going to tolerate whatever you did, and it's terrible.

But what do I do now? It is totally frustrating.

Matt and Danny and all were planning to go to some kid's house party—they "said" they weren't going to drink, but I guess it doesn't make much of a difference.

This stinks. I'm not sure I could say no to them if they ask me to hang out again. I hope they don't. I hope I can just wave to them in the halls and pretend this never happened.

I wish. But everything's complicated like it is with me and Scott and. . . I totally wish I could disappear.

October 8, 2005

I don't feel like writing—I don't really know what to write, but I really like the color orange tonight.

I think it's lame our minds come up with the same old reasons why, when we're sad. . . or upset. It always gives you the same run down of all the same circumstances you can't control. We're looking for blame really. Then you think it's you. And that's why I'm confused. I'm TIRED of feeling over-whelmed. I'm tired of listing all my problems/feelings.

I want to be happy.

I know how to be.

So I have nothing to say.

I'm lazy. That's what.

October 9, 2005

I fasted today. Dad says I have Depression. I decided to try some medicine. I hope I will finally be able to take some control of my life. I do not want to go back to school tomorrow. I'll try to keep perspective though and trust I will survive. I'm sorry there's nothing more I can say to you. I should go to bed now.

October 10, 2005

Dear Tim,

The air is so breezy. It feels thirty times better than sitting in your living room. There are bees humming beside me and I am sitting on the perfect bench. A woman walks up to a huge beige Blazer and chuckles, "I am over this gas guzzling car!" and politely waves goodbye to her friend. If I hadn't arrived here so early I could've had her parking space. Never mind, she was a teacher.

A twenty-something sits beside me for a smoke. I never really minded the smell of smoke. Honest. Anyway, the guy has this really slow drawl, but he was polite enough to assure me I needn't mind him sitting there. I have my back toward him 'cause I'm sitting on the bench sideways—I guess that's not very friendly—but I'm sure he appreciates the privacy. There is not a cloud in the sky, but he tells his friend Doug, "Dad is hiding money from her. He said, 'Christmas is gunna be tight this year' or something. She don't know how much money he got. She doesn't make nothing. The freeloader. I'm serious! She's just as bad as I am. At least I work though. She don't do anything."

I see people filing out the college doors, and it makes me feel like class will start soon. It almost makes me furious, the thought of sitting inside a concrete classroom.

The guy is finished on the phone, apologizes for it and makes polite conversation. I mention the weather, and it's a shame because I really did mean to discuss the weather, and he asks my name and says it should be easy to remember. I laugh a little—someone else will say the same thing—but I turn to write again. Awkward, he phones another friend.

The fake palm trees planted on campus cast great shadows though. They're terrific.

Two voices race down the concrete corridor outside the building. The women talk about stress because that is what women always talk about. There are voices beneath me at the vending machines but they are soft and distorted, just like the underwater vibrations whales make.

A lawn mower goes by, but I can hear the older women say, "It happens (snap) like that and today was the first day I noticed anything because you know. . ."

And of course everyone knows, so she ends with, "I just . . ."

Anyway, yep. You take care.

And I'm by myself. But I can hear now yet another voice, complaining, looking for a sympathetic nod from a frizzy blonde woman wearing a soiled baggy t-shirt and holding a chrome coffee mug. She can barely get her two cents worth in, but whatever she says won't matter anyway.

It's 12:47 p.m. Class starts in three minutes. My friend Bill will think I'm not coming again because I missed class last week. It's 12:48, and it makes me want to punch someone because I have to go inside.

Allegedly, I mean algebraically. And I don't think that function is odd, because it looks quite normal to me.

October 11, 2005

I'm so glad I took some medicine. It has made such a difference. I should've taken it a long time ago. Yesterday, I met this guy from my Earth Science class. He graduated in 2002. . . so he's a little older than me, but surprisingly Dad didn't seem to care. Anyway, he's a really nice guy and we're planning to study Thursday.

October 12, 2005

I couldn't concentrate on my math homework so I'm really in big trouble. I hope I make it to Seminary.

October 16, 2005

I feel a need to write something. I'll try not to think too hard, because anything I'm about to say I don't feel needs to be said. That sounds strange. Anyway, I talked to Sarah on the phone yesterday—and what a strength she is to me. THAT DOES need to be said.

I'm depressed. I fasted last Sunday and felt I should try taking medicine. No results yet, but I'm. . . surviving. It's a burden I wish desperately were lifted from my shoulders. It's been so long now—two and a half months doesn't seem like a long time, but two and half months in endless misery is. I just need to be happy again. So bad. It hurts. It's frustrating. I can understand how the elderly must feel—how frustrating memory loss is—because I can't control my mind to make myself happy. In my mind I know I'm supposed to be happy if I do the right things, but I'm not, so it's frustrating. It's like working without getting paid. That's why some quit.

But I'm hanging in there. I try not to think or let my mind wander. That's tough to do, too. I feel like quitting everything. Ugh. This is exhausting. Don't think too hard about this. Forget the stupid working thing before—I'm just saying—I feel like dropping Algebra and Earth Science at OWC. I feel like dropping all my events for Districts (Drama). I just want to study some gospel and be happy. I can't handle this. I'm so confused. I feel guilty and lazy and insecure. I can't trust myself. I don't know what my conscious is telling me. I'm tired. I can't endure.

I've stopped writing Tim emails.

Dad said the feeling I had Monday was just a spike in mood. That you don't get normal that quickly. It takes time, sometimes weeks for medicine to start working. I was sort of disappointed. I'm confused even more.

It's funny. How ironic it is I chose to name this journal, "The Things I Like About Life."

October 17, 2005
Dear Tim,

*I like it when I surprise myself and actually DO my homework. On the drive here I thought for sure I'd go home and discuss dropping the class with Dad. I'd use my whole "insanity" plea. Not to say I'm not. Honestly I am and sometimes I feel like telling every single person I know just so they'd stop judging me, 'cause they don't know anything. They're just a bunch of high school kids. They're going to wake up one day and realize none if it matters. It's stupid really. I feel like a twenty-three-year old in nursery sometimes, if you know what I mean. If there's no one around to relate to, it's lonely. You even feel left out. But the sad part is knowing better. I read the creepy story Mr. McLaughlin told us to read (*The Yellow Wallpaper*, *if you're wondering), and it creeped me out.*

I wish a lot of things never happened.

Countless flyways and pocket lint and paper clips and dust bunnies hop everywhere. I have no control of my life. I am happy somewhere. Maybe underneath the nail polish on my left pinky. I like that one. Otherwise I can't bring myself to say anything. I just have to sit there and take it. They say, "How many have you been to? That's what I thought," and smirk like they're kidding, but you know they really think they're better than you because they've been to a couple of football games.

But sometimes I don't feel like I'm better than that. I admit. But it's okay 'cause I'm alive, I got up in the

*morning when it was still dark, I smile and try to be nice.
I try. At least I am trying. I could press exit anytime and
no one knows it. Isn't that scary? Isn't that terrifying for
you? For me too! At any moment we could push someone
over the edge. Don't worry. I'm stronger than that. I'm
nowhere near the end. I just want people to notice I have
a reason to be, that I'm not plain stupid. He'd read this
and laugh, but that's the point isn't it?*

*I don't like the way she impatiently stabs the white board
with black Expo. It's frightful.*

*I'm always surprised at how unfamiliar the ceiling looks.
It's too bad most of us think we look ridiculous looking
straight up. But little kids do it all the time.*

*Glass is a funny thing. It separates the world without
blocking our view. Tricky. It's the strangest thing to be
outside and look through a glass door and see outside
again. The reflection is the giveaway. It's the only thing
that reminds us we know better.*

*Two coats last night and it's already chipping. Or I guess
it was Saturday night. Still.*

*Scott almost made it awkward like always, but he took
some. "It tastes like Christmas," he said. And he smiled
too. And just because the guy next to him hit on me on
the first day of eleventh grade, he convinced him to put
me on the list. That isn't why—I mean, I don't really
know—but I thought you'd like that little bit about the
guy next to him. I'm honestly indifferent to whether my*

name is on that list, 'cause I'm not the girl I was last year. It's a letdown, I know. I'm the one letting everyone down, remember? Sam let me down. And everyone else back there. Pathetic. In every aspect of the word.

"A and K" days were just freedoms we've never felt before, and it felt great but you can only live new once. The second time is always disappointing. If you try the third, you won't even remember.

I wish I could wake up one day and have pancakes for breakfast. No, I wish I could wake up on a Monday and have pancakes for breakfast.

Gosh. The sky is so blue. I wish I could put a pinch in my pocket.

Then I could say, "Here. I love you. It's a piece of the sky."

I think hand soap that foams out the dispenser nozzle is absolutely wonderful. I could wash my hands chap with foam soap.

I wish everyone walked down the street blowing bubbles. Everyone would be three notches happier.

October 17, 2005

Monday. Today was awesome. I met April at Barnes and Noble and we hung out all afternoon. We just chilled. Just laughed and talked a little bit. Then I went over to her house and we ate steak with our bare hands and watched a little *Young Frankenstein*. I had never seen that movie before. It was funny. I had a lot of fun.

October 18, 2005

Tuesday. I went to Ihop with Kim this morning and we had pancakes. Then I picked her up from school and we stopped by Yardbird's 'cause they're the best! Then we went to her house and by crazy chance Jake came over too, and so I spent the whole day with them. It was so fun. I haven't done homework in so long. . . but I don't care! And there is curry rice!

October 18, 2005
Dear Tim,

It's Tuesday, I know, but I had pancakes for breakfast today. Not a cloud in the sky.

April didn't ask any questions. Neither of them did. She just chilled. She was exactly the way she was to make me forget. And Jeff, the twenty-one-year old at Starbucks, had half of his cheese cake devoured (by me), but it's nice we connected as perfect strangers. It was new and it felt good.

It's been crazy, Tim. The pieces are everywhere. My dad says the medication should start working this week, and I'm hopeful. It's been too long. The last I was happy was before I turned seventeen. That's August twenty–sixth, 'cause I know you'll think September something. Anyway, I'm not working at Target, and I've stopped caring about homework for my sanity's sake. . . haha. No really. I'm sorry this is weird. I have been hesitant, because for a while I had nothing to say. I was just depressed, and I

*didn't want to be a downer. I love, love, love you so much.
I hope you have pancakes for breakfast sometime.*

October 19, 2005
Dear Tim,

*It's Wednesday in Music Theory. Nowhere else. I guess I'm
writing you now since I spent so long typing. This girl in
front of me is picking at her bloody nails with clippers.
She's one of those with an Orlando Bloom purse. I almost
disappeared in Death Cab for Cutie. Man, I forgot how
amazing music is. Yesterday was another "new" spent.
Who knows what I'll do tomorrow. Friday will be death
day. Oh, I have to babysit tomorrow.*

*I think I dreamed about him yesterday. I think I dreamed
about Alex. I've been having uncomfortable dreams.*

*She goes, "And remember I don't give them back, I send
them straight to the colleges." This music makes me want
to kill myself. Seriously. It's this awful piano that makes
you think you're standing at the edge of an infinitely high
cliff and there's nothing but you and the sky. Clear, blue
sky. And the breeze kisses your face and everything is
perfect.*

*That story we're reading makes me want to rip my face
off. Maybe I'll quit. I mean to quit everything, but I
might not. I can't take it anymore. I'm starving.*

*I don't want to be this way when I wake up tomorrow.
I don't want to live this way. I don't want to go to class,*

I don't want to eat, I don't want to listen to awful piano music. I don't even like the thought of going to Dad, because he can't fix anything.

I wish I could sing. Her shoulders aren't covered. She must think she's cute. It's not due tomorrow, Barbie.

October 20, 2005
Dear Tim,

Sing me a song. I'm getting the sniffles, and my voice is like steel.

Let's play with Legos and build robots that love plants and cookies and hugs and animals. The bad guys are dead. They got their heads chopped off. That's funny. I'm the dog; you're the owner. Say, "That's too many, Santa! No more!" Did you shove it? And I say, "No. I'm just bigger than you, so I eat faster."

So my Music Theory teacher is writing the key signature for Ab major and says, "I'm telling y'all flat out. . ." She didn't even know what she was saying! I let her know. I hope people let me know when I'm funny.

Size me up. I'm a perfect 100, vintage wash, and two extra belt loops. Oh hey, and Stephen King called. I used to know a kid named James Bond.

October 21, 2005

Wednesday was scary. It was really bad. Thursday, I took some medicine. Today I was feeling a little better. AND I made audition cuts for solo musical and monologue today.

My voice was totally shot 'cause I'm sort of sick, but I still made it! I'm really proud of myself.

October 22, 2005

The fall festival was fun. I emceed the whole thing and helped decorate and did a cake walk and helped Sis. Church. I went over to Kim's house to see her room and also to change her light bulb. . . I broke the glass cover (oops), but they didn't care. I just chipped it and the base will give 'em a new one if they want it. We started a movie but I didn't get to finish. I left to make curfew.

I came home on time, and Mom and Dad were sleeping. I think that's rude.

First of all, I could've been late and they wouldn't have known. Second, what if I didn't come home? They'd be sleeping! Third, I wanted to tell them about today. I understand they're tired, but I mean you always see in movies the parents waiting up for their teenager.

I'll ask them tomorrow, I guess, to wait up, 'cause I think that's important.

Saturday, October 22, 2005 10:38 PM
From: tim
Subject: Fried Ham

I love you!

October 23, 2005

One step at a time. I invited Mary Vaughn to come to the fireside today, and she did! I'm taking her to TOPS Thursday.

I can't drop my OWC classes, and life isn't happy and gay, but I'll work through it. I also need to apply for BYU-Idaho tomorrow. This is a nightmare. I wish it were all over.

October 24, 2001
I hate everything. I've been thinking about suicide, but that'd be giving up on life. I think I'm stronger than that.

October 25, 2005
I found these in a book in my No Class period. There were 88 symptoms for Bipolar Disorder. I have Depression, but I was just curious. I copied down how I feel.

5. Excessive distress when separated from loved ones

8. Has marked changes in appetite

9. Often craves for carbs or sweets

10. Experiences periods of extreme sadness

11. Experiences elevated or irritable mood greater than 1 hour a day

14. Experiences depressed mood greater than 1-2 days in duration

19. Has thoughts of suicidal behavior

21. Has difficulty getting to sleep at night

26. Thoughts race/many ideas at once

27. Wide swings in mood

28. Takes excessive risks

33. Often blurts out answers to questions

40. Often fidgets with hands or feet

41. Often leaves seat in classroom

42. Has difficulty waiting their turn

44. Demonstrates inability to concentrate at school

45. Frequently attempts to avoid school

50. Experiences panic symptoms

51. Has anxiety that causes impairment in social functioning

61. Repetitive mental acts, ex. counting

75. Is often truant from school

81. Is often angry and resentful

The majority of Borderlines have concurrent mental illnesses, such as depression, Bipolar, or other mood disorders.

This makes correctly diagnosing BPD difficult, especially if those illnesses aren't treated with medication first.

Symptoms can overlap. The things that I listed are symptoms that apply to both depression and BPD. For example, number five, which described my fear of abandonment.

October 27, 2005

Dear Tim,

I can hear them count envelopes from across the room then con the librarians for passes. They deserve them I guess. I like his brown velvet bow. I'd like to have a home in the 1960s with a whole couch made out of that brown velvet. I never liked the '80s.

They walked out the conference side.

She's a little embarrassed so she says, "No, I think it looks cute on you. I just don't want to put my hair up." She pleads with the sideways ponytail girl. That girl says, "You promised me last night. Plleeeaaassseeee!" She's won and they've left too.

The China doll sighs softly as she sees her boyfriend walk in. As he sits down she gives a sideways glance at the floor with a soft "hey." He's left-handed and writes immediately, but is sincere in his concern for her and her health. She nods her head no and continues to write. She's right-handed.

I feel bad because it looks like everyone else is doing their homework, but maybe they think and observe the same things I do. Coaxing themselves to "FOCUS!" but they end up spending an entire period on one word, or you have those who just flip profusely. Those are the ones who didn't study and have become desperate because they have a test in 3rd.

Now the China girl rummages around her purse for a cough drop as lefty coughs violently. "Here, you want a cough drop?" She croons. "No, really I'm fine. I just have to get the cold outta me."

It would be sweet to see them married. I'm sure they've thought about it. They could break up tomorrow, but I don't think so. I hope not.

Everyone is handsome and young. Striking, I should say. The idea is wonderful, but we're all too little inside to know it.

I'm hungry, but I'll wait until I take Mary to TOPS. Mary is 15 and will turn 16 in January. She is blonde and sweet and I like her a lot.

October 28, 2005
Dear Tim,

Yesterday was bad again. I try to be patient with myself, but it just isn't going anywhere. I took Mary to lunch. I like her. She doesn't talk enough and I like that. She is Drew Barrymore when she speaks, she is Mary when she laughs. I dreamt deep and mysterious. There were multiple CD players and multiple boys who played the same role in the same scenes. You were not there. I'm in front of fiction, and I suppose a part of me is fictional. That girl wears the same clothes every day with the same idea that smaller sizes will make her small. She smiles at herself because she took the picture angry. She has black eye liner. I'm nauseatingly hungry but I forgot to bring bags of cereal I made this morning. They are on the living room table next to September and August.

It felt nice to talk to him at the airport. He left one of those Livestrong bracelets with her to give to me. My wrist is too small. My mom can be real nice sometimes. She sat down and played that game April and I made up. I call it Grog Art. It's pretty cool and it's the only thing I look forward to everyday besides Seminary, now that he's gone.

I wish I could give some kids a nice haircut. You ever feel that way? My hair is dirty, but lately that's how it's been. I'm not wearing Chucks today for the first time in a long duffing time. If you took all the paint off I think it would be nice.

China doll looks especially professional today. I like her sweater. The two girls behind me are still talking about their car accidents, trying to outdo each other. Authentic Cadence Notation doesn't sound as impressive as he makes it. Words you don't know just sound impressive because you don't know them.

I'm going to ask my artist friend if we could Grog on here. I've never seen you draw before and now I'm very curious. I know you'd immediately fall in love with Grog Art though. I can hear your excitement gasp right now. I can see us in New York or Paris or somewhere like you say; you'd be drinking coffee—I'd rather you wouldn't smoke, you look cooler than everyone else in the room already—and I'd be drinking milk, and we'd sit under a lightly-shaded tree and talk about shapeless things and go back to the attic to paint Grog. We wouldn't have to stop for dinner because we'd never get hungry, and we'd fall asleep like kids again.

And what would we dream about?

October 28, 2005
Dear Tim,

I am a bright and shining star. Today is the big game, but I'm babysitting for Sis. Church. There are people who helped me remember, friends I will be eternally in debt to. Music has helped me too. I hadn't really listened to music since ninth grade. I'll pick up my guitar today and play something "Kristen." I feel change finally. I drew a picture for April since she rekindled my passion for art. That's important to me. You've been the only thing holding me together sometimes, and I'm not afraid to write anything, and I can do flipping anything life offers me. I love you like we knew each other before life even began. Wouldn't that be something? And here we are. Red orange yellow green blue purple homes I've loved. Lucky ladybug, drop a penny for that sad stranger. I have ten pennies.

After August and September and much of October, I can finally ask myself, where will I be in five years? Every dream is safely tucked into my train. Like Stargirl. And they helped find them from beneath dark closets and creepy things.

March 6, 1997
I went to school and played outside and taught Daniel how to climb a tree. Dad is coming home tomorrow so goodnight!

October 30, 1997
My dad's gone to Korea now. He left three months ago.

February 16, 1998
I wish Dad were here.

March 1999
My dad is on TDY (out of town) for a month.

September 5, 2001.
Dad has to leave tomorrow.

March 2, 2002
Guess what? DAD IS COMING HOME!

July 24, 2002
And I kinda want Dad home for my birthday. But he won't be back til August 31st so oh well.

October 3, 2002
Dad came home today.

February 8, 2003
Today is the last day my dad will stay here, til tomorrow when he leaves. I don't know how long he's going to be gone. He doesn't either.

April 1, 2003
Mom said Dad might be coming home in a couple days for one whole day. Yeah. But at least I'll get to see him. I get to ask him how the War is going.

April 6, 2003
I was thinking. About stuff. People usually do at 2:17 a.m.

We picked up Dad from the airport today. Well, this morning. Midnight really.

I've been thinking a lot about Kayla. And Robert and Alex and Zach. Where will we all be within the next few months? Life is changing already, I can feel it.

With this "war" going on I don't know what will happen or where I will be going. Everything is all the sudden. . . unplanned, unscripted—random. I don't know what will happen next.

April 6, 2003

I had pancakes for breakfast and cheesecake later. Cheesecake is Dad's favorite. Mom makes it for him on his birthday. I just wish he could stay longer. He's leaving tomorrow afternoon.

April 7, 2003

It was rainy and cloudy today. Dad left this afternoon, so I got to see him one last time after school before he left.

April 9, 2003

YW tonight was fun. We had this Daddy-Daughter Party thingy, and I got paired with Bro. Lindsey 'cause Dad's gone of course, but Bro. L was cool! He turned out to be an awesome person.

May 4, 2003

Today was pretty boring. I still don't know where I'll move to yet. Gosh I'm so lazy. Oh well.

Dad came home Friday. There was this huge airplane—I mean, bigger than a C-17, and Mom and Dad and I waited for his luggage. I saw Colonel Kyger there, and Alex's mom came up to me and gave me a hug.

So I guess the war's "over" or whatever? But Dad left again. Some conference in San Antonio. Love, Kristen Jex

---

My dad has contributed a ton to the Air Force as a flight surgeon, and had crucial responsibilities in the Iraq war. He's a respected leader, and is good at what he does. People come up and shake his hand for defending our country. I'm proud of him.

Unfortunately, being in the Air Force meant my dad was gone on duty a lot. I usually didn't keep track of when he left, it was so commonplace. I just counted down the days til he'd be home. Leaving for weeks at a time was typical. When I was 9, he moved to Korea for a year, leaving my mom and me in Texas. After September 11th, my dad was absent more than he had ever been, and even when he was at home, he kept late work hours.

I don't resent him for it, it's just a fact: He wasn't around half the time.

Dad comes home today! How happy he will be that I can too. There is nothing more clear to me now than what is really important in life. I can't wait until Christmas because everyone loves each other more then.

I wish I could play the piano like you, Tim. It's so nice. If rain were music it would be piano. It's water, life. Rushing, rushing in the thrilling way you feel when it's breezy. Yeah. When the sky is so blue. It almost hurts it's so infinite and deep and heavenly. Who's up there? Is there any way to color the sky? I'm glad there isn't and every day is a new picture. Every day is another portrait of us.

Sometimes when I listen to music I feel my heart could burst. It's overwhelming. It's happy and sad at the same time. It's a realization that you are ALIVE. Like, when it's quiet at night and there's only the light from beneath the door and the bed sheets, right before you slip into the dream world, you smile.

Yeah. Just like that.

Saturday, October 29, 2005 11:54 PM
From: tim
Subject: I never knew how much of you was a missing part of me.

Just send me an email to let me know you're okay and feeling better and I'll be content to leave you to your own emailing schedule. It's just hard to worry about you from afar. I tend to get email happy.

With an upside-down grocery list,

Timothy (a bestest friend)

October 30, 2005

Sunday.

Wednesday I felt sick. Thursday I asked the Seminary class to pray for me. It helped a lot. Friday I babysat for Sis. Church. I gave April a drawing I drew for her and stopped by Scott's too. Saturday I took Mary and Stephen King to the Tri-Stake dance. I had some fun.

Today was a bad day. But I'm learning and getting better. Friday Erika L. asked me to cut her hair, so I did in the school parking lot behind the old drama room. Then we got caught, so we drove down to the Marina and did it. It was awesome. It was SO random. She liked it too!

Tomorrow is Halloween. hm. What should I wear? I'm listening to the CD April burned for me last Thursday after that one really bad Wednesday. It has Death Cab for Cutie on it, and they're really soothing. I love them.

April won't be at school tomorrow. :(

November 1, 2005

The rain made the leaves look like broken ceramic under the streetlight.

I promised April I would go to her church if she'd come to mine. Scott, Kraig, Russell, and Stephen did something really mean to me today but I won't talk about it.

I went over to Sis. Church's today and helped out a little. That helped me a whole lot. I went Trick or Treating with Duffin, Amanda, Erika L., and Meagan L. yesterday and we got TONS of candy. And Kim and I drove to Erik's house this morning before school and bombarded him because he wasn't at Seminary.

He'll be there tomorrow.

November 1, 2005
    Dear Tim,

    It's cold and bright and cozy even though my legs feel bare and exposed in thin denim. The fumes of my car are calming down. You haven't written back yet, but I know you will by Thursday. Just in! 24 to 0: Jamba Juice! I never found out what the patch of grass behind the window was for. I remember when I was young, being disappointed when Dad told me grass had no nutritional value to us, only to cows. I'm sorry I can't spell nutritional, but it's all about the "delishional" value anyway. Kim and I went and bombarded his house today. He hasn't come to Seminary on time—once—since August. He will come tomorrow. I'm so glad April is back.

Scott came and sat right across from me. He doesn't know, everything he does tastes like Christmas to me. It's enough just to sit. Yes. That is enough. And things will be better than they ever have been. Even better. He doesn't know. He really is infinite inside. It's in his voice. I hope he becomes something great. Really great. Honest. So many of us deserve things beyond what this life can offer. He's trying hard. Just like me.

I had a great idea for our project—I hope I do a good job because it will be a surprise to him. And surprises have to be good. I like how he doesn't match today.

China doll has her glossy black hair down. It is perfect. It falls in perfect locks at the ends. She is so quiet.

He hates his life and I know it. I wish I could play Connect Four with him or something. He might like Hungry Hungry Hippos. He wants the things we had, and I mean all of us, last year too.

He'll listen to my music and he's wearing the pants he did when we went on that thing this summer when we fed the ducks. He's a lot like me, I swear. He lets the skin get to the best of him. But only he can free himself. I wish I could take him to Big City Cafe. He'd like it. It breaks my heart to see him look down.

Thursday, November 3, 2005 2:41 PM
From: tim

Hey, I wrote you a poem called Ode to Melancholy.

There's a small man sitting on a hard-backed chair in a white room. On his left is a door marked "Do Not Exit." On his right, a very similar door reading "Do Not Enter." For this, he simply sits in his brown suit and holds his hat, waiting for something to change.

He does not get bored or sad or tired. He simply waits.

He does not wish for something more. He simply waits.

He holds his hat as the years pass and nothing ever changes.

And that's it. Hope you like it.

Timothreet

Friday, November 4, 2005 11:37 AM
To: tim

"Focus," she says, "It's just an illusion," and stares straight ahead.

Her heart has a gash and the tears are sliding down. "love" is soaked on his lips, his hands touch her neck, and someone tells her he is familiar.

Tiny whispers hang from above. Rage in a fist grabs the man's hair. She holds the necklace he gave her. It reads, "s" after lie.

"No, this is reality." And she stands. Trying to make him listen with her hands.

The necklace fell.

She cannot speak or sing or scream, and she runs out the room like it was a dream.

And there it was. A piece of the sky. The tag said, "I love you." She ran as fast as she could toward the stars on the beach. The water was chill and air was still. The sand held her close and the dark made her think of when she was twelve. "The first time I saw my escape," she explained. And space understood what she meant and why.

The telephone can't reach that far, but she knows it is waiting, listening still. She loves that.

Time to go back, her piece ran out. Back to the room, back to reality. And when she came back, it was all gone. The walls were white and blank and clean, and there was a man holding his hat. She said, "What's your name?"

He smiled. He grabbed her hand tight and they ran through the fields. They never looked back.

We never looked back.

~kristen

sawdust song

"I'll make you okay and drive them away,
the images stuck in your head."
- Elliott Smith

November 7, 2005 (Monday)
Dear Tim,

She said, "I want to start over," and rested her head on
her chin. The room is so loud, the echoes are splashing
all over the place. 50 minutes and then she will be able
to visit Dad. She has no quiz, but she's past the point of
worry anyway. Everything is numb. "My heart hurts,"
she thought to herself. None of the boys pay attention

to her anymore. It was like the show was over now and people were wandering out the theatre. And there she stood in the spotlight, emotionless. Every once in a while a child innocently asks, "What's wrong with you? Make me laugh," and the girl can only cry. She is shameful and shameless, shameless she is shameful, and the battle inside her always wins, and the other half loses. There are the ones who mop up her tears every week so that the stage doesn't spoil; or maybe they hope she will sing again if they eliminate the chance of slipping.

Every week is the same. Her fellow cast members, now long gone and performing elsewhere, give her lines to say on her own, but she is alone. She sits and thinks about what is important. She starves herself because she doesn't have the courage to kill herself instantly. The pain helps her escape her mind. Her room backstage has mice and spider webs and dust and wood and metal saws that have rusted. All the costumes are yellow and the zippers broken. Some are wet.

The air drives her mad but it's not cold or hot, just right. Her face is drawn in chalk. Each tear erases a line. Sawdust collects in her throat and her hands are cramped and useless. Five people sit and watch. She imagines twenty more, but all that's left of them is gum and paper. She is past the point of "Do you remember," past the point of "I'm moving on." She is like a favorite song that you've listened away and every thought has been analyzed and spent. They hate that song. What a shame. Who would've thought she'd end before five people. She's never even been outside.

The division of reality and fantasy is sideways in her brain. Both sides are diluted. The pills say, "get well," but they're only plastic beads she takes out of habit. They keep her from floating beside the curtain. She doesn't care about murders or failures or heinous crimes. She shrugs a little and looks away. She wishes there were no corners of her world. She wishes her corners would disappear into an infinite plane to paint on. Sometimes she says to herself, "You ought to stand today."

The same song plays over and over and over and over. What will change unless she sings? Maybe she'll sing her sawdust song and six hundred people will love her again. Maybe her five people will yawn. A cell phone rings, and one of her imaginary people walks out forever. She doesn't know the one that stands behind her. He is watching. Patiently, smiling. Her knees are blue, her elbows purple, and there isn't any position that doesn't hurt. She can't sleep at night. Her mind is screaming like an infant. She counts until six hundred then starts over. She falls asleep at twenty five, but her dreams don't know when to stop. She loves light blue that is shockingly bright, shirt pockets, and letters, and things that are simple. She has it all rehearsed in her head what she would say if that quiet boy with a girlfriend said hey. But he has a girlfriend. He laughs softly at her jokes when no one is listening. She hasn't seen him all summer. He says, "You should do that more often," and later they feed ducks at the pond.

She hates that memory because it makes her angry. She likes to watch, but that's always lonely, isn't it? She thinks someone who will smother her will make her feel wanted. She wouldn't feel wanted anyway. "You can't just drop out of life," the phone said. She sat up in her bed and sat for an hour. It breaks her heart the sky is turning grey. She fears the mistakes that are permanent. They infect her sense of will. There is no erasure for Sharpie. She likes to watch the ink bleed. She is jealous of the past. I'm going crazy. I want to start over. I wish I could start over. I know it's you behind me. Will you take it away?

It hurts. My heart hurts.

I really wanted out. Living was hard. I cried even when I didn't want to anymore. My body cried, and I couldn't do anything to stop. I felt heavy, trapped. Like I'd never see the light of day, or walk, or feel any emotion besides overwhelming sadness. I was tortured and exhausted.

Killing yourself is hard to do. It's easier with a gun. Pull the trigger and it's over in one swift, painless exit. Otherwise you've got to wait until you run out of air, bleed out, overdose, or hit the ground. Sometimes I think if I had access to a gun I would've done it. Because otherwise it was too much effort to plan a suicide, and I was just too depressed to put that much energy into anything.

But maybe I wouldn't have. Meeting my maker prematurely was unacceptable. He'd be so disappointed in me. Maybe He'd understand though. Maybe I was strong enough to give it one more day.

Wanting to die.

I once learned during some uncivilized period of time, prisoners were exiled by being dropped into a deep well. The shaft barely wide enough to fit a torso. They were dropped feet first, so that they could starve to death standing on their broken legs.

That's how bad I wanted to die.

It's difficult for me to read what I wrote when I was depressed. Because I remember, and I pity that girl. I want to save her. I don't think I've ever tried to do anything harder than to endure that depression. To bury my yearning to die.

November 9, 2005
  Dear Tim,

I'm writing this on the back of a "Questions on Hills Like White Elephants*" worksheet.*

We sat outside and for one moment, nothing else mattered. For a moment, my two sides collide. The barriers melted away, 'cept one sat in the shade and one sat in the sun. But I was between them, and for a while, they made it okay. I was falling apart. That random sweet girl offered me a chocolate chip cookie, and man, it was good even though I almost choked on it from the hysteria. I hate how crying makes your face all puffy. I can't even think far enough ahead to next period. I don't have one.

I'm six years old. April tells me so. It's just a momentary flutter of when life was a lot more simple and dumb; we didn't know stuff then. She kissed my last option. I wish I had something better. I mean something better I could bring for show and tell. I have the world in my eyes— they're green, don't cha know? But I can't be that girl. I shouldn't be ashamed. The other one glances at the mirror a lot. She is pretty but slutty also. She is my friend. Hey, at least we've got good memories. They're happy reminders. A sugar rush. It's always bad on the backside. Is nothing long lasting? Nothing except this stupid rock. I'm Kristen in slices—thin slices of effort. I wonder if anyone is home. I'll run out of gas real soon.

November 10, 2005
Dear Tim,

I'm restless, that's easy. So what if I'm not in the mood. I need food. I'm not sleepy, just loungey. Loungey. I'm lounging on a table of round red waves. It looks like one of those Keebler Shortbread cookies we had over at Matthew's house. His cat had a problem with me and we couldn't solve the newspaper. His face was glued on infinite dimensions. I had detention once for saying, "nit-noity."

Give me a floor, a canvas, and paint. I'll paint you a mood that'd make some people faint. Don't ever stop breezing and kissing my face. Take me with you to a different place.

I hug lots of people and I pretend that they're you. I hope
you do that also. A pine cream cone just fell from the sky.
I like to sit like a kid who is five. Hello Fly, why did you
fly down here. Do you like the corner because it is corny?
Are you reading what I write with those big red eyes?
I'd wager it ain't bad being a fly. Just live for a day and
then you'd die. He said it's boring without me, and that
felt outrageously nice. I got a hit of that cinnamon spice.
Goodbye I said to the fly, but he's still there. I could keep
you as a pet even though there's not much to pet. Pity.

November 11, 2005

It seems like forever since I've written in here. I switched medication this week.

Monday I freaked out and threw a hammer at the living room mirror—as well as my Miss F-dub trophy at one of the framed pictures. Dad said I could eat wherever I wanted to, so he took us to Cracker Barrel for dinner that day.

Tuesday I told Scott I was depressed, and Wednesday was another meltdown and I cried in AP Music Theory. April sat outside with me, and Scott came out there too. Thursday he sat at our lunch table, the first time that's happened this year. Today is Friday, no school and I'm exhausted, but I'm feeling a little better now 'cause I'm writing.

I've been to Yardbird's 3 times this week.

November 13, 2005

Sunday. Dad and Bishop Boyd gave me a blessing to get better. Sarah left a message on our phone. Fender is right beside me.

I'm in Mom and Dad's bed. My room/car is a mess. Dad says I should start taking a pill at night as well.

We had a hayride Saturday. It was not a good experience, but Hunter was really, really nice to me and I appreciated that. I am exhausted. I took Sabre, Kim, and Lindsey to Waffle House this morning. We listened to Something Corporate in the car.

I have strange dreams.

November 14, 2005
Dear Tim,

F major, ¾. Don't talk about it. It's immature and mean. I think we just need to move on. So what can I do to move on? It's her birthday and I haven't even thought about it. I want to give her my laughter, but I can't. I smell really bad and my hair is greasy. Nothing is easy. But I try to make it like the glitter wishes into the well. I'll be well. You made fun of my cheeseburger wish on the porch, and I silently wished for the world after. I want to go home. I want to give her happiness—but how can I? I have none left.

How I wish I could make magic into a box, I'd wrap it in chocolate sounds. I miss music. I'll go home today and try to play 'cause I'm die-dead-ing. Your rules suck, Mrs. Brink. What are you talking about? Did they tease you back then? If you gave us water we might be all right. I want to go home. Where is home? Where can I turn for peace? And the girl with the Orlando Bloom bag is still writing. Stop please. I have to sit next to you now. I hope you smell me. Life is so boring. I hate waiting for Dad to come home. He understands, but I don't believe he knows. I'm anxious right down to my toes. Who knows? Can I go home? I'm thinking some therep' might help. My shirt is sour. I've stopped wearing the flower in my hair, I'm sorry. My arms hurt 'cause I carried Twinkie all the way home. Her paw bled a little. I don't think at all. My mind is mush. Mushy. I dream about strange things. I'm looking real hard and I'm in a store. Mrs. Brink is a whore. My hair is sad, too. I hate it. I hate a lot of things. I want things I can't have. I need to be right now. I still like Danny, and I hate myself for it. Stop playing sad piano. I could kill myself. Sounds sometimes make me sad. I guess I'm not going, not trying. I guess I'm missing out. My dad says I can't drop out of life—I'm sorry it fell. Honest.

Oh my goodness. It's in the band room. Dumb band kids. One of you rat us out. They think they know everything. I know it's late. I did it though. I flipping did it. All geniuses are on opium. All of them are freaking insane. It makes me so mad. How ignorant. How selfish. I did it in 2 minutes. I was the first one finished. I got a 50/60. I'm amazing. Too bad it's only a quiz. I rule. I rule cupcakes. Sugar makes me sick. I hate food.

His "Opium Dream." Eff that. People are stupid. He was a genius and he deserved every note of music he composed.

November 15, 2005
Tuesday. Today was a good day.

271

I organized my binders in my No Class period, so I actually did something productive. I felt I did a really awesome performance in Improv today. I think I played it better than Danny! I made an origami bunny for Scott in Music Theory. I really wish I could make Scott and April and Kim a little happier—I hope I do in some way.

Then on the way home I noticed Sis. Church was back, so I gave her her mail and talked with her a little. I should've helped her with the dishes, but at least I swept her kitchen floor.

November 18, 2005

I had a hard time getting up this morning. I'm sorry I'm too tired to write, I babysat. I'll finish in the morning.

November 19, 2005

I slept in until about 4:00 this afternoon. Dad said I was probably just catching up. Let's see, oh yeah, so Friday Kim brought breakfast to Seminary and we all read 6 chapters in Mosiah. I babysat for Sis. Cowart. I met this cool kid, Sean, after school. I'm going to babysit for Sis. Church tomorrow morning while she goes to Ward Counsel.

Fender is sleeping in a little ball beside me. She is so cute.

November 20, 2005

I stopped by Yardbird's and picked up dinner for the family last night. Everyone liked it. I ordered just the right amount, too.

Pat wrote me! Pat from the cruise. I was so happy. I love Patrick so much. It floors me how personable he is. I totally wish I was older and Canadian so I could be his very best friend.

November 23, 2005

Wednesday.

Listening to: Death Cab for Cutie—*Plans*.

Given to me by: Joe.

Tomorrow is: Thanksgiving.

Tim wrote me an email. I love Tim! Oh my gosh, I really love this band. Tim would die. I miss that kid so much.

I'm so hungry! But there's nothing in the kitchen. I took Joe to the skate park and the Marina. OH MY GOSH. Arrrggghh! I LOVE THIS BAND! Ugh! They are amazing. I did laundry when I woke up, and then I picked Kim up and we cleaned Sis. Church's house. I finally met Joe. Joe is nice. He is a little quiet. He sounds like he should, like it didn't surprise me or anything.

November 24, 2005

Oh my goodness. I'm exhausted. I cleaned and cooked all day. I can't even remember too well. I just remember the Turkey was finally done and we ate and then The Churches and Egberts and Kim came over for dessert. Kim, Joe, little John (Sis. Church's son), and I came into my room and John played my guitars, and I made him stop after he almost broke my top E string. Anyway, after that Kim and I went to the skate park and watched Joe, and then we all went out to the Marina. It was fun. Joe is really adorable. I just can't get enough of that kid. He says things and makes funny noises that make me want to hug him. He's just Joe.

I'm so exhausted though. I cleaned my whole room. There was a lot of work to do. I hadn't cleaned my room the whole time I was depressed so it was just. . . gross. I washed all my clothes, my whole bed and everything.

Fender is sleeping on the beanbag 'cause I don't want the bed getting "Fendered" on.

I was reflecting the other day, I am so blessed. I am so glad I survived that. It was so scary. I can't even remember how it was. It's like waking up from a dream and the more you try to recall the faster it slips from your mind. It's weird. I was me, but I wasn't. I'm so grateful I can feel happy again! I love it! Man, I dunno. It is just so weird. I took a vacation from the real world and now I'm like, what happened?

November 26, 2005

I am seventeen again 'cause of Kim McKay and Reliant K, and Death Cab for Cutie. April and that giant Strawberry Latte in Barnes and Noble and Joe 'cause he wrote me every day. Tim 'cause he was there.

November 27, 2005

I feel really sad. The kind of sad you feel when you can't have what you want. Well, I guess that's the reason why anybody would be sad.

My tummy is a dark cauldron of mixed thoughts and feelings I can't decipher. I listened to a little of *The Tim Sound* tonight. It's like a giant fist squeezing my heart 'til it suffocates. I want to let out something, but I don't know what it is. It's just there and it's because of Tim.

I've been having a lot of "I hate guys" comments scrolling through my head today 'cause Joe did something real jerkish. I told him exactly how I felt about it too, and he just made me feel even worse. He gave me some emo response I didn't really get and it was frustrating. I just hate guys. I hate that I can't date Danny or Sean or Scott or whoever the heck I want to.

I know better, and that's excruciating. It's just that the older I get, the harder it is for me to be close to a guy without him expecting me to be a girl. Does that make sense? Ughr. I'm frustrated 'cause I love Tim, and I wish he were here, and I wish I could hug him, and I don't care if he's gay.

Ugh! See, it's just stupid and pathetic. How can I love a gay guy? But I don't. I love Tim and that is totally different. I love Tim. I just feel mucky. I feel dumb. I hate all guys except Tim, and that makes me hate them all. I need to forget about it. It's inconsequential and pointless.

November 28, 2005

Today was a good day! Dad and I had a meeting with all of my teachers and we worked some stuff out. I went to *Shakespeare Abridged* rehearsal and that was really fun. It seriously felt so good, and Scott and I were like we used to be, and my life is all pieced back together. Tim wrote me too. It was the highlight of my day.

November 30, 2005

I'm just sitting in the kitchen reflecting a moment. Just basking in the in-between of now, then, and will. It's a weird feeling. I remember when I was seven, counting all the years of school I'd have to take. I actually remember looking forward to 5th grade. I do remember thinking after high school there would be college and that scared me. It's not as scary as graduating from college though. I'm terrified to have to work. I'll be honest. I don't like thinking about it. Geez. And even when I was a freshman I thought being a Senior was so far away. It was—but now I'm here. It's weird. I think I WILL miss high school.

December 4, 2005

Finals are next week, and I'm withdrawing from both OWC classes. The year is almost over! I am glad we get to spend Christmas at home with Mom and Dad for once. We'll have a Christmas Tree! 2006 will be insane. I can't wait.

Saturday I had lunch at Big City with April. It was good to spend some time with her. Then I had Sean meet me afterwards, and we drove to Destin and played our guitars in Destin Commons. I hope we do it again.

December 11, 2005

I don't feel like I'm spiritually progressing, and I've been thinking about the whole dating thing a lot. It's frustrating thinking about it. I hate it, and I feel like I can't talk to anyone about it. I really wanna learn how to play drums one day. Anyway, I feel really stupid and I shouldn't feel stupid. But I do. It's all kind of confusing right now and I don't like it. I want to know exactly what I'm doing, and love to do it. I want to be happy with no worries, no insecurities.

For some reason I attach my happiness on a cool reputation and a hot boyfriend. I sound so dumb! You'd think after going through something like Depression I wouldn't worry about stuff like that. Little things like reputation or rejection aren't as detrimental as they have been, but they still drive me crazy. It's frustrating 'cause I don't want to spend any part of my life feeling negative if I don't have to. You can't blame me. It's never easy being the only one. It sucks. It's embarrassing. I'm curious, I'm jealous, I'm sick of it.

And another thing. BYU-Idaho. Bleh. I hate applications. They intimidate me. I'm a nice person, just let me in. Thanks for the kiss Fender.

Man, I really wish I had a sister. I could talk to her about stuff like this and she'd understand. Even a brother would work. I've been writing for almost an hour, just thinking, writing, being mad at myself, daydreaming.

December 12, 2005

Listening to Death Cab for Cutie, just flipping through old journals.

I feel all lonely and sad like I did when I moved away from Sumter. It's like I never got over those things, I just learned to hide them. It surprised me. I didn't realize I LOVED Alex Kyger. I really did. Scott comes nowhere close to Alex. I loved Alex so much. I cried when I read pages about him.

I don't care if I was only fourteen. I'm flipping seventeen years old and I'm still writing about him. I still wish I had that chance. I loved him so much. But everything is changed now. We're all older and different. Everyone is. I'm still crying over it! Alex Kyger, you broke my heart. Fix it! No one wants me.

Junior year was really tough. It's lonely. Maybe I just want to feel unconditionally appreciated.

I had grown to make myself forget; now I remember and I'm astounded. Seventeen years old. And I'm still writing about Alex Kyger.

Love sucks.

December 13, 2005

Today was fun. I slept in, took a shower, then drove over to Matt's house. Amanda was there. Then we went to Sonny's. It was all right. Sean made a face when I asked if he could spot me $2. He made me feel bad. He asked Amanda out. What a jerk, huh?

December 14, 2005
Dear Tim,

I'm sitting here in the chorus room watching Scott rush back and forth from his seat to the piano as he corrects his paper for the millionth time.

It's all right though. No one really cares. I can feel a little pride emanating from some of us who feel we've been honest though, or maybe it's just me because I can see Nathan's paper from where I'm sitting, and I know I got my end cadences all wrong. They're backwards. Shoot. Oh well. It's not like Scott's helping his grade anyway. I'm sure he's got a D or something. I dunno. I guess I can't say anything 'cause my grade is probably just as bad. Only one more exam to go and it's Drama 4. I've got to perform my district pieces and I haven't at all since. . . since district cuts. I'll have to come up with a new take on "Taylor the Latte Boy" 'cause I'm sure I can't remember the chord progression. (sigh)

Kraig is taking me to see King Kong *in half an hour when we can leave. It's got Jack Black in it. Kraig's a nice friend. If you were to meet any one of my friends down here, I'd like you to meet Kraig. I think you guys would appreciate each other's wit. Kraig has really smart humor and then some stupid humor, like making a funny noise or something. You guys have those in common. I found a bracelet by the piano when I came in, one of those plastic letter bracelets everyone had in 8th grade, that spelled "Amanda." I'll wear it for a week or so when school starts again. I do have a friend named Amanda though, so that might be awkward for us. . . but it matches my Hello Kitty stamp ring so I don't care.*

There is nothing more visually pleasing to me to see something perfectly match. I love that. I found the coolest sneaks from Goodwill the other day. They are from the '70s, I'm almost positive. My dad thinks so. They are brand new, but the rubber is all hard and stuff and the glue is yellow.

Oh geez. They're playing Rent. *Scott and Nathan are belting it out.*

See you, Kristen

December 15, 2005
Dear Tim,

I have to address this to you, or else I will feel like there is no purpose in writing at all. I'll feel like there's no purpose in feeling the feelings I feel, or feeling like I'm lacking some feeling. My thoughts are all jumbled up like Krispie Kremes? There's no beginning and no end, and at the end of the day, after you've battled your mind, it let you win and you ate it all. And you feel sick. Even after you've drank some milk.

Do you feel like there's anything wrong with being bi? I was randomly searching MySpace with whatever names I could think of, however many people I knew, used to know, and I typed in Sami's name. I didn't know she was bi.

279

What is that anyway? bi. So. . . you like guys and girls? Are you just a confused little puppy that can't decide?

I don't understand how she could veer so far away from what was before. And what was it before? Why is this so hard for me to understand? Why am I angry? Why am I upset? Why does it matter to me? What do I care?!

Why does it make me sad?

What am I missing out on? Is there some central theme here everyone gets to experience but me? Why am I so flipping special? It's like they're saying, "Really Kristen, are you really that lame?"

Why do I feel this unexplainable drive to become NORMAL? Everyone else has their way of dealing, hiding their differences. It's like they can't figure out why they're different, so they make up some acceptable excuse everyone accepts. Of course. 'Cause it's acceptable. Why am I not acceptable?

Am I intimidating to you? Anybody? Am I? What scares you? Or maybe it's what scares me. And it is scary. The whole thing is. The whole dang Krispie Kreme is.

I FEEL BETRAYED. I feel left behind! People aren't who I want them to be, and my friends are turning into people I don't want to know anymore. And they're all going in the same direction. So why am I going upstream? Were we all going upstream before? I didn't think so, so how did we end up this way? Why can't I have the things I want? I want everyone to feel infinitely happy over the same thing.

Three whole years. Three flipping years, and I still write about it. I cry when I read what I used to write. I loved him. Yeah, I really think I did. I don't know how I dealt with it. It was the ultimate betrayal even if it does sound dumb to anyone else. It was like everything was planned, it was clean and neat, and we were counting down the seconds. . .

And something goes horribly wrong. And no one knew whatever happened. We can't fix it. He punched the hole, and now it's a cycle that never ends.

I don't think my parents are as affectionate as I'd like them to be. To each other, and to me. I dunno.

Sometimes I go to people's homes and everything is messy and lived in and it's warm and it's chaos and people are hangin' all over each other, and I feel like there are no mistakes. There are no accidents, there is no one to blame, feel no shame.

My parents were strict. They had high expectations. That was fine, I guess. I mean I think it's okay to be strict. Kids need rules you know? But you can't expect them to be adults. They're still kids. If I made a mistake, I was blamed, and harshly. I think that's unnecessary. There is never a good excuse to make a child feel guilty. They're children. They feel guilt on their own, naturally, because we're all born with that ability. There's no need to rub someone's face in it.

I think it contributed to my constant need of approval. Bad behavior made me feel guilty, and good behavior was simply expected.

On top of this, neither of my parents were affectionate. To each other or to me.

June 22, 2005
Mom. I think it's funny whenever I try to give her a hug—she's limp. Her arms are just dangling. You feel like you're hugging a rag doll. You have to insist she hug you back until she does.

They were pretty affectionate to our dogs though, and sometimes they talked to me like that. (Which really messed me up, because in college I'd talk to my boyfriend in the pet voice, since it was the only example of familial affection I had.)

It's true. I hate giving casual hugs. I hate that. I'm not going to give you a hug if it doesn't even flipping mean anything to you one way or the other. I want people to love me, and to show it. I want people to be sincere. I want people to apologize. I'm not stupid. I'm not a doormat. I don't know what people think I am, but for some reason, I'm just not normal. And he took me for granted.

I am a nice person. Does anyone care?

Yeah, and when Sean and I were in that coffee shop and he asked me why I don't drink coffee I told him why. I told him everything. I set aside my whatever it is and was bold enough to tell him. And you know what he said? He said he respected that. He said he bet I had more faith than anyone he knew.

So he asked my friend Amanda out instead.

My peers can't relate to me, and when I find an adult to talk to, they tell me they wouldn't have related to me as a teenager either. That's not their fault but it doesn't help.

After testimony meeting Fast Sunday, at least six people came up to me and told me they had Depression too. They were all like, 40 and above. I felt like I had Alzheimer's or something. A lady last week pulled me aside and told me her little "tricks" to not being depressed. I wanted to cry. I wanted to punch her in the face. THERE ARE NO EFFING TRICKS. I WAS DEPRESSED. CLINICALLY DEPRESSED.

Dad says most people have chronic depression and are just sad their whole lives. But it wasn't like that. They'll never understand what it was like. No one will. April was the only person who saw the real me when I was depressed, and she doesn't even believe in it.

Everyone thinks that you can just do better. Buck up. What are they thinking?! I'm not having a BAD DAY. geeeezz!

You're watching yourself go insane. You're seeing the most beautiful thing in the whole wide world and it doesn't make you happy. Nothing makes you happy. Imagine not feeling happy. At all. Even for just a day. Not one thing. Imagine a time when you were really hurt and cried and cried and felt your heart was about to burst.

I felt like that every second of every day for three whole months. I was mentally ill. I really went insane. I can't imagine anything more horrid than being trapped inside your own body. I can't imagine anything more horrid than being trapped inside your own mind.

A girl sat down next to me last week and said she hated Japanese food. She made this disgusted face and said, "All it is, is sushi."

Maybe it bothers me so much because my friends are making permanent choices. They are making choices I'm afraid they'll regret, but there is no restitution. You can't give a life back, you can't GO back. You only get one flipping chance, people. Yeah right. Living life with no regrets. I just don't think they know the way BACK is ten times more upstream down there than it is up here. If you would've stayed by me in the first place, it wouldn't be so hard for all of us. At least it wouldn't be so hard for me.

Don't tell me you're bi, don't tell me you drink, don't tell me you smoke, don't tell me you kissed another girl, don't tell me you lied, don't tell me Dad isn't around, 'cause I KNOW AND I CAN'T DO ANYTHING ABOUT

IT, don't ask me what I am, don't ask me have I applied, don't ask me why I can't do it.

And yet, why do they make me feel like I'm the one letting THEM down?

I wish I didn't have to worry about why Alex Kyger chose Emily Chance over me. Or why Scott Smiley didn't choose me either. Or why Sean asked Amanda instead. In the back of my mind I always wonder.

And I wonder why you are gay.

December 15, 2005

Oh my goodness. Where do I begin? My mind is a bucket full of heavy sand. I helped Ben move. (sigh) Then we went to Danny's house. Danny and I kissed. I stayed until almost 1:00 a.m., then rushed home and got a speeding ticket.

Yeah.

I'm sitting on my bed thinking. . . "What am I going to say in my prayers tonight?" I honestly am too clogged up to think. There are a thousand things wrong. I made a big mistake.

My greatest fear has always been disappointing people.

It's been the main motivator for decisions I make in life. That fear, and the craving for approval, some assurance that I'm doing the right thing. In the eyes of my friends, in the eyes of teachers, in the eyes of my parents, in the eyes of God. And they rarely ever want the same things. For instance, here:

June 23, 2001

(sigh) Boy. Did I blow it. BIG TIME. Dad just gave me a new book to read today and let me go to Maddie's. Mom wanted me home by 5:00 and when it was 5:30 Mom got mad but he just told her to let me play a little longer. I just came home and it's 10:30. Dad has lost total trust in me. AAAAAaaaaRRRRrrGGGhh! It makes me so mad! WHAT THE HECK IS WRONG WITH ME!!

Okay. . . I'm crying now. . . I hate being like this! Why is it so easy to forget or, or to think everything's ok; to push limits with your friends? I mean, it's like your brain isn't even there. It is SO hard to remember who you are as a Saint and to choose the right with friends doing different. I could've been happy. But no. I had to watch some STU-PID SHOW ON TV! AARRGHGGH! It's just not fair.

I feel like I've hurt someone or betrayed them. Do you think Dad will ever trust me? It hurts to hurt someone. Gosh this is pitiful! I know they think I'm talking advantage of them. Time after time they've let me go, they gave me another chance. How am I supposed to apologize? How am I supposed to ask for their forgiveness? How much longer is this going to go on?

So, I stay at my friend Maddie's house because the alternative was sitting in my room alone.

By disobeying my parents and staying at her house, I get the attention and love I want. But it comes at the expense of my parents' approval. Whom I do not want to disappoint. I also throw in God, because of course when I disappoint my parents, I disappoint him. And then God hates me. Because back then I didn't know I was worthy of being loved, regardless.

Realizing that we're all worthy of being loved was a huge turning point in my therapy process. The idea that I could literally do anything, and would still be worth loving, was such an epiphany.

I wish I would've known, because the guilt was exhausting. Disappointing my friends because I couldn't hang out with them, disappointing my parents because I needed love from my friends, disappointing God because it never felt like I was doing the right thing.

I wish someone had talked to me about boys. I tried to suppress my sexual feelings as much as I could. I genuinely thought it was a sin. I would pursue boys for their attention, but I didn't really think that far ahead in the instance they would actually like me back. I just thought we'd hug or something. No one had actually told me what was and wasn't appropriate for me to feel or act on. Maybe it was a religious teaching of abstinence, but I think it's because my parent's didn't talk to me about it, and I was scared to come to them. No one had ever given me permission to have romantic feelings.

I thought kissing Danny was the greatest sin I had ever committed. It was so frustrating having these impulses I didn't feel I was allowed to have. After Danny, I just tried to bury it.

December 16, 2005

I walked down to the pier tonight and called Sarah Brown. She listened, I cried. I feel horrible, but I feel better than I did this morning.

I need to talk to Dad.

Talking to Sarah made me recognize how horrible my actions were. I seriously messed up. I love Sarah. I love her with all of my soul. Thank you for Sarah Brown. I'll never be able to tell her enough so that she'd know.

I hate thinking about it, but it happened. It's a memory. I let myself down and that's the worst part. What will they think of me now? I betrayed myself and everyone else I cared about.

I love Sarah. I'm so grateful. She didn't judge or anything.

I really, really hate what I did. I'm embarrassed. I need to fix it. I'm going to.

December 18, 2005

I told Dad Saturday. It wasn't so bad. He said he'd take care of the ticket and stuff. I think I'll retrieve my jacket from Danny's tomorrow. Yikes.

December 19, 2005

Two years ago on this day I was in South Carolina, and it was Friday, and Joanne and I were playing a show at the coffee shop. Duffin made me a MySpace page today.

I got my jacket. It was awkward. It smells like Danny. Egh. Please help me! I want to start over. Can I just escape everything? I had no clue Senior year was going to be this difficult. I'm out of my mind! I can't live like this. Frustrated right now. Why can't I just be spiritual and forget everything? Why is this so hard? I need help.

December 20, 2005

Listening to: Death Cab for Cutie—*Photo Album*.

Feeling: Bad. Discouraged. Not confident. Crummy. Really clingy.

Kristen, honestly, why do you feel this way? Just let it go. . . Stop feeling sorry for yourself and stop trying to make up for it. I'm. . . jealous. Ashamed. Competitive. Needy. Materialistic. I feel. . . like screaming. Hate these battles with the mind. Agh. Please. Go back. Go back. No! I'm not happy! I want to be happy and do the right thing. I can't live like this . . . I don't trust myself. . . I feel really suffocated.

I wish I could spend a weekend with President Hinckley*. I wish I could tell him everything. I wish we could walk around Temple Square and he'd tell me I am a daughter of God, and I'd remember, and he'd smile and encourage me and he'd be really proud of me. He'd understand how hard it is. For one moment I wouldn't think, and I'd feel loved. I wish he could embrace me and believe in me and convince me I AM righteous. I AM wonderful. That I can do it.

* President of the LDS church

Tuesday, December 20, 2005 11:04 PM
To: tim

I went to the mall to buy gifts for friends today, but ended up getting a skirt from AE ($5, thank you very much) and a jacket from Old Navy (another $5, 2 points) and another journal, 'cause I'm almost done with the one I have now.

Okay. So this is going to be long, and really, like. . . girlish but I have to spill and I am starving for your say.

I kissed a guy Thursday.

See, I have this friend Amanda. This guy Sean who I liked asked her out instead, and I wasn't mad at Amanda but I really let it get to me . . . I mean it was like Alex+Scott+Sean fused together and I just became really bitter. And I did something stupid. Since Amanda got Sean, I wanted to get Danny, 'cause she liked him and he didn't like her. I don't know, it was my way of justifying myself somehow. I was low on the self-esteem and I wanted control.

The other side of it is. . . I really do like Danny. He drives me crazy, but I really wish we could just be together, but at the same time I know we can't. He's a jerk. You know? Have you ever read The Outsiders? It's like Cherry and Dally. This nice pretty girl falls for this badass even though he's a jerk to her. Danny just gives me a lot of attention and I like that. But, he's a jerk. I mean, in person, when no one is around, he's fine. Even nice. I kinda like that actually, but it just isn't right. I dunno. So anyway. . .

I went over to his house, and I was going to go home at ten, honestly I was, but Mom said I could stay out an hour later anyway, so I did. So it was me and Danny, with a weird scary movie on, in his room with the door closed, lights off, under lots of blankets on his futon bed fighting over a pillow. . . yeah. And he kissed me.

He put his hand on my back though, underneath my shirt, and when he did that, it scared me. I was like, holy crap. What am I doing? I'm better than this. I don't even like this guy. I mean, I had a crush, but geez we don't even know each other. It scared me. I was over there until 1:00.

I felt awful. Horrible. One, because I have higher standards than that. I just felt. . . unclean. Two, it was stupid to do just out of spite. And three, I left my jacket at his house. I mean, how slutty is that? Leaving an article of clothing at a boy's house!

It was awful. I felt so guilty I told my Dad. Yeah. I did. I felt better afterwards though.

But when I went back to get my jacket, it all came back to me and I wanted to stay so bad, and he looked so sincere and he wanted me to stay, I know he did, and I know I hurt his feelings no matter how tough he tries to be, and it's all so aggravating!

And I tried contacting Danny once, through MySpace, and I said something totally dumb and stupid. I dunno. They were filler words. Words people say when they have nothing to say, but want you to give them something to say, but it just comes off as being elusive, like they really don't want to talk to you, instead of, "Oh my gosh I have a million things to say to you but I'm scared and don't know where to start."

He didn't or hasn't, prolly didn't, write me back and it bugs me. I just want to know if he really did like me, or just made out with me 'cause there was a girl in his room late at night.

I did this to feel better about myself, but I don't. You don't win. It's awful. I made a horrible, horrible mistake.

I just want a solid thought to hang on to, you know? Nobody really cares, but secretly in my mind and heart I'm screaming and it IS a HUGE deal and I want to know, but I'm afraid that's not going to do anything for me even if I did.

It just felt good, you know? There were no emotions. It was just. . . mechanical. I felt nothing. All that drove me was the fact that a guy, ANY guy, wanted to kiss me. Wanted me. And I didn't have to give it to him if

I didn't want to. I had control. I was playing a game, and I felt like I was winning. I felt like I could prove something.

It was stupid.

It just makes me mad. Everything around you is feeding the drive to have someone love you. Every song and book and sentimental moment on TV and movies and just peer pressure and gosh, I couldn't take it. I let it get to me. I felt like a loser when I shouldn't have. I had respect. But this time around I just wrote that off as being a goody-goody two shoes.

It's haunting. It was so late I just can't believe it happened, but there it is. I remember. It's a memory, so it must've happened. I keep seeing myself kissing Danny on his bed and it makes me furious. I can't believe that's me! It's NOT me. That's not who I am!

I called Sarah and just cried and cried. I dunno. It's all crazy. I'm a messed up kid. I don't know what's gotten into me.

Sooo. . . that's it. sigh.

~me

December 21, 2005

12:15 noonish. . . So yesterday, I went to the mall with Amanda and saw Kraig there with what's-his-face. We didn't speak, we just stood there and stared at each other. Then he walked away. We were both smiling inside though.

Sean stopped by later, and the three of us took a picture in a sticker booth. We were supposed to be all serious and emo, but you can see I'm about to crack up and Amanda is almost smiling too.

Oh! And I cut Amanda's hair! That is my handiwork, thank you very much. Bye.

Wednesday, December 21, 2005 2:14 PM
From: tim

Every time I tell a story to my friends here, I always say stuff like, "My best friend Kristen. . ." or, "My best friend who writes really great music . . ." or, "I was with my best. . ." and they all say, "Kristen?" and I'm like, "Ah. . . yes. . . I've told this story already." It's very funny. Today is my four month anniversary outside of the United States. I have five months and one week left, I believe.

Wow! Bravo-duffing-o on the sales shopping! I'm so terrible with money here, I've decided. I find sales, but like nothing that's ON sale, so I end up buying the 40 peso shirt that I really like instead. It's so bad. I spend it on other things as well, but we'll discuss that when we get to the "this is not me!" section of the email.

So you kissed a guy.

That's cool.

First off, I can totally understand your reasoning after Sean asked Amanda out. Alex with Emily, Scott with. . . whoever, me with gayness, whoever else with whoever else, then Sean with Amanda. That's justified to me. Maybe not "right" as far as the duffed-up rules of friendship/dating go (i.e. you can't date your best friend's sister/brother), but justified. It was conveniently symmetrical and easy and you thought it would feel right and then be evensies. I get that.

The fact that you sort of like Danny is a little deeper. I mean, I'm not going to play therapist or anything (because I definitely do NOT want to come off as Katie M.), but if he's a jerk to you and you like it, that's something to figure out. It's like you say, if it's that he gives you attention, that's great, that can feel so good. But relationships can't work like that. His face will explode after giving everything he has.

Instead of lingering over the details of that fateful night (you've been playing it over and over in your head enough, I'm sure), I'll talk about me. I'm gay but I've never made out with a guy in my life. That's been said. When I got here in Argentina, I'd never made out with a girl, either. I'd never smoked cigarettes. I'd never been so drunk that I forgot things from the night before or vomited. I'd never been high on marijuana. Now, four months later, I've done all four, pretty much every weekend. And although I've enjoyed (and continue to enjoy) those things, I feel so. . . empty about them. Guilty.

I just shake my head when I know you'll read this, because I've always been such an admirer of your strength in a pretty spineless world, and here I am buckling to peer pressure like I have no morals, like I CARE what they think of me. I'm half tempted to erase this paragraph, but I know it might bring you a little. . . something, I don't even know. It might make you feel better, or it might make you feel worse. So I'm just saying it. I've pretty much lost myself, but at the same time, I hope I'm finding myself. I should have the strength to say, "I don't like doing any of those things, so I'm going to stop," but instead I'm just hoping I don't die in some freak accident while I'm here so that I can make it back to my normal sober/clean/girl-free life, haha. I guess what I'm trying to say is that, although you're not in a foreign country, you can still go back home. You didn't break the world or yourself by doing that. Sometimes things happen, mechanical and empty, but you don't have to join the robot army.

But you told your dad. That's a step. I haven't told either of my parents any of those things, and I think I'll feel weird around both of them until I do. At least my mom. I've lied to my dad for years about being gay, so that's not hard to do, I'm sad to say.

What I find interesting is that you wanted to stay once you went back. Temptation can be such a siren. The things that I know are bad for me (my lungs, my brain, my liver, my psychological health) are the things I continue to do and continue to feel guilty about. And I KNOW it's weak to say, "Oh, when I go back to the United States, I'll go back to how I was." I'll go back addicted to all those things and then kick myself for being so . . . like this in Argentina, but. . . but nothing. I can't finish the sentence because I don't even know.

When I arrived here, I was at a party with my host sister, Chechu. We were with Spanish-speaking friends from school, there was alcohol, whatever. The conversation turned to sex, as it often does with a large group of 17- and 18-year-olds and she asked me, and these are direct quotes because it ran through my mind a million times, "Tim, are you a virgin?" "A what, I didn't hear you?" "A virgin." "Oh, yeah, actually. I am." "Ha! You are a loser!"

"You Are A Loser." The anthem of my life. And I let it get to me too. It's been getting to me since that party at the beginning of September. That word has been getting to me for years. So here I am, acting like someone I'm not and I'm not winning either, Kristen. So honestly, the only solid-solid thought that I can give you is that you aren't alone. And you are by far not any worse off than I am.

So. That's all. I guess you didn't think I'd flip it all around on you like that, huh? Haha. I'll be thinking about you, and I hope to hear from you soon. Have a fantastic Christmas!

– yesterday's hero. today's villain.

December 21 (22), 2005

Wednesday (Thursday) 1:50 a.m. . . ish. SOOOO I'm probably going to get my car keys revoked, BUT! I have to admit I had a blast.

So Kraig and I saw *Narnia*, but on our way out we saw friends and they were going to see *Dick and Jane*, so we decided to sneak in. So we DID! I told Kraig I'd prolly regret it, but he laughed and said too late now, and I giggled too, and the movie was great, and then he spilled a giant Sprite all over me. So then we went to Wendy's, and then made a really wise decision and went over to Scott's house. But his phone is broken so we weren't sure how we might go about contacting him.

I peeked in his house and Kraig called Nathan, 'cause his car was in the driveway. Kraig wanted to peek through Scott's window so we were climbing over junk trying to open the gate. Kraig went first, and just as I was entering, a car pulled up and Kraig and I hurried up and "Shhhhhhh!"-ed. Kraig was still gnawing on his hamburger, so I couldn't hear anything but his chewing. Then Nathan left and it was just Maggie and Scott. Kraig and I felt REALLY awkward. Then Kraig silently threw his Wendy's wrapper in the giant green garbage bin we were hiding behind. That was funny. Then Maggie left and Scott went in the house and Kraig and I went up to the door and softly rapped. Scott looked so good. He'd just come from seeing *King Kong*. He didn't like it. I was sort of offended.

Scott, Kraig, and I stood outside as Kraig and I recounted the whole thing, and Scott's mom opened the door and told us to come in and exclaimed, "Don't keep that poor girl out in the cold!" Then she offered us cookies and so I had cookies and milk, and Scott loved my hair, must've said it twice. He asked me if it got darker, if I had cut it, he touched it, he ASKED IF I LOST WEIGHT. ???????? What? I have no idea. But he was flirting with me the rest of the night, which is confusing 'cause he just came home from a date with Maggie, 'cause rumor has it they're an "item" or something. But I did love the attention. He put his arm around me.

April 10, 2003
This morning during 1st block, by some lucky fate of the stars or higher power—Alex put his head on my shoulder. ♥

Chris (a senior) was telling me about this one story when Scott (Alex's brother) turned out the lights while Alex was taking a shower and it was REALLY embarrassing for Alex (apparently) because he dug his face in my shoulder. It was a really funny story.

Man. I really like Alex. Sarah thinks Quentin is cuter, but whatever. I still like Alex. That's that. I am utterly, sincerely devoted to Alex.

Not that there's anything wrong with Quentin, I'm just in love with Alex.

Kraig is such a good friend. I always have a blast with him.

But so anyway, Mom finally called and was mad of course, but I got really annoyed when she said, "So did you kiss someone again?" because it's just like her to make me feel awful.

What a cheap shot! It was low, but so are my excuses for not calling her. So I'm in MUNDO trouble. I had way fun and I seriously don't feel bad about it. I had second thoughts about this, I mean whether I SHOULD be feeling bad, but I don't. I didn't call. That's it. That's my offense. But whatever. They didn't call me. Lame, but still. If they ground me, fine. Hey, they're my parents. I trust them. They know what they're doing, mostly. I just hope their punishment won't be hard enough to crush the optimism I've got going here. It's Christmas.

Things between Scott, and Kraig, and I are finally almost exactly the way they were this summer. Things are the way they're supposed to be. Tonight was really fun. I laughed so hard! I laughed so much.

Change. Lots of it. Happened, s, ing.

I am sad, but I am more sad about the fact that I'm getting used to it.

First, the contrast between Scott's mother welcoming me into her home and feeding me, and my own mother who assumed I had recommitted an act that had brought me the most shame and guilt I had ever felt in my life, is troubling.

My dad never really showed any respect for my mother. He wouldn't take her side, he'd coddle her by taking every financial and legal responsibility, and chastised her like a child for her mistakes. So I didn't really respect her either.

She was insulting towards me. She loved to harp on my faults—I couldn't sing well, I had acne, I was ruining my friends—in a way that was self-congratulatory because she thought she was doing me a favor.

When my dad was home, I was disciplined in a very sterile, strict way. When he was not, he instructed my mother to do so, but her punishments for my bad behavior were inconsistent and hasty, because she acted on emotion. She was hardly the parental authority. It felt like an older sister punishing me for something arbitrary, because she wanted to win. We'd fight and slam doors. We would hit each other.

I never got any empathy from my father. I didn't receive any from my mother either, because it was she who always needed the empathy, and somehow she'd always turn it around and manipulate me into giving it to her.

It's hard for me to write these things because I know it will hurt when she reads this, and I love her. But I want other mothers out there to know that if they are broken, their children will be also.

My mother had a violent and traumatic childhood and never received counseling for it, and as a result had several emotional and mental problems. As a victim who was never treated, she unknowingly contributed to creating a new broken home, because she was a broken individual, who became a broken mother.

In 17 years, I learned all her attributes. I have all her beauty, tenacity and spirit, but I also have her addictions, anger, fear and dysfunction. My mom imprinted all her repressed problems onto me.

She was also hilarious, and fun. She was and still is, a best friend. But back then I needed a mother.

Second, I don't know what the big deal was, but my parents hated giving me a ride home from anywhere. They thought it was THE most impractical thing in the world. It was my responsibility, they said, to find a ride home. I can't think of a single time that they picked me up from Drama rehearsal. I rode in the back of a police car in middle school once. I missed the bus, and it was the only vehicle left to give me a ride home.

I hated finding rides. Youth leaders, other parents, friends with a car. They always politely agreed, but I knew it was a pain for them after so many rides. And you know how much I wanted them to like me.

The other half of the problem was that I never wanted to go home. I wanted to spend as much time as I could with my friends. It put me in a miserable situation. I wanted to be cool, I wanted to hang out. I didn't want to be the girl who drags a friend out of the party so he/she could take me home for my 10 o'clock curfew, especially when theirs wasn't until 12. My friends hated it. For them, it'd take 30 minutes to drop me home and then another 30 to get back to the party.

If I was late, I was grounded. It wasn't my fault that my friends didn't want to keep my curfew. "You should've planned ahead and found someone who would," my parents would say. If I couldn't find a ride, and they had to pick me up, I'd get a long reprimand on responsibility. "Don't depend on us to bail you out."

That's why I never wanted to call them. I knew what they'd say. "Come home immediately." I didn't want to hear that. I didn't want to leave, and I didn't want to force my friends to take me.

One night, after a teen activity at church, my mother had to come pick me up. Halfway through the customary verbal onslaught of guilt, I blew up. We had a huge argument, and she kicked me out of the car miles from the house. In the dark. I was so mad.

Half an hour later, my dad pulled up beside me and told me to get in the car. I refused. He freaked out.

He parked the car, got out, and yelled at me to get in. Scared and stubborn, I continued to refuse. Fighting against my thrashing and screaming, he picked me up and bodily forced me in the car. There were no apologies, no hugs, no discussion. Just silence. We went home, that was it.

I was expected to take on adult responsibility, but I was punished like a small child. Physically picking up and throwing someone in a car is not a way to treat an adult. It is a standard example of how my feelings were not acknowledged or validated.

December 22, 2005

Thursday. I feel closer to Tim than ever, like he should be strumming his guitar next door or something. Something about today sheds a little finality, a definite closure. It's weird. I feel spaced out. I feel evenly spaced out on a silver platter. All done up and presentable. Organized.

I've got it figured out, I just haven't got it together.

Me and Tim. We are so much alike. We live on different planes, but there is a common feeling we share that no one has ever touched before. It's so unexplainable, almost paranormal. I've often wondered why God has lit this part of my soul, blessed me with this amazing person. It's almost annoying how I can't define this incredibly intense connection to him. Love, yeah. But what is that? Do we share a love no one else has experienced? Maybe. Seriously. I dunno. I feel like Tim and I would be just as intensely drawn to each other even if I was a 95-year-old woman from India, and he was a Dutch schoolboy. The connection, it'd be there. As sure as sugar, it'd be there. I know it.

I wouldn't say Tim is like family. Maybe just as important, but not like them. I think we just call it love because there isn't a stronger word that describes us. It's like looking in the mirror sometimes. Other times, it's like I'm talking to the greatest human being alive. But it's never the opposite. I never ever feel ahead or above him, ever. And though I don't necessarily look up to him, I respect him, and he respects me. I've compared this to a relationship I imagine my husband and I will share, but I can't compare. It's like they're two incompatible mediums.

I feel more comfortable with Tim than I do my own parents. Yet, I feel like I know my parents. With Tim it's like an infinite well to draw from. Like, his personality is undefinable and endless. There is no end to Tim Threett. It's both comforting and chilling. I've got everyone else I love in my life figured out. Tim isn't a puzzle to solve. He just is. It's fantastic. And real. I have this, I get to experience it, and I don't think anyone else could quite get it. Which is a shame. I could spend eternity with Tim and be perfectly complacent.

I'd be happy.

But this and my vision of an eternal temple marriage seem totally opposite. I want a family, I want a marriage, and a husband. . . don't I? At the same time, I tire at the thought, and feel relief to think of a life where there is no romance. I mean, this sounds weird, but, where there is no sex. I just want it to be like it was when we were kids. It's all very weird and confusing, I know, but it's what I think about. I feel very awkward picturing a family and a husband and still a friend-ship with Tim.

But then again, I can't bear to picture a future without Tim. I never want to lose him, ever. I just want to be with Tim. That's all. This is what I think about and it's so bizarro! I love him. I don't know. I just do. I realize how much thrill Tim brings into my life. My heart beats a little faster every time I think of him. My heart just sort of skips.

We can't explain it. It just is.

Today was very nostalgic and emotionally numbing.

I just want to sit next to Tim Threet and talk.

chapter eight

and those in life that change

"I don't want you to know where I am, 'cause then you'll see my heart in the saddest state it's ever been."
- Relient K

December 23, 2005

It's been awful and scary, dark and lonely. Life's been confusing. Life's only been five months and I've failed more than once. I've shattered. I saw myself die, trapped in my mind. I've made mistakes I regret, there have been tears that I cried.

I fell and bled.

But I have survived.

I know the truth—and it is insane.

The things I like about life,

and those in life

that

change.

December 24, 2005

Saturday, Christmas Eve 3:24 a.m. I'm still struggling with myself. It's hard not to get carried away with the superficial. Honest, it is. I start caring, and then I've got no confidence. I stop thinking. So I got carried away with Kraig the other night. But I really don't feel bad about it. Dad is telling me I should, but I don't. I don't care about much these days—and I should. I still don't trust myself. I can't believe how hard life is becoming. Life comes hard and fast.

Kraig stopped by today and gave me a Christmas gift! The only wrapped gift I'll probably receive. It was a Mars Volta CD! It was perfect. Exactly what I wanted and totally Kraig. I haven't listened to it yet. Ugh. I'm starving. Sorry.

I don't know why I can't sleep. Who knows.

I hate Christmas. I haven't enjoyed it in a long, long time. I hate our family 'cause of the way we are. We have no traditions. There are no gifts under the tree. I had to beg them for a tree. I've got no siblings. I dunno, it just seems to matter, and Christmas is boring with Mom and Dad. I hate it. I absolutely hate it.

Of course the idea and spirit of Christmas isn't so bad at all. I love hearing the Tabernacle Choir sing hymns and all that. I love the scriptures and devotionals centered on Christ. I like that.

I just hate the way our family doesn't celebrate it.

December 23, 2001

I'm so mad 'cause all my relatives agreed not to exchange gifts on Christmas this year. They're ruining my childhood. I want the excitement of waking up on Christmas morning to open up mysterious packages waiting under the tree. To finally kill the suspense. To wake up, realize it's Christmas, and rush out into the living room.

This sucks, man. I miss my friends, I've got no more batteries (they ran out) for my CD player, and my freaking parents are driving me crazy.

January 3, 2003

I didn't get anything for Christmas besides my board.

I understood it was a big present, and like, Dad told me it was the only thing I would be getting for Christmas, but I did not expect to spend Christmas Eve in middle of nowhere, Canada, at some last-minute Chinese buffet. It was so boring. I silently cried in the back seat of the rental car and listened to "There Is" by Box Car Racer on repeat until the batteries ran out. I just wanted to be with Sarah and Robert and Zach and Meagan and Sami and all them so much. I just wanted a Christmas, way more than I wanted a snowboard.

I understand it's 3-something in the morning and I'm not thinking straight, and it prolly makes me depressed, so I won't write much more. I can't stand my friends.

December 25, 2005

MERRY CHRISTMAS!

The most exciting present I got was the apple air freshener Mom got me for my car. I got $100 too.

We had pancakes this morning and played Clue tonight because it's my favorite game, and my parents only agree to play it with me on my birthdays and stuff. It was really fun. :)

December 27, 2005

Tuesday, chewing gum.

I'm sad. I feel this huge hole in my heart and I feel lonely and unsatisfied. I don't feel loved. I don't know why that is, 'cause I should. I don't know why it is so hard for me to do the right thing, but it is. I don't know what I want to do with my life. What do I want? What is wrong with me? What happened to Kristen? I'm still not over Danny. I'm still not over myself. I'm so messed up. It's frustrating! I hate it! I hate writing stuff like this, but I'm going to anyway. This is MY journal.

I really hate life sometimes.

December 28, 2005

School starts again Tuesday. I'm not happy. I'm obsessed with MySpace, I'm obsessed with my friends. I want to go back to not caring about anything.

I hung out with April today. We rode bikes and that was a thrill. I'm thinking too fast for my pen to keep up. What the heck do I want in life? I feel like everyone else. Lost in a sea of thousands of others. Why am I so. . . lame? I'm totally lacking confidence. This is all very complicated, and I feel nauseated and anxious all at the same time. I imagine the next guy I could kiss. I HATE THAT. Why can't I let go?

I think my parents are going to give Fender away. That sucks.

I have no concern for the future, and I worry about inconsequential things. I feel very separate from everyone. I hate life.

I found my phone in the washing machine. It's broken.

I like Kraig though. I wish I could spend more time with Kraig. Scott bit my face today! I hate that. I like him so much. WHAT IS WRONG WITH ME?!

This life is surreal. I'll be graduating. Weird. Something needs to change. I need to change.

I'm lazy. I'm bored. Hungry, my room is a mess, and I feel unproductive, overwhelmed, and not confident. Where are my parents? Geez.

I stopped by Amanda's house for about an hour. FINALLY I was out of the house. I'm disgusted with myself. I dunno. I just hate everything.

January 2, 2006

Life is still sucking for me.

Tomorrow school starts. Dad came home today. I went over to Sean's place and watched him and his band record their song. I wish I were as talented as they are. Scott threw a football at my boob during rehearsal, and I hated watching him smooch Maggie. Gross. (sigh)

Tomorrow is gunna suck. I'll see Danny. I HATE my life right now. Seminary is tomorrow too and Kim won't be there.

On the way home from church, I saw a sign another church had posted and it read, "Maybe He will come in '06" It's looking bleak. I hope he comes soon.

January 3, 2006

I'm getting there. Today was a good day. It felt so good to be in Seminary again. Scott is in my improv class now. Yay! But he still with Maggie.

January 5, 2006

NOT a good day. Mr. McLaughlin patted me on the shoulder today though, and for some reason it made me feel better for a little while. I hate Scott and Maggie. They totally suck.

June 9, 2003

11:59 p.m. The last minute of the day. Thank heavens. Today sucked real bad. But I cried it all out. I can't stand to look at Alex or Emily. I can't handle it. Makes me want to scream!

January 8, 2006

I can't have the things I want. We'll probably have to give Fender away when Mom and Dad move into the new house. I love Fender so much.

Tim wrote me an email today about how his friends love my music! That was nice.

I can't have what I want, but I have Mom and Dad, and Tim, and Fender. I have Sarah and Rob. I have Kraig, and yeah Scott, even if he is with Maggie. I have Duffin. I have April. My life isn't over over. (sigh) Still. I get discouraged. The pressure is still there and it's not going away. I don't think, but I hope. I really want everything. I want to keep Fender. I WANT TO KEEP FENDER!

I wish our favorite pens never ran out.

January 10, 2006

Today was so boring. I did nothing.

January 17, 2006

Tuesday. I didn't have a good day. I cried a little around dinnertime 'cause I was freaking out. I dunno. I just was. I hope I can stop worrying about dumb stuff soon. Like, tomorrow.

I hit my knee and I know this one is gunna be a real big bruise. It hurts.

January 22, 2006

So Friday and Saturday was ITS. I did awful on my monologue and judges didn't like "Taylor the Latte Boy." Kraig came Saturday and I felt more comfortable. We went to Waffle House afterwards, and I ate a whole chocolate chip waffle and a sausage, egg, and cheese wrap. Someone asked me if Kraig and I were going out, but we're not. He did hold my hand down the hallway, but it sounds a lot mushier than it was.

January 24, 2006

I went to the beach and thought about nothing and everything, and I went to Waffle House by myself.

January 25, 2006

Dad said if I missed a day of Seminary he'd ground me for a week. So I'm going to bed. BYE!

January 26, 2006

I went shopping for groceries yesterday. I don't think I mentioned that. I bought a lot of junk food.

January 30, 2006

Tonight was Striking Viking and I was Kraig's escort. I was really cute! I borrowed a dress from Amanda and wore the "velvet sleeve thing" over it. Kraig won! And he won best talent. I missed the X-games though. :(Oh! And David called me today. He left the cutest voice message ever. He was really nervous.

January 31, 2006

Tuesday. Stephen, April, and I went to Big City Cafe and went to The Sound, a music store/poetry reading coffee shop. They trade/sell used music. Then we went to some bar, (it was empty) and played the jukebox, and pool. It was so much fun. April and Stephen had a blast. It makes me feel all warm and fuzzy inside. Dad comes home soon.

You know what we could really do away with?

Gender. I HATE gender. It's awful! Gender makes EVERYTHING complicated. The misunderstandings, the stereotypes, the preferences, the sexism. I really hate it. It's such a pain.

Why can't we just all be neutral and share crayons or something?

And why can't all buttons have colors? And, and a different musical note? What if every step were like a piano key, you know? And the soda machines played some cool song as the soda fell down, or like what if it made a goofy slide whistle noise like you were in a cartoon! Yeah! That'd be great! And I think bubbles should emerge from every air vent.

This could quite possibly bring about world peace. No gender, more music, and a few bubbles. Brilliant. I love it.

February 1, 2006

Today was sorta dumb when I got home, so I took a nap. Then I watched some *Law and Order* and *X-Files* and made

Pad Thai and went to YW. I felt GREAT when I called David, 'cause I hate talking on the phone but he makes me laugh.

January 29, 2002
I haven't done anything since I got home from school today. Well, I made Rice Krispie Treats. That's basically it. I've just been sitting on my bed thinking and listening to music.

February 2, 2006
I went to IHOP with Stephen and April after school, Stephen's treat.

Friday, February 3, 2006 4:19 PM
To: tim

I totally haven't written you in forever and I've been dying to sit down and write you.

First off, while I'm driving to Seminary, I pass by an elementary school that's across the street from my high school. The other day I saw their bulletin sign outside, and it read: "Congrats to school faculty member Angie Clinkingbeard". . . Angie Clinkingbeard—is that not like the most perfect name ever?

Second, I've been a lot happier lately, and I totally think it's because I've been going to Seminary every day and on time. I am totally convinced that I'm always so happy because of the Church. The gospel makes me happy. When I'm unhappy it's almost always because I'm not doing what I'm supposed to.

I wanted to share with you my favorite scripture in The Book of Mormon. It's in Alma 37: 6-7

6. Now ye may suppose that this is foolishness in me; but behold I say unto you, that by small and simple things are great things brought to pass; and small means in many instances doth confound the wise.

7. And the Lord God doth work by means to bring about his great and eternal purposes; and by very small means the Lord doth confound the wise and bringeth about the salvation of many souls.

My absolute favorite. This is just so true for me.

Okay and third, I finally wrote a beautiful song, I mean I'm really proud of this one, for you. Here are the lyrics:

Wishing Well

I see a perfect light in your eyes
Our hearts and thoughts leak
to keep us alive
Soft chairs and soft drinks softly remind us of
Pause. And reverse, we spent all of our first times
in May

In my mind I'm held by your fingertips
in an open reflection of pennies
we had thrown from our hopeful lips
Is there a reason to what we did right
Will I ever miss you like I missed you that night

I see a perfect light in your eyes
Our hearts and thoughts will
Will keep us alive

Our hearts and thoughts
Will survive

I miss you, miss you, miss you, cannot wait til you write back, so write back soon. ~kristen

Friday, February 3, 2006 7:32 PM
From: tim

Write back soon? I scoff at you, silly girl, and write you back IMMEDIATELY.

Angie Clinkingbeard is not a real name. It can't be! It's fantastic, and I think I may have signed an email like that once.

Sometimes, when I write the word "signed," it comes out "singed," which always makes me happy because it's nicer.

I really like that verse, too. It's a sort of English that directly makes me think too hard, so I've given myself the liberty of rewriting it.

"You might think this is crazy guys, but check it out: sometimes tiny things—the most miniscule of ideas or thoughts—can bring about something great. Sometimes they can even make really smart dudes scratch their heads. So that stuff that the Lord does that everyone always marvels at? Well sometimes they're brought about in tiny ways as well. So keep your eyes peeled—big things come in small packages."

And scene.

I love you so much.

Candi Rattlingmustache

February 3, 2006

I cut my hair today. Stephen stopped by Target today while I was working 'cause he's a sweetheart. Oh yeah, Dad comes home tomorrow, hoorah! I lucked out today 'cause I didn't pack a dinner for work, but it was potluck in the break room so I totally stuffed myself with free food. It was way good, especially 'cause I was starving. Today was the "crunk" rally. I liked seeing Krage dressed up as a robot with my turntable strapped to the box of his costume.

February 5, 2006

So yesterday I cleaned my room a little, did some laundry, then I went to the movies with Kraig and back to his house for cold pizza. Then I went home, took a quick shower, and headed on over to Amanda's. I wasn't paying full attention on the way there and a car stopped right in front of me. I swerved into the other lane so I wouldn't hit him, but I swerved too much and I tried to straighten the car out, but over-compensated and kept swerving until finally I had sense enough to hit the brakes and I spun around. I ended up on the opposite side of the road. All the grass was pushed and uprooted. I could've died if there had been anything around me. It was just one of those "whoa" moments where you stop and take a look at your life.

But anyway, I got to Amanda's—we had a little girl-time to get ready and went to White Sands bowling alley. Kraig, Stephen, Stephen's friend, and Joey were there. Somehow I managed to get a movie date with Joey at the end of the night. Whoo hoo! 'Cept that I was really tired and slept in and missed church this morning. (oops. . .) So I'm grounded now. So I can't go to the movies with Joey.

February 9, 2006

Twinkie ate all the pizza. There were, like, 6 pieces. I really don't like that dog.

I made muffins for Sabre and brought them to Seminary Tuesday 'cause it's her birthday, but she wasn't there and Jake was the only one who took any. Wednesday I made oatmeal chocolate chip cookies, and today I finished an art project and a song. Joey is sick but I made him laugh, and that made me feel good. Joey is cool. David just called me. Hmm. . . I think I'm leaning a little toward Joey. . . agh! I'm such a horrible person! Oh, and Sis. Church came by yesterday, and I saw baby Emma for the first time.

February 11, 2006

I am exhausted and have a headache. Today I ran into Mom's car. Mm hmm. Yeah, I didn't feel so hot. Neither did Dad.

I saw Joey! But really, today pretty much sucked. I hope Kim is doing well. I miss her. Haven't heard from Tim in a while, but he's on vacation. He's such an adult now—it's crazy. Tonight as I was walking up and down the street looking for Fender, I remembered thinking how weird and old I would be when I became seventeen. So now I'm convinced I'm going to be completely the same at nineteen or twenty-one. Am I going to stay this crazy and insecure and ME forever?

February 12, 2006

Sunday. Finished two songs and uploaded a new picture onto MySpace. . . sorry. That's not important. I still have "facial" problems. hm. Yuck. But I do like my eyebrows. They're a nice feature. And a lot of people say I have nice teeth.

Tomorrow I'm supposed to make a V-day dinner for Mom and Dad since Dad has to fly Tuesday.

February 12, 1997
I gave daddy a Valitine House that I made yesterday. But he didn't like the candy. I guess dads don't like candy.

February 14, 2006
I made April this huge Valentine card and it made her day. Scott gave me a Power Rangers Valentine, and that was nice too. Then I came home and tried to record, but it turned out crappy and I got frustrated with myself.

Then Dad came home and I showed him the song from yesterday, and I said, "I've gotten much better huh?" and he said, "No."

I was so upset. I am crushed. Then Target called, so I went in for work for four hours then David called—and it was awful. Ugh. This is why I hate talking on the phone. Well, eventually our conversation led to religion, and so I told him about the Church and he told me he drinks and he felt weird now 'cause he wanted to impress me but I'm all "perfect," and I HATE it when people tell me that! Ugh! It's awful! It was downhill from there. It was a huge wall, and I feel like I've been dumped. By Dad and David. I felt stupid, that's all.

So here's the thing about my dad. He doesn't value things that he isn't interested in. Examples: He wasn't interested in the childish aspect of Christmas, because he was an adult. He didn't think Drama was a worthwhile curricular, at least not on par with football, (which is silly because I feel you have equal amount of chance making a career out of either), so he had no problem grounding me from it. He didn't think writing music was very important, so he probably didn't think saying "No" was offensive. He didn't like to eat candy, so he didn't eat my gingerbread house. Things that weren't congruent with what he liked just weren't practical, and this is how he views the world.

You can see why I developed such an intense attachment to my friends and other adults. Because they encouraged me. They told me I was beautiful. Regardless if it was true, they told me my voice was amazing. My friends were everything my parents couldn't be.

February 8, 2004

In the deepest depths of my very soul, I've always and still want to make it with my music. Sis. Sampson came over today and we talked about that. She believes in me. 100%. Not only does she like, LOVE my music, she believes in me. She believes in me. She knows I can do it. I can do it. I'm gunna make it.

February 15, 2006

This morning was way awesome 'cause I gave Jake a ride to school (I usually don't), and we got to talk about the whole-David thing and how tough it is to be LDS out here and stuff, and we were sharing stories. It was such a strength to me. It made me feel a lot better.

February 16, 2006

David left the most awesome comments on my MySpace. It was a real confidence booster. He's such a heart. I dunno.

Anyway, Joey and I hung out today. It was only an hour, so that sorta sucked, but hanging out with him was cool. He's adorable. I like his hugs. . .

I had to do my monologue today and I cried on stage! I cried because I was so nervous. That never happens! Mrs. White pushed me though, and I finally made a big leap and did it. It was so exhilarating and real and scary, but amazing. I don't take emotional risks, so it was hard for me, because the emotion was real. Anyway, that was really cool.

February 20, 2006

This morning I went to the mall and bought a shirt for $4, then went to American Eagle and bought April a pair of jeans. Then I went to babysit, ($30) then Joey and I saw *Narnia*. I found a super short message from David, "I miss you so much" ♥ yay!

I told Stephen I was totally playing two guys at once, and he goes, "live it up, playa!" He said eventually I have to choose, but it's still early, I know.

February 22, 2006

Hahaha! Fender just flopped down on my bed. She's so cute. Every night before I go to bed, I wonder how I'm gunna fall asleep without her at BYU-I. I love Fender.

I was really cranky today. Made cookies for YW tonight. My life is sort of boring. I have a slack attitude. I feel really numb to the college thing. I mean, I think, is it really ever gunna happen? But it HAS to. I mean, I don't know what

I'll do if I don't get in to BYU-Idaho. I haven't even thought about the move. The truth is—I've got a lot of things to worry about, but I don't like to worry, so I'm not gunna. College seems so far away. (sigh)

February 24, 2006

Stephen, Joey, April, and I went to T.G.I.F. I really hate that place. Then Joey went to work, and David met us at the bowling alley. It was awesome. He was wearing a "Les is more" Gibson guitar shirt with red chucks. We all had a fun time.

April and Stephen both agreed David, and I think I'm going for David.

I'm planning to hang out with David tomorrow. Ugh. He's so amazing. Like, I can't believe this is happening. Finally, after all that heartbreak, not one, but TWO! Anyway, this is very new to me.

February 25, 2006

David picked me up today and we drove toward his house and I saw a TOPS, so we stopped there and it was POURING rain and so we drove to his house soaked. We played songs back and forth on his guitar, and I met his Mom and Dad and dog Patty. She looks a little like Fender 'cept really fat. Then he took me home as it was getting dark and we listened to really sweet songs, and then we sat in the driveway and he was looking at me, I KNOW he was, and I was trying NOT to, and then he goes, "Do you mind if I kissed you?" and I could've DIED. I did die. It was so sweet and then he said, "So will you be my girlfriend?" and I died again, and he walked me to my door and held my hand and it was so amazing and unexpected.

I'm exhausted now, I spent it all squealing and screaming.

In the car after he asked me out, I gave him a high five. He's really sweet and charming, very gentle. He makes me feel pretty. I just can't believe he likes ME! Agh! It's all too good to be true. I love being with him. And he's way hot. He is. I don't know. I don't know. I don't know. Sarah would TOTALLY approve though. She would. She totally would. It's very rare to feel so indescribably happy. I'm totally high. As April says, Live in the moment. So I will. Go me.

February 26, 2006

Sunday! I GOT ACCEPTED INTO BYU-IDAHO! Life could not get any better. New house, great friends, David, Sarah, BYU-Idaho. It rocks! And I talked to Joey today. He's such a sweetheart. He was totally okay with the whole David thing, which broke my heart. He even said congratulations.

I went to the new house. It's SO far away. It's really big and nice though. It'll be different. Last night seems forever ago. Alright. Goodnight. I love you!! (whoever you are)

February 27, 2006

School was horrid. After school I cut April's hair and Stephen's hair out on the pier. It was windy, but somehow I managed to do a decent job. I think Stephen looks much, much better now.

February 28, 2006

Awww. . . Fender fell asleep with her head on my pillow. Today Kraig and I reached 180,000 miles on his car mileage. We've been waiting for this since, like, LAST YEAR.

Ahhh. . . stole the pillow. Sorry Fender.

March 1, 2006

Today in Mrs. White's class, Zach was doing his monologue. It had to do with gay rights, and Mrs. White was using her Stanislavski method. She picked two people Zach loved and trusted and she said, "Girls, you're going to sit on either side of Zach and say, 'I tolerate fags.'"

Before he even started, he started tearing up. Once he started his monologue, it was so real. I cried the entire way home. I love Zach so much. To see him, to see the pain he suffers, it was just, heart wrenching. Our world today is so messed up. No one should have to carry around that sort of pain for being who they are. I don't understand. I see both sides. Homosexuality isn't natural. But it is wrong?

The point is, I guess, that we are no one to judge. By not giving them rights, I mean, what harm do homosexuals create? They are just like us. Why should they be punished? It's awful. It really is. I just, today really made me think. Zach made a sharp impression and a heavy impact in my heart. I don't think we can judge whether or not a person is wrong for being homosexual.

It's just, overwhelming.

March 4, 2006

Sis. Church might take Fender! Isn't that awesome? I hope so. We went out to eat at Golden Corral, and Dad forgot his wallet, so I paid for dinner. So, then I went over to Kraig's, then David came over and we watched *Marx Brothers* and then *RENT*. *Rent* was good. So sad! But so good.

March 8, 2006

Wednesday. Sunday I dropped Fender off at Sis. Church's. I was sad.

July 12, 2000

My dearest Diary,

Today was probably the worst day of my life. Today Mom, Dad, and I went to the pool. While we were gone Grandma couldn't find PJ. We came home and found out he was lost and went looking for him. We finally found out that PJ had been shot. Some cable guy had a gun. We made a grave for him, and I will miss him with my deepest heart. Sometimes I wonder why Heavenly Father would do such a thing. But I guess that's part of life. I will miss him. In honor of Prairie dog Jex, known as PJ.

I really hope she likes Fender though, because I wouldn't want anyone else to have her. Monday I went over to April's to work on McLaughlin's paper. On the way home I saw David. We went to the park.

March 13, 2006

Monday. So, this morning/last night at 4:30 a.m. David and I broke up. It really is a shame. But he told me that he drinks and that he wasn't about to change that, so I told him I didn't want a boyfriend like that. So we broke up. I'm kinda relieved. I came home and called April and Sarah and vented to them about David/my standards. That took, like, 4 hours. Then I went to Target, and I totally found out I missed a shift Saturday. It was awful.

March 15, 2006

Wednesday. Joey and I hung out all day. We went over to Amanda's place. David and I talked again tonight. It was rough. But. . . yeah. Joey is going to prom with me now 'cause he's a nice kid.

March 19, 2006

Sunday.

Thursday was pretty crazy. I went grocery shopping, stopped by Sis. Church's house, read to Elementary kids with Kraig, then went to work.

Friday I was stressing out big time. Went to the mall, bought prom shoes and earrings, then went home, took a shower, freaked out some more, April came over, then Amanda came and I did her hair. Then Mom totally pulled through for me and made dinner 'cause I was a total failure. Stephen came, Joey came, Kraig and his date came and we all had a blast.

Prom itself was really fun. The decorations were all city-like and there were trees and stuff. I danced all crazy. I saw everyone there, and they had a punch fountain. That was cool. Kraig dances even crazier than I do. So we left at 11:30, then Joey and I walked around the block and looked at houses til midnight, and I gave him a kiss on the cheek.

I talked to David tonight and I didn't tell him, I mean I pretended like Joey didn't like me, but we both know that's a lie. He's totally jealous. You and your drinking.

Today I ate April's leftover cake she brought for prom.

March 27, 2006

Monday. Today I went to Kraig's house. We went to the post office, grocery store, watched *Titanic* at his place, went to

Scott's, and then I went to April's.

Saturday was pretty intense. Mom and I talked about what we've never talked about before.

August 14, 2001
I'm not sure things are going too well in my family. Things are kinda "tense" right now.

Serious stuff. Like, she was talking about what would happen if she and Dad got a divorce. Yeah. I don't think I've ever sobbed so hard in my life. I felt so much love and compassion for Mom. She is amazing.

September 5, 2001
Mom came back today, and Dad has to leave tomorrow. I've never seen her so sad or cry so much. It's not so much her father's death that makes her sad, it's her family.
Her aunt accused her of causing all of it. Saying that she could've visited more often, and she only cared about herself when she left Japan to marry my dad. She didn't believe my mom loved my grandfather, 'cause if she really did she should've stayed in Japan. It was pretty harsh.

June 14, 2004
Today Mom was telling me about her family growing up and it just made me relieved I live in the situation I do. I'm so blessed. So, so, so blessed.

She told me about her family, how her parents had problems.

There was domestic violence. Mom told me that when she was a girl, her mom said she might run away with the baby, but Mom would have to stay with her dad, because her mom didn't have the money to take both kids. So whenever Mom came home and saw that her mom wasn't there, she'd always check her mom's dresser to make sure her mom's clothes were still there.

I cried so much.

March 29, 2006

Tuesday. This morning I went over to Kraig's house again and had bagels. We drove to the F-dub library and read to 20 or so kids. It was cute. I also explained to him today how I noticed I say "that's cute" all the time. I use it profusely. Back to Kraig's place briefly, went home, took a nap. Woke up, and then washed the fence with Mom and Dad. I'm the luckiest girl in the world. I really am. My life is going really well for me lately. I don't know where all this joy is coming from, but I don't mind.

I went to Joey's house. Joey's mom loves, well, his parents love me. I like that. I liked being loved by his parents. I love his Mom and Dad. They look a lot like Joey. (well, duh. But yeah) His mom is adorable. She thinks I'm really cute. Before I left, Joey gave me a kiss on the forehead. Isn't that cute? It's so cute!

David called while I was in the car with Joey and his friends. It was awkward. He hates it. He totally knows I'm hanging out with Joey and he absolutely hates it. I can tell it really hurts his feelings.

This morning I made the family sit down and read family scriptures. I was glad we did that.

March 30, 2006

Joey suggested we take a walk around the neighborhood so we did. We held hands and said hi to all the puppies that were being walked, and we picked up a frog. And we sat and talked about silly things. I like Joey a lot. He's like my best friend. He makes silly stuff up. Like, tonight he said, "If you were a civilization, you'd be 'cuteopia'."

I've been really blessed with good friends. I love April. She is such a relief. I really am grateful for her. She is a unique spirit. I know God loves her. He loves me enough to send her to me. Oh! And Mom says we're going back to Japan this summer!

March 31, 2006

Friday.

The things I like about life,

and those in life that change.

I'm shorn apart like cloth. I don't know really. Mom and Dad might be separating. I've spent a good hour crying downstairs. Mom and I had a talk in the kitchen. It's overwhelming! I have a million thoughts racing through my mind. I never thought I would have to deal with this. It's intricate and complicated.

My mind is just swimming. I wish I could write it all down, but it's just so much. (sigh)

I got paid today. $200! I was so excited and giddy. I went shopping this morning and bought these really cute orange All Stars and jeans from AE and some perfume and a grey polo. I'm glad I'll see Joey tonight.

It's just unreal to me. I can't believe we have these problems. I don't know what to feel. Just a few moments ago I was enraged and now I feel so mellow. I feel sad and. . . it's so frustrating. (sigh) I don't know, Kristen! Life just never ceases to surprise me.

It's so tough. I feel like I should write more, but I can't. Not now. I need a hug though. I wish I had Fender. I'm trying to follow God's will.

April 2, 2006

I made cookies for Colby—he's the kid next door— 'cause he helped clean our fence.

I have this vertigo feeling right now. I really have no idea what I'm doing. I'm just going for the ride. My life is insane. It doesn't feel like I'm living one day at a time. I mean, I am, but it's continuous. It's jam packed and crazy and it overflows into the next. It's confusing. It's so WEIRD. Growing up is the weirdest sensation. I don't want to get all teen-angst, but man. It's crazy.

April 3, 2006

Monday. I missed Seminary this morning, so Dad put a lock on the computer.

ugh.

My tummy hurt all day. I went through this crazy depressive state today.

April 8, 2006

Saturday. Thursday I babysat for Sis. Church til 11:30. yikes! But I got to see Fender. ♥

You know what? I like Joey. He's got a little bit of Alex in him.

And it's not awkward with him either. I can just play. That's what I like. He doesn't try to make a move or anything.

We just hold hands, sometimes a kiss on the cheek. It's very sweet.

I can't believe I'm a senior. Creepiness.

April 9, 2006

Sunday. I am SO totally bored right now. I can't go on the computer 'cause Dad is home, there's nothing to eat, I can't find the crochet needle I was looking for, and my room is clean. so.

April 10, 2006

Monday. Today was really long. I went to Seminary, I went to school, then I went and got a burger at McDonald's with the change I had in my car 'cause I was starving. I came home and sold my guitar Brody for $150. Not bad. I'm glad it worked out. Then I took a nap, and when I woke up I was starving again, so I waited until Dad came home, but we ended up eating at T.G.I.F. I ate a lot.

April 15, 2006

ugh. Work today was SO depressing. I don't want to talk about it. I came home and read some *Perks of Being a Wallflower* and went over to Joey's. I was really boring. (Sorry, Joey.) I was just depressed.

April 16, 2006

Happy Easter! Sis. Church gave a wonderful lesson today. I look up to Sis. Church so much. I really hope to be an example like that. I love my Young Women leaders. I've loved pretty much all of them. How profound of an impact these women have made on my life. I am so grateful for the guidance they've given me, the love they show. I hope our Father blesses each of them forever. Anyway, I bought those dyeing kits so Dad and Mom and I could dye eggs today. It was fun. I pretty much made Easter happen.

April 20, 2003
What an Easter. I did nothing. No special dinner, no eggs, no candy, no bunnies.

April 20, 2006

I've been really cranky lately, and I have no idea why. Like, I want to throw temper tantrums everywhere! Bleh! Grrrr. . .

April 23, 2006

So. . . today was depressing and I don't know why. Well, I might just be emotional right now. Yeah. . . I'm really bored with my life. I haven't played guitar in weeks. I'm just not inspired. In any way. I feel like I'm doing nothing with my life. I miss something. I miss a whole lot of stuff. I dunno, like today, after the *Suessical* show, I felt left out 'cause all the other seniors are in the cast, and they shared this bond and it was a moment for them. I don't feel any of that.

I sat next to David today during the show, and he definitely still likes me. I don't know what I feel right now. I can't wait to see Sarah this summer. I hope that happens. I have a lot on my mind.

David brought up the fact that I wasn't as enthusiastic as I usually am. . . yeah. I don't know why. My thoughts are more or less focused on my future, and I'm getting that vertigoish feeling again. Like, I'm just free falling, nothing really tangible. I'm totally bored with my life right now.

April 26, 2006

Joey came to my house, and I drove 'cause I needed to vent. It was storming on the way home and I said, "Look a plane! It's so gunna crash!" and Joey was like, "OMG Kristen, that's awful! Knock on wood!" so he was desperately flailing around looking for wood and finally he realized he was holding a toothpick and tapped it. He's so funny. He was dodging raindrops back at my house and it was the funniest thing I've ever seen in my life.

April 29, 2006

Saturday. So today was awful. I was stressed about Kraig's birthday present and the Stake Talent Show. . . so I started painting. I spent the entire day painting 'cause I decided that was going to be my talent. I didn't get Kraig anything. So I went to Kraig's party, which is pretty much the only highlight of the day, but I did feel really crummy for not getting Kraig anything.

So I go to the Stake Talent Show, and I totally disappoint Sis. Harris 'cause she wanted me to perform something, and I knew that, but I had a talent! Didn't matter. So I just left without doing anything. I felt terrible.

I can't play guitar. I can't do it anymore. I've lost it.

But anyway, so I went back to Kraig's party, and it was nice, finally being able to hang out with Scott. I left before they showed *Hostile*, and Joey tried to kiss me for the first time tonight.

AND IT WAS AWFUL!

And you know it was if I just spent five minutes writing out "awful" and making it all important and stuff. Seriously the worst experience ever. I feel bad saying it, but yeah. I just want to sleep.

Bye.

May 8, 2006

For Family Home Evening tonight, Mom and Dad taught me how to play hearts! It was my idea. I thought I should know how before I got to college.

May 12, 2006

Today was awesome. I signed yearbooks and had kids sign mine today.

I went to work and It. Was. Horrid. It was truly awful. I'm glad I didn't bail and call in. They would've HATED me.

But what made my day so awesome was two things. First, while I was on lunch, I drove over to the high school just in time to watch the Senior Slideshow. I mean, my timing was perfect. I even had a couple minutes for Grant to give me my senior box! He covered it with guitar picks, and he got everyone to sign a pick. I love it. There was a ton of other stuff, candy necklaces, glow sticks, suckers, but the last thing he pulled out was. . . well he goes, "And last but not least I got you a BIG paperclip for all your BIG ideas." Isn't that sweet?! All the girls went "awwwww!" The second is: Seminary this morning was a whole lot of fun. Sis. Cowart is, like, the best Seminary teacher ever. But anyway. I'm SO TIRED. Like, seriously, I'm exhausted. I'm about to fall asleep right here.

May 17, 2006

Today was our "Senior Luau" thing. Tomorrow I'm going to lunch with Kraig.

I've been really cranky lately. Mike Boyd left a message on my phone. He wants to know if he could take me out on a date. I think his parents put him up to it. How could he really like me? I've been awful to be around these past Sundays. I've just been down. And like, I don't feel "worthy" or something. I dunno. I guess I'm just being weird. I've been so bleak lately. Whatever.

Oh yeah. Sami's four months pregnant.

May 20, 2006

Yesterday I worked. Kraig called me and was like, "I don't know about you, but I'M graduated," 'cause I didn't go to graduation yesterday.

August 13, 2006

I saw Sis. Church and Kraig and Amanda and April before I left. Ugh. It was weird leaving. I was fine until I went over to April's house Friday night. . . I kinda realized it then. . . and then I started to feel the numbness of it all. When I said goodbye to Mom at the airport, all of the sudden I felt like crying and I got that huge lump in my throat.

College. Everyone going their separate ways, making our own lives. It's crazy.

a concrete sky

*"I've got a story, it's almost finished. All I need is someone to tell it to.
Maybe that's you."*
- Jimmy Eat World

The realization started when my husband Shane pulled me aside one Sunday during church to express his discomfort in the way I talked and acted like a child in public.

I would play with his tie and lay on him and lick his nose. I'd slap his butt when we'd walk down the hall. I would use this cutesy baby cartoon voice all the time. It was weird and nauseating and inappropriate. I did not transition into adulthood very well. I guess I thought the longer I was an innocent kid the longer people would adore me. Which is the opposite by the way. But mostly I was scared. I was a helpless soul, looking for someone to take care of me, to nurture me, to baby me. Because apparently I had missed the boat on that account.

My parents aren't mentioned often in my journal entries, and I think that's the point. While most people's idea of a broken home evokes images of outright physical or sexual abuse, neglect is the subtle blight that can wreak equivalent damage.

Not only was I emotionally neglected, my parents were literally never home.

December 28, 2005
Where are my parents? Geez.

My dad was usually gone for work, and my mother attended college in another town, and I was the only child.

Don't get me wrong, I think my parents did the best they could. But they didn't have all the information, nor awareness of what was really going on.

And so, as a result of neglect, my main motivation in life was to seek out assurance, affection, and praise from whomever and wherever I could. It was a compulsion, an obsession, an addiction, and I was indiscriminate. I needed approval. Because otherwise I'd be thrown away, abandoned. I was frantic to know that people I love loved me back, because they defined my self worth. I desperately needed love.

Sometimes I still feel like, if I were just a little nicer, maybe if I were more interesting, maybe if I did something incredible with my life, they'd want to know me. Maybe if I gave them all of their favorite things they didn't think I would remember, maybe if I loved them and idolized them, and worshipped them more, I'd be worthy of being loved.

I just didn't want to be alone. I needed to feel that people loved me unconditionally, and so I possessed an over-attachment to people around me.

And this is why moving was so traumatic.

I didn't have a solid, structured home life. Yes, moving around from place to place coupled with my father's frequent deployments didn't help, but the military is not wholly to blame. My parents held the responsibility of ensuring a family household I could call home, instead of a city I depended on for love.

It's like that book, *Are You My Mother?* A mother bird leaves her nest, and in her absence an egg hatches. The baby bird does not know where his mother is, so he goes from one thing to another asking if it's his mother. He asks various animals and objects who each reply, "No." In my case, I believed everyone was my collective mother. So every time I moved, I was lost, and felt abandoned again. Time to search for my new mother.

September 8, 2004
I've often compared my pain with the pain someone would feel from their mother's death, because that is the only thing that comes close to what I go through when I move.

When I moved, I couldn't process the change. I was helpless against a world that was entirely out of my control. This perception of impending separation made me exercise what little control I did have to compulsively preserve everything from my past. I salvaged what pieces of my life I could and tried my hardest to keep them intact.

Without my friends, I felt empty, a shell. The people around me were who I was. I didn't just miss the past, I wanted to live in it. Which is also probably why I refused to move on into adulthood.

October 30, 2007
I don't know why I still feel the same way.

We've all grown up and found our different lives, but I still feel like I'm fifteen. I still feel like what we had was something beyond friendship or love or family, beyond independence, beyond responsibility or regret, something that would bind us together beyond life.

I can see it in your faces. The slow acceptance of what we never wanted to be. And now as I'm facing this same reality, I find that I miss your friendship more than ever, and as I grow older my memory of you becomes more and more distorted, more perfect with every trial, with every year. I don't know why I refuse to move from this spot. Maybe you feel the same way. Maybe you've learned to deal with it in an ideal manner.

Maybe you're as scared and terrified as I am.

I wish we could be together again. I wish we could pause life with what we had and renew our souls. I wish it would feel the same, but I know better. I wish I could do great things, I mean really great things, so I wouldn't feel like a failure. I wish I could do enough to make you proud. I wish I could do enough to make you want to know me your entire lives. I wish you would read this and understand what I mean, but you won't because we don't know each other anymore.

Then my parents divorced, finalized shortly after my wedding.

This crushed the sliver of a foundation I had of who I was, or where I was from. There was now no geographical or metaphysical place I could call home. The feeling worsened when I found out nearly a year later that my dad had remarried a few weeks after the split. I felt betrayed that he didn't tell me. I felt thrown away, like he literally traded Mom and me for a new wife, and a different kid.

I felt more empty and numb than I had ever felt before. I think the soul can reach the maximum threshold for processing grief, and when that happens it shuts off all systems. Like a reflex. All the sudden you feel extinct. You need to feel physical pain, you need some proof.

I cut myself, and the feeling was euphoric. By pressing knife to skin I could actualize the torment, some kind of emotion, because I felt I had none left.

I could see it sliding down my arm. A blood letting of an intangible affliction. An exorcism of evil from my soul.

The divorce was the fulcrum that created my dramatic drop backward in time. I was regressing. I was looking for attention, stability, unconditional love. I wanted reassurance, validity for my opinions and feelings.

I became super clingy to Shane. I desired nurturing and attention, and would scream, hit, and manipulate Shane to get it. I basically cast my husband as my father. I expected him to love me, and hated him for not loving me enough at the same time. My anger was incontrollable. Our lives and our marriage were falling apart.

When Shane confronted me about my new, kid-like tendencies, I became afraid. Being a child was easy, comforting. It was my defense. The thought of being an individual human adult being was terrifying. I was under so much anxiety I made myself throw up.

I kept making myself throw up.

In the moment, shoving my finger down my throat seemed so normal, natural. It felt good. Much like cutting myself, it was a way to purge all the bad feelings inside. But later I always felt horrified at what I was doing. I didn't know why I felt so compelled to do it and why it felt so good. It's not like I had body image issues. I had to be crazy.

Before my forced vomiting became too advanced, I decided to see someone about it. I found a wonderful, qualified psychologist, and she correctly diagnosed me with Borderline Personality Disorder.

There is no medication for BPD. There is no "cure." Psychotherapy is the only effective way to cope with personality disorders, though taking medication for any concurrent conditions (in my case Bipolar Disorder diagnosed in my early twenties, and anxiety) helps a lot. Treating BPD takes time—years—and frequent visits. It feels like a sacrifice in the beginning, mentally, emotionally, fiscally. But it's an investment. Because what you achieve is worth more than you could ever pay. It takes patience from everyone involved, and all the humility a person can muster as the patient. But the transformation is a gift.

I like to think I'm functioning normally these days. Therapy has worked miraculously, though I never forget I have BPD. It is a constant battle, but a battle I'm winning. I can say I have a life I'm living.

I can't express how much I wish I could have gotten help as an adolescent. I wish I could've been that professional help to my friends. But we were just kids. We were just trying to figure life out on our own. We banded together to make sense of it all.

I'm grateful for those kids, all of them. All the friends I didn't mention in this book, but who are in countless pages of my journals, supporting me, telling me to keep my chin up. They were the glimpse of hope I needed to keep going, and I love them more than they'll ever know.

October 28, 2001

I better go to sleep. It's getting late. I feel like I could write forever though. That'd be cool if this were published. Hey everyone who might be reading this if it ever gets published! I really doubt it. I mean REALLY. I've got a pretty lame life.

I think the most beautiful thing in the world is the sky. I guess it's because it's so big and deep. It seems like it would go on forever and ever. I forget about everything else in the world when I look up.

October 17, 2005

The sky is so blue. I wish I could put a pinch in my pocket. Then I could say, "Here. I love you. It's a piece of the sky."

Love you all,
Kristen.

playlist

chapter one: the scarlet crayon
1,000 MILES PER HOUR (OK GO)
FOIL LETTERS (KRISTEN JEX)
TICKETS, PLEASE: A COLLECTION OF STORIES AND POEMS
(D.H. LAWRENCE)
HATE TO WASTE (KRISTEN JEX)
PANCAKES (KRISTEN JEX)

chapter two: in boxes
TRANSATLANTICISM (DEATH CAB FOR CUTIE)
CATCHER IN THE RYE (J.D. SALINGER)
THE PERKS OF BEING A WALLFLOWER (STEPHEN CHBOSKY)

chapter three: pages of me
THE OCEAN (THE BRAVERY)
KNIFE PARTY (DEFTONES)
LOST IN YOU (ASH)
ON KEEPING A NOTEBOOK (JOAN DIDION)
ON THE ROAD (JACK KEROUAC)
BRIGHTON BEACH MEMIORS (NEIL SIMON)
THE SECRET LIFE OF BEES (SUE MONK KIDD)
COLLEGE IS A WASTE OF TIME AND MONEY
(CAROLINE BIRD)

chapter four: the art of rumination
LAST NIGHT (MOTION CITY SOUNDTRACK)
THE THINGS THEY CARRIED (TIM O'BRIEN)
ETERNAL SUNSHINE OF THE SPOTLESS MIND (2004)
THE YELLOW WALLPAPER (CHARLOTTE PERKINS GILMAN)

IF I *(KRISTEN JEX)*
THE MAGICIAN'S NEPHEW *(C.S. LEWIS)*
BLACK AND WHITE *(KRISTEN JEX)*

chapter five: the things i like about life
OKAY I BELIEVE YOU, BUT MY TOMMY GUN DON'T
(BRAND NEW)
CONVICTIONS *(KRISTEN JEX)*
YOU LOST AND IT DIED *(KRISTEN JEX)*
A CLEAN, WELL-LIGHTED PLACE *(ERNEST HEMINGWAY)*
STARBUCKS *(KRISTEN JEX)*
NINE STORIES *(J.D. SALINGER)*

chapter six: letters to tim
NOTHING GETS CROSSED OUT *(BRIGHT EYES)*
HILLS LIKE WHITE ELEPHANTS *(ERNEST HEMINGWAY)*
THE BOOK OF MORMON
STARGIRL *(JERRY SPINELLI)*

chapter seven: sawdust song
BETWEEN THE BARS *(ELLIOTT SMITH)*
THE OUTSIDERS *(S.E. HINTON)*

chapter eight: and those in life that change
WHO I AM HATES WHO I'VE BEEN *(RELIENT K)*
THERE IS *(BOX CAR RACER)*
WISHING WELL *(KRISTEN JEX)*
RENT *(JONATHAN LARSON)*

chapter nine: a concrete sky
THE WORLD YOU LOVE *(JIMMY EAT WORLD)*
ARE YOU MY MOTHER? *(P.D. EASTMAN)*

Kristen Jex lives in New York City with her husband and two ferrets, Peanut and Grizz. *A Concrete Sky* is her first book.

www.ingramcontent.com/pod-product-compliance
Lightning Source LLC
Chambersburg PA
CBHW072108270326
41931CB00010B/1493